Speaking Persuasively

Speaking Persuasively

Joseph A. Ilardo

Herbert Lehman College of the City University of New York

Macmillan Publishing Co., Inc.

New York

Collier Macmillan Publishers

London

Macmillan Publishing Co., Inc.
866 Third Avenue, New York, New York 10022

Collier Macmillan Canada, Ltd.

Library of Congress Cataloging in Publication Data

Ilardo, Joseph A
    Speaking persuasively.

    Includes bibliographies and index.
    1. Public speaking.   2. Persuasion (Rhetoric)
I. Title.
PN4121.I47   1981   808.5'1   80-19513
ISBN 0-02-359620-1

Printing: 1 2 3 4 5 6 7 8   Year: 1 2 3 4 5 6 7 8

To My Parents

Acknowledgments

I wish to acknowledge my gratitude to my wife Roberta, and to my children Janine and Karen Leigh, for their understanding and encouragement. Their support has made an otherwise difficult task pleasant and satisfying.

Abne Eisenberg has been, as always, a source of good ideas and practical advice. His intelligence and wit have been a source of inspiration.

Lloyd Chilton, Executive Editor, Macmillan's College Division, has been helpful and conscientious. His efforts on behalf of this manuscript have improved it tremendously. So, too, have the efforts of Elaine G. Irizarry, a most meticulous and insightful production editor, and Marcia Schonzeit, a copyeditor whose careful attention to detail and to the nuances of style have done much to improve the accuracy and readability of this text.

Preface to the Student

This book has been written for upper-level students taking courses in persuasion and persuasive speaking. The product of two years' work and a decade's experience teaching such courses, the volume is intended to be an introduction to theory and a guide to informed practice. It rests on the premise that the most effective persuasion stems from an understanding of the persuasive process. I do not believe a person must have a gift in order to be effective as a persuader, nor do I think it advisable to follow blindly and unthinkingly the prescriptions of others. A knowledge of theory and of the practice principles theory can generate seems the most reasonable assurance of persuasive effectiveness. Accordingly, this book is grounded in current theory. In addition, however, it draws freely on two other sources of knowledge: traditional wisdom and practical experience. Traditional wisdom refers to the rhetorical heritage of the speech-communication field. In my view, it is a mistake to avoid completely the fruits of this ancient and rich heritage. In addition, it would be foolish to ignore the insights of those who practice persuasion professionally, though they may lack academic degrees in the subject area. Hence, I have drawn on the experience of salespersons, attorneys, advertisers, and others who are involved daily in persuasion. I think that the combination of theoretical knowledge, traditional wisdom, and practical experience affords a comprehensive purview of persuasion and provides the tools for success.

The book is divided into three parts. In Part One, Introduction to Persuasion, I present a rationale for the study of persuasion, pointing out individual and social benefits to be derived from studying the subject. I also address myself to the question of how we learn about persuasion. I present an original learning model that explains the importance of theoretical understanding.

Part Two, The Science of Persuasion, is devoted to the scientific side of persuasion. I show the applications of the scientific method to the study of persuasion and discuss the tools used to measure attitude change, as well as the concerns of researchers in the field. In Chapter Four, I summarize five representative theories of persuasion, pointing out the practical applications of the theoretical principles discussed.

Part Three, Practice and Criticism of Persuasion, offers a review of preparation and presentation strategies, and blends traditional wisdom, research findings, and the fruits of practical experience. It also includes material on speech criticism, for which an original model is offered. I maintain that rhetorical criticism, properly undertaken, contributes directly to both theory and to effective practice.

Throughout this book, I have attempted to integrate theory and practice, as shown particularly in the Student Activity Options. These include enrichment materials, exercises, and projects to do alone or with others. They serve as springboards to individual writing projects and class visits by researchers and practitioners in persuasion. Each of these options has been tested in the classroom for interest and learning value. I think you will find using them both exciting and informative.

Preface to the Teacher

I undertook to write this volume because, as a teacher of advanced courses in persuasion and persuasive speaking, I have sought in vain for a text that meets my students' needs. In addition to teaching students how to prepare and deliver effective persuasive speeches, my courses are designed to introduce students to the theory of persuasive communication. I try as an author, as I have done as a teacher, to integrate theory and practice and to show the relationships among theory, practice, and criticism.

The ultimate aim of this volume is to foster the informed practice of persuasive speaking. To that end, I have offered a book that is both theoretically sound and practical in orientation. I have tried to approach the subject of persuasive speaking from a broad perspective. First, I wanted to convey to the advanced undergraduate student the many aspects of the field of speech communication and to show its interrelationships with other fields such as history and political science. Secondly, I have taken this approach in order to permit the instructor maximum freedom to determine the thrust and orientation of the course. The flexibility deliberately written into this text permits branching off or emphasizing subject areas of special interest to the instructor and class.

A unique feature of this text is a set of Student Activity Options that appear in each chapter. These options provide enrichment materials (readings, class activities, home study projects and such); they also serve as springboards to individual writing projects, group reports, class visits by experts in particular subject areas, and interviews conducted outside the classroom. The range of activities suggested by the options is limited only by the imaginations of the instructor and the class. While some activities are quite comprehensive, in others I have deliberately avoided spelling out precisely what is to be done or in precisely what manner. The instructor and the class therefore have the opportunity to formulate their own learning plan, in keeping with the emphasis and interests the instructor wishes to stimulate. Further, I have hinted at and suggested many other activities that can spring from the options appearing in the text.

The options appear not at the end of the chapters nor in an appendix, but as part of the textual material within the chapter. As soon as an idea is discussed that lends itself to an activity the option appears. The location of the options within the chapter itself allows for maximum student involvement when interest is likely to be highest. Moreover, the options often expand on chapter materials in such a way as to stimulate further interest while providing useful additional information.

The accompanying teacher's manual provides important information on the philosophical premises from which the book springs. It describes the varied uses to which the book can be put. Further, it includes general and specific objectives for each chapter, class exercises, exam questions and instructions for the use of Student Activity Options.

Speaking Persuasively was born of a desire to improve upon existing texts. I have tried to avoid both excessive abstract theorizing and naive prescriptions. A decade's experience with students of wide-ranging ability levels has afforded me the opportunity to try many different approaches to teaching this material. I believe I have found a satisfactory solution. I hope you think so, too.

Contents

Speaking Persuasively

PART ONE

Introduction to Persuasion

Chapter 1

Why Study Persuasion?

I. The Pervasiveness of Persuasion

You live in a world of words. You are bombarded constantly by messages designed to influence. Advertisers urge you to buy their products. Preachers stress the need to reform your life. Instructors attempt to persuade you about the desirability of study in their field of specialization. Salespersons prevail upon you to purchase their service or product. In turn, you are constantly striving to shape the attitudes and behavior of others. You urge your roommate to assume an equal share of the housekeeping chores. You try to talk your parents into letting you borrow the family car. You persuade your boyfriend or girlfriend to act in a way you'd like. Persuasion is, in sum, an inescapable fact of life.

The systematic study of persuasion goes far back into antiquity. It began, so far as is known, in ancient Greece. And it extends to this very moment. As you read these words, researchers around the globe are striving to understand better how people influence each other.

You certainly have a general idea of what persuasion is. As a sender of persuasive messages, you know that it involves exerting influence in order to change a person in some way. As a receiver of persuasive messages, you know that persuasion involves changing your way of thinking or acting so that it is more in accord with the urgings of another. It is desirable, however, to arrive at a more precise working definition of *persuasion* as the word is used in this book.

Persuasion is a communicative process of altering the beliefs, attitudes, intentions, or behavior of another by the conscious or unconscious use of words

3

and nonverbal messages. A careful reading of this definition reveals that it contains several important components.

1. *Persuasion is a form of communication.* As such, it involves a sender and a receiver who interact. Relatedness is essential to all persuasion. If sender and receiver are never brought into contact, it is impossible for influence—in either direction—to be exerted.

At times, you are simultaneously both sender and receiver of your own persuasive messages. You can persuade yourself, for example, by muttering encouraging words as you attempt a difficult feat: "I can do it! I can do it!" Most often, you function primarily as a sender of your own messages and a receiver of others'. It would be a mistake, however, to overlook the mutual influence exerted in a persuasive situation. Some great speakers have argued that their alleged eloquence was largely a product of their audience's emotions rather than any persuasive words they uttered.

It is important to realize that as a form of communication, persuasion is subject to all the potential breakdowns inherent in human interaction. A persuasive message is subject to distortion and misunderstanding. A speaker's motives can be misinterpreted. A persuader may fail to select words properly to convey the desired message. A host of potential problems can affect the persuasive message from the point of conception to the point of interpretation by an auditor.

2. *Persuasion is a process.* Persuasion is not static. It is not an event, an object, an action. It cannot be seen, touched, or directly measured. Like the process of baking a cake or playing a chess game, it is something in which we engage. It is ongoing. Processes are bound not by space, but by time. It is possible for ease of instruction to trace the origins and evolution of a persuasive process, to divide it up arbitrarily into steps or phases. But in nature no such divisions exist.

3. *Persuasion involves change.* A persuasive message is like a therapeutic intervention planned and carried out by your medical doctor. Such an intervention begins with an objective (say, to lower your fever). As a result of the intervention, the target is supposed to change in some way. Success or failure is gauged by the extent to which the intended effects are achieved. This raises two questions: First, what are the targets of persuasion? And second, how is change measured? These questions are addressed in depth later, but for now you can think of the targets of persuasion as an auditor's inner state (beliefs, attitudes, or intentions) or outward behavior. Change in these is measured by comparing inner state or outward behavior (or both) before and after the intervention.

4. *Persuasion may be conscious or unconscious.* A persuader may consciously intend to bring about specific changes in an individual or a group. This is the case when a persuasive speaker plans and delivers a speech with the specific purpose of changing an audience's attitudes. When a company plans and carries out an advertising campaign to induce the public to purchase its product, this is also conscious persuasion. In addition, however, persuasion

may go on outside the awareness of the sender. Parents may encourage obedience by inducing feelings of guilt ("Go ahead and laugh at me! I'm only your mother!") or ignorance ("Why don't you ever help out around here, huh?"); but challenged directly, they would deny any such intent.

In this book, we will focus on persuasive messages consciously and willfully constructed in order to bring about changes in a target audience. But it will be impossible to avoid discussing many subtler forms of influence.

5.) *Persuasion is brought about by the use of verbal and nonverbal messages.* You know that words properly put together can have a persuasive effect. In fact, between these covers, I will concentrate on the verbal aspects of persuasion. However, I would be remiss if I failed to note the importance of nonverbal messages. The look in someone's eye, the posture the person assumes, the furrowing of a brow—all these can have a tremendous impact in an interpersonal situation.

A spate of recent books has touted the desirability of winning by intimidation. While I don't advocate the manipulative use of space, body, and voice to intimidate others, I think it is important to recognize that such factors as these do have a major impact on the outcome of a persuasive encounter.

As I have implied, persuasion is related to coercion, manipulation, intimidation, and brainwashing. In many respects, the dividing lines are slim. Some people have even suggested that a good speaker is similar to a hypnotist. But in order to place limits on what you'll learn here, let me state explicitly that I will not discuss the use of coerion—violence or the threat of violence—as a "persuasive" tool. I will discuss brainwashing, propaganda, and manipulation, but only as interesting aspects of the subject of persuasion. You may pursue your interests in these subjects by following up on recommended readings and by completing Student Activity Options. But do not expect this book to tell you how to manipulate, coerce, or con others.

One last point remains to be discussed. The orientation of this text is scientific. All persuasive events are different in important ways; never are the variables the same. Nevertheless, the task of the behavioral scientist is to find common truths among apparent diversity. We seek generalizable conclusions—those having applicability to a wide range of circumstances. Insofar as I am able, I will provide you with guidance that will be valuable no matter who you are or whom you are talking to.

OBJECTIONS TO THE STUDY OF PERSUASION

For several reasons, some people object to the study of persuasion. Two of the most common objections are that it is unethical and that it is unnecessary.

The argument that training in persuasion is unethical comes in two varieties. The first runs like this: Teaching persuasion gives people the tools with which to manipulate others. It is wrong to provide such tools, for in the hands of the wrong person, they can be misused. Look at Hitler, say such opponents. If he were less effective as a persuader, would he have rallied the German people behind him? Others object on the ethical grounds that teaching persuasion conveys a power, and they are uncomfortable with the fact that power exists at all. Charles Reich, writer and former Yale University law professor, has observed that evil inheres not in the misuse of power, but in its very existence (Reich, 1970, p. 125). Hence, we may infer that teaching any skill that conveys power is wrong.

The argument that teaching persuasion is unethical dates back to antiquity. As early as the fourth century B.C., the Greek philosopher Aristotle felt a need to respond to this argument in his lectures on rhetoric. Skill in speaking, he observed, is a tool; and like any tool it can be misused. What distinguishes a rhetorician—a practitioner of the art of persuasion—from a mere sophist—a glib talker who misuses knowledge of persuasion—observed Aristotle, 1355b, 16,* "is not his faculty [i.e., the mere knowledge of persuasion and the ability to influence others] but his moral purpose" (*Rhetoric*, 1954/c. B.C. 330, p. 24).†

The mere fact that a tool can be misused does not constitute a reason for outlawing instruction. Rather, responsibility for ethical use of competencies lies in the practitioner. Members of the police force, trained to shoot a handgun, can use this skill for good or ill; the choice is theirs. But certainly no one would deny them the skill needed for the safety of society, simply because it can be misused.

The second objection to the study of persuasion is grounded in the belief that training in persuasion is unnecessary. "Good speakers are born and not made," say the holders of this view. "Furthermore, any speaker can rise to the moment. Inspiration is sufficient to carry even an untrained speaker to heights of eloquence!" And finally, they contend that we are living in an age of mass media. "Training in conventional, person-to-person persuasive speaking is outdated," they say.

The first argument falls under the weight of common sense and research evidence. Good sense reveals that innate talent can always be nurtured. Mozart showed signs of genius as a child. But had his talent not been nurtured, could he have achieved the artistic heights he did? In the same way, outstanding speakers from John F. Kennedy to the ancient Greek Demosthenes have profited by conscious, careful study of persuasion and persuasive technique. Further, research indicates that courses like this one do make a difference in level of performance, regardless of the native talent brought to the course by student speakers.

Inspiration—of which the root word is *spirit*—certainly plays a role in true

---

*These numbers, called Bekker Numbers after the person who first used them in cataloguing each line in all of Aristotle's works, are a traditional way of citing Aristotle. The numbers remain the same, regardless of which edition, reprint, or version you have in hand.

† Throughout this text, I have reported the copyright date of the reprints and translations actually used in my writing. The original date of publication for any work is the date that appears to the right of the slash.

eloquence. The Greeks even had a name for the spirit responsible for bringing eloquence to a speaker. She was Peitho, the goddess of persuasion and a companion of Aphrodite. Alone, however, inspiration is insufficient. Only training and practice can provide the assurance of reliable levels of competence.

It cannot be denied that we are living in an age of mass media. Nevertheless, in politics, business, religion, and any other area of endeavor you can name, there is no substitute for the impact of personal encounter. Anyone who has ever attended a rock concert can recall the excitement that only a live performance can engender. Furthermore, students of media cannot afford to remain ignorant of what persuasion theorists and researchers tell us about influencing others by the spoken word.

But, you may say, to demonstrate that the study of persuasion is neither unethical nor unnecessary is not the same as showing its positive benefits. What can I gain from the study of persuasion? This is a reasonable question; it deserves a serious answer.

BENEFITS TO YOU AS A SENDER OF PERSUASIVE MESSAGES

A knowledge of persuasion can help you meet your individual needs. This deceptively simple statement implies more than it says. Whether you think of needs as did the humanistic psychologist Abraham Maslow (see Figure 1.1) or more prosaically, a knowledge of how to persuade others can help you satisfy these needs. None of us lives in isolation, and only by talking, making your needs known, and influencing others to cooperate with you in their satisfaction, can any degree of contentment be achieved.

Consider the following cases:

1. You have a big date Friday night and need the family car. You must talk your parents into letting you borrow it.
2. You've missed two of your recent classes in biology, and you have an exam coming up next week. You need the notes from those classes to prepare for the test. You must talk a classmate into letting you borrow them.
3. A candidate for student government, you must convince a campus group to endorse your candidacy. You must convince your classmates to vote for you.
4. Driving home for the weekened, you are pulled over by a state trooper for speeding. You must talk your way out of the ticket.
5. Your teacher in another course has graded you unfairly on a written exam. You must convince him to raise your grade.
6. Your new job entails supervision of five workers. Your boss has told you that for the past several weeks your five charges have been goofing off and not getting the necessary work done. You must motivate them to perform up to par.

You can doubtless think of other instances in which persuasive skills are required to meet everyday needs.

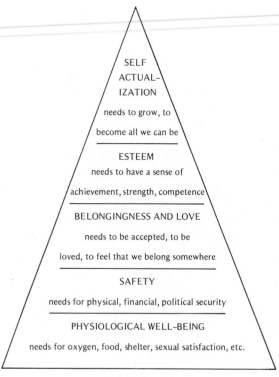

Figure 1.1.

Student Activity Option 1.1
Planning for Persuasion

INSTRUCTIONS

This activity provides training in situation analysis and strategy planning. In order for it to be beneficial, it is important that you follow the directions completely and accurately.

1. List and describe two current, real-life situations in which you must persuade others. You may choose one or more of the examples given above, but only if it is really descriptive of what is going on in your life now. Having chosen those two instances, do the following:

2. Describe the background of the problem. How did the situation evolve in such a way as to require that you persuade another?

3. Specify exactly what it is you want from the other person.

4. Give an estimate of how willing the other person is to give you what you want. What is the source of his or her resistance to your persuasive efforts?

5. How do you plan to go about persuading your hearer?

6. Why have you chosen that particular strategy?
   a. What about *you,* as an individual with a unique history and personality and a certain manner of speaking, makes you choose that strategy?
   b. What about the receiver as a person, a group member, makes you choose that strategy?

7. Consult with your instructor as to the form in which you are to complete this option. You may wish to submit a written report.

8. Discuss your persuasive choices and options with your classmates in a small group or with the entire group.

9. Your instructor may arrange to have you role-play the persuasive scene. In the event that a role-play is scheduled, I recommend that these descriptions be submitted anonymously in writing, both to assist your instructor in planning the role-play and to ensure that no one's privacy is violated in class.

Student Activity Option 1.2
Learning from Experience

INSTRUCTIONS
The preceding option focused on planning for an upcoming persuasive encounter. This one is a bit more like Monday morning quarterbacking. You are asked to look back on a persuasive situation of which you have been a part, and to try to determine the reason for your success or failure in achieving the results you sought. Please follow the instructions carefully. Consult with your instructor on the format for completing this activity.

1. Recall two recent attempts to persuade others, and analyze them along the following lines:
   a. What was the problem you were attempting to solve by using persuasion? How did it arise? What was your place in the problem situation? Who else was involved? How were responsibilities allocated?
   b. Did you succeed in achieving what you set out to achieve? What strategies did you employ? To what degree were the strategies a matter of conscious choice?
   c. At what point in the persuasive encounter did you begin feeling things were going to go your way? At what point did you feel you were beginning to lose ground?

The preceding discussion and Student Activity Options dealt with the benefits you receive as a sender of persuasive messages. Now let's turn to the ways in which a study of persuasion can help you as a recipient of persuasive messages.

BENEFITS TO YOU AS A RECIPIENT OF PERSUASIVE MESSAGES

The pervasiveness of persuasion can also be looked at from this perspective: Not only are you always in a position of wanting to influence others, others are always trying to influence you. Friends, classmates, political candidates, salespersons—all attempt to change your beliefs, attitudes, or behavior in one direction or another. Some of these attempts at influence are explicit and forthright. When political candidates urge you to vote for them, for example, their efforts are explicit. Other attempts at influence are less explicit; a person might wish to change your mind not so much by giving you reasons but by playing on your guilt, your fear, your sense of loyalty, or other emotions.

The following Student Activity Option focuses on your characteristic way of responding to persuasive appeals in a one-to-one situation.

Student Activity Option 1.3
See What You Made Me Do

INSTRUCTIONS

This activity is designed to facilitate self-scrutiny regarding yourself as a persuadee. Please note that a number of suggestions follow the questions to which you are asked to respond. It would be a good idea to follow one or more of the suggestions. Consult your instructor for input as to which suggestion might be most profitable in light of the thrust of this course.

For this activity you are asked to recall a recent instance in which you allowed yourself to be talked into something you didn't want to do. You might have subscribed to a magazine you didn't want; perhaps you agreed to drive a friend somewhere, or to lend a sweater you'd rather not have loaned out. Think back over how you allowed yourself to be talked into doing it. Here are some questions to guide your thinking:

1. What was your state of mind at the time of the persuasive encounter?

2. What is (or was) your relationship with the person who persuaded you?

3. What appeals were used by the person to persuade you?

4. How did you feel during the persuasive encounter?

5. How did you feel afterward?

SUGGESTIONS

Discuss your answers with your classmates, either formally or informally. See whether you can discover any common elements in your experiences.

An important part of this course involves learning to be sensitive to how others go about persuading you. See if you can begin describing those conditions under which you are most persuadable. Consult with your instructor on the desirability of starting a "persuasion diary," in which you keep a record of those persuasive encounters of which you are a part.

In the diary keep track of the things suggested by the questions that follow: Who was involved in the persuasive encounter? What were the characteristics of the interpersonal relationships involved? What was the occasion of the encounter? What was said by each party? What appeals were used by each person? How did you feel before, during, and after the encounter? What was the outcome? Questions like these can help you learn about yourself, your relationships, and about the process of persuasion. Ask your instructor about the specifics of this assignment; he or she may have preferences based on the design of the course.

Consider the possibility of inviting to class a member of your school's department of counseling, social work, psychology, or guidance who has had experience as a leader of assertiveness training groups. Consult with your instructor as to the desirability of extending such an invitation. The visitor might be willing to conduct a few basic assertiveness training exercises with the class.

SUGGESTED READINGS

You may have recognized similarities between the questions asked in this Activity Option and assertiveness training exercises. It might be profitable to read one or more of the following books on assertiveness and to report back to the class on what assertiveness trainers have to say about such topics as these: (1) the relationship between persuasion and manipulation, (2) how to resist manipulation, (3) coping with criticism, (4) aggressive vs. assertive behavior.

Bloom, Lynn Z., Karen Coburn, and Joan Pearlman (1975) *The New Assertive Woman.* New York: Dell.
Fensterheim, Herbert, Ph.D. and Jean Baer (1975) *Don't Say Yes When You Want to Say No.* New York: Dell.
Smith, Manuel, Ph.D. (1975) *When I Say No I Feel Guilty.* New York: Bantam.

THE INFLUENCE OF GROUPS

It has been said that we are living in an age of groups, and that as members of groups we are subject to the influence of leaders and comembers. Because the influence exerted by groups is so profound, it is important to spend a moment surveying its kinds and extent. We will begin with the subtle but enormously powerful influence of the family.

The family: a source of primary influence

Psychiatrist R. D. Laing has advanced the thesis that a primary legacy of family living is the definition of one's self as a certain kind of person. It is from your family that you get a sense of who you are and what you're like. Have you ever wondered why two children raised in the same family see themselves as very different from each other? One considers himself shy, another sees herself as outgoing. One sibling is bright, another dull. One is likable, the other unfriendly. Such self-perceptions frequently determine the kind of person you become, for if you believe yourself to be a certain kind of individual, you will call forth responses from others that confirm your self-perception.

The popular explanation is that innate capacities or propensities account for the differences between siblings. But Laing (1967) poses another alternative. He suggests that a sort of hypnosis occurs in family living, as a result of which individuals come to see themselves in one way rather than another. This, he declares, is less a function of inner propensities than of usually unconscious choices and decisions on the parents' part. They "decide" that one child will be successful, another less so; one youngster will be neat and organized, another sloppy and careless. While his explanations of the reasons behind these decisions are fascinating, they are of less interest here than is his discussion of the persuasive strategies used to communicate these messages to the persuadees. He identifies two principal strategies: attributions and injunctions, both of which, he asserts, are far more powerful persuasive tools than conventional forms of coercion or persuasion.

Attributions are labels that serve to define a child as one sort of person rather than another. They are usually issued directly to the child, as when a parent says, "You're so clumsy!" But attributions may also be issued indirectly; when, for example, a parent or another adult in authority describes the child aloud to another in the presence of the youngster: "Johnny is such a polite boy!"

Because children have no clear sense of themselves, of who they are or what they're really like, they have to accept these attributions unquestioningly. Without realizing it, children begin to think of themselves along the lines sketched by their parents. To use an analogy, a youngster can be thought of as a glass of clear water; the parents' attributions are like vegetable coloring. Because water is colorless, it tends immediately to take on the tint of the color added to it. Attributions influence the child in that way, exerting a pervasive and lasting influence on the youngster's self-perceptions.

The other persuasive tool Laing identifies is the *injunction.* This, he asserts, is a command that the child not be a certain way or not do a certain thing characteristically. Injunctions are prohibitions. Most often they are implied, hinted at. When issued directly, they are issued humorously or in anger: "Don't smile!" says the parent with a gentle laugh to the unhappy child. On the surface it sounds like an attempt to encourage the child to break out of a glum mood. In fact, it may well be an injunction, a prohibition against being happy. Another example of an injunction is the message a mother might give her daughter, indirectly, not to enjoy sex. Mother might allude to men who "only want one thing"; she might make it seem that her daughter must ever be on guard lest she allow the bestial side of a man (and, by implication, of herself) to hold sway over her behavior. A host of other injunctions could be identified: "Don't think!" (issued usually to a woman who is being programmed to be helpless so that she conforms to sex-role stereotypes), "Don't show anger!" (often issued in households where much hostility is beneath the surface), "Don't be idle!," "Don't have fun!" and so on.

It should be noted that injunctions and attributions often go hand in hand. They are often issued simultaneously, as when a parent says to a child, verbally or otherwise, "You are reserved and mild-mannered [attribution] and you don't show anger [injunction]." Together, injunctions and attributions survive childhood. Like a birthmark, they grow with the youngster, exerting a lasting influence on the course and destiny of his or her life.

The kind of influence exerted by injunctions and attributions can be called primary, for it does not involve the alteration of an existing set of beliefs, values, perceptions, or attitudes. Childhood and other times when a person is like a *tabula rasa* (e.g., when a person is uprooted and thrown into a completely alien culture or situation) are the only occasions when primary influence operates. Later in the chapter we shall discuss brainwashing, and you will see that one of the steps in that process is the stripping away of the prior identity of the individual so that he or she is in a psychological position roughly equivalent to that of the child. Once that point has been reached, the person can almost literally be born again as a new person.

Secondary influence, as implied, refers to influence exerted against the weight of countervailing forces. When a person already consciously believes herself to be "good" or "moral" and a preacher sets out to show her that she is a "sinner," then the preacher is attempting to exert secondary influence. Thus, the hypnotist's suggestions can be considered a form of primary influence, whereas the conventional persuasive speaker may be said almost invariably to be attempting to exert secondary influence.

Before turning to other ways groups influence us, you may wish to complete the following student activity.

Student Activity Option 1.4
Injunctions and Attributions

INSTRUCTIONS
This activity demands careful self-scrutiny. Its goal is to help you become aware of the way you define yourself, of the origins of that self-definition, and of the effects of that self-definition on your day-to-day behavior. In column one of this activity, you are asked to list four personal attributes, qualities, or characteristics that you possess. It would be best to select qualities that you regard as enduring, those that have been a part of you for as long as you can remember. They can be positive qualities (for example, friendly, intelligent, optimistic, genial), negative ones (moody, hot-tempered, stubborn, inhibited), or relatively neutral ones (athletic, conservative dresser, fashion-conscious).

In column two, you are asked to speculate as to how you learned to identify yourself as a person who possesses the corresponding quality in column one. For example, if you say you are shy in column one, in column two try to determine how you happened to come to think of yourself as shy. Some questions to ask: (1) Did any family members ever refer to you as shy? Do they continue to do so? (2) What do you and your family argue about most often? During explosive family arguments, if they occur, are labels applied to you or to other family members? What labels are they? (3) What is your recollection of what your mother, stepmother, or other adult in authority used to say about you most often when you were a child? Did she (or he) tend characteristically to refer to you in certain terms when talking to you or when talking to others about you? (For example, one college teacher, asked to complete this exercise, said he recalled that as a youngster, he wore glasses from the second grade onward. Each morning he would go off to private school, uniformed, wearing glasses, and carrying a leather school bag. He looked very erudite. His mother often joked that she was sending her "little professor" off to school every day. It came as no surprise to this teacher that the "little professor" had grown up to be a full-fledged college professor twenty years later!)

In column three, you are asked to discuss the pros and cons of your accepting the label you applied to yourself in column one. What are the advantages and disadvantages of defining yourself as shy (or helpful, fashion-conscious, thoughtful)? How does this label shape your life and experience? What kinds of things *can't* you do because they contradict the terms of your self-definition? What kinds of things *must* you do to retain that self-definition?

Note that these three columns appear in the book only as guidelines for making your own chart.

1 Personal Attributes, Qualities, or Characteristics	2 Origins	3 Effects
1. _____	_____	_____
	_____	_____
	_____	_____
2. _____	_____	_____
	_____	_____
	_____	_____
3. _____	_____	_____
	_____	_____
	_____	_____

Nonfamily groups

Not only families, but other groups of which we are a part, influence us in a variety of ways. It is a cliché to observe that members of groups tend to act alike, to dress alike, even to think alike. Picture a motorcycle gang. Consider your instructor and his or her colleagues. Look at your own peer group. The similarities in styles of behaving are obvious.

Social psychologists have studied what they refer to as the homogenizing effects of groups (Cartwright and Zander, 1968, p. 139). In a classic study replicated many times, Solomon Asch has demonstrated that a person's behavior can be influenced by group pressures to conform, even when those pressures are not exerted directly. The study involved a group composed of several members whose task it was to view four lines projected on a screen and to make a series of judgments concerning the length of a particular line compared to three other lines that were grouped together. In turn, each subject was asked to gauge which of the three lines was closest in length to that of the single line. There was a twist, however. A surprise was in store for one member, called the naive subject. Without the naive subject's knowing it, the other members of the group had been coached beforehand. They were told to agree during certain of the trials that one of the three lines was to be repeatedly and unanimously identified as the line closest in length to that of the single line, even though it was not. The naive subject was thus placed in the position of being part of a group whose membership frequently and unanimously offered judgments that contradicted the evidence of his or her own senses. Interestingly, most naive subjects yielded to the group pressure, despite the fact that at no point did group members interact verbally; nor was any pressure to conform exerted directly on the naive subject by the others. Replications of this study have shown that roughly three quarters of the subjects yield to the unanimous judgments of the others on at least one trial, and that one third of the naive subjects yield on at least half of the trials.

Clearly, groups exert influence. Consider especially that in the Asch study and its replications, group members are strangers to one another, and the matter is of little consequence. How much stronger the pressures to conform must be when people are among friends or acquaintances whose opinions they value and whose liking for them and respect for their judgment they cherish! And when the matter about which the judgment is made is important! And when pressure is applied to conform!

Grim testimony to the validity of Asch's findings was provided on Friday, November 17, 1978, when the Reverend Jimmie Jones, head of a cult of disaffected dropouts called the People's Temple, orchestrated a mass suicide in Guyana. Under duress, under the nearly hypnotizing influence of the then-psychotic Jones, and under the influence of tremendous group pressures to conform, over nine hundred persons took their lives. No rash, impulsive behavior can account for the debacle. The entire ordeal took several hours, as cyanide-laced Kool-Aid was methodically ladeled out of a huge vat and administered to People's Temple members. They obediently waited in line for their cup of poison as they watched their fellows stagger from the dispensary and writhe in agony as they slowly died. It is a scene almost beyond description, almost beyond comprehension. It would perhaps be less frightening if we could satisfy ourselves that everyone in the People's Temple was mad. But these were not insane people. They were, in fact, really not so very different from you and me. Poorer, perhaps, and more desperate; but really not so different. "What!" you ask. "Me? Certainly *I* wouldn't act like that!" Perhaps not, but the research of Asch and others suggests otherwise. Were all the Nazi concentration camp commandos madmen? All the kamikaze pilots? The lines between sanity and insanity blur at some point in the life of a group gone mad. Research in organizational behavior demonstrates that a person's membership and place in an organization, be it a corporation, a prison, or a religious group, strongly influences his or her perceptions, values, and behavior. When we discuss audiences (see Chapter 6), we shall return to the matter of the effects of group membership on audience behavior and on responses to persuasive messages.

Before leaving the subject of group influence on individual behavior, however, I want briefly to discuss the topic of brainwashing, for it is among the most mind-boggling and fascinating subjects within the area of attitude and behavior change. The term was coined by journalist Edward Hunter in his book *Brainwashing in Red China* (New York: Vanguard, 1951). Prompted by the bizarre changes in personality and behavior that characterized American soldiers captured by the Red Chinese during the Korean War (1950–1953), Hunter's book was designed to account for such phenomena as the apparently total rejection of their friends, family, and country by once-loyal and courageous American soldiers and officers. Surely, mused Hunter, some strange and mysterious power had been unleashed by the Red Chinese in order to bring about such radical transformations.

It took ten years of study, involving interviews with victims of brainwashing, before a reasonably thoroughgoing analysis of mind-bending was completed. In their 1961 book, *Coercive Persuasion* (New York: W. W. Norton), Edgar Schein, I. Schneier, and C. H. Barker identified several features characteristic of brainwashing. Among them are (1) intensive study of the dogma to be inculcated, in a setting completely sheltered and free from outside interference (a prison camp or retreat facility, for example); (2) public self-examination sessions, where change targets confess their wrongs and recount their flaws, hopes, fears, and disappointments; (3) intense group experiences that provide a great deal of support for changes in the desired direction; (4) in punitive settings such as prison camps—less obviously so in nonpunitive settings—the targets of change are ordinarily subjected to anxiety-provoking experiences, to endless harangues, and to incessant questioning.

It is a matter of tremendous concern to some that the techniques dubbed brainwashing in the 1950s and 1960s are now being utilized methodically by such seemingly innocuous change agents as religious cults and psychological self-help groups (Conway and Siegelman, 1978). No longer is coercive persuasion the sole province of psychological mind-benders in military uniforms. Now it is part of the stock in trade of nonmilitary persuaders. Think for a moment of the young adults who have dropped out of conventional society to don saffron robes and to chant ancient Eastern mantras. Or think of the urban-bred business executives who have left their jobs, families, and homes to raise sheep and vegetables on failing farms in Maine. Or, more specifically, think of heiress Patty Hearst, kidnapped by the Symbianese Liberation Army and subjected to psychological and physical assaults. Reborn again as Tanya, the machine-gun-toting revolutionary, Patty denounced her parents and participated in at least one major bank heist in the name of liberation. Think, too, of the thousands of young people who willingly attend weekend retreat seminars sponsored by esoteric religious groups, and who never return home. Swallowed up by the cult, they become, in effect, new people; they are lost to their families and social acquaintances forever. Deprogrammers, Ted Patrick the foremost among them, recognize that such radical transformations of self indicate that something immensely powerful altered the beliefs, values, and very personalities of these people. It is as though they had adopted an entirely new set of instructions for living. The term "deprogramming" itself suggests the mechanical and profoundly influential nature of the process.

One of the most insightful discussions of sudden personality change is provided by Conway and Siegelman, a team who combines extensive training in communication with sophisticated research and writing skills. Their recent book *Snapping* (Philadelphia: J. B. Lippincott, 1978) provides a tentative but impressive explanation of the phenomenon of personality rebirth. The influence of group pressure on inducing sudden personality change is critical, say Conway and Siegelman. In the proper group setting, systematically deprived of conventional reinforcements, subjected to a barrage of intellectual challenges and psychological assaults, provided with enthusiastic reinforcement for desired changes, and continually reminded that all this is being done in the interests of love, caring, concern, and brotherhood—under such conditions, each of us can snap. Each of us can experience a radical rupture with our past. Each of us can be made to shed our identities and to take on new ones. Each of us can become new selves. The rebirth experience is the same, according to Conway and Siegelman, whether it is the experience of the Apostle Paul on the road to Damascus, or of the Watergate conspirators (at least one of whom apparently underwent a religious rebirth experience while doing time for his part in the cover-up), or of a college student seduced by an Eastern cult, or of a business executive whose participation in a self-help group results in his dropping out.

As I noted previously, primary influence occurs when an individual is devoid of a set of attitudes, beliefs, or behavioral propensities. Whether these traits are absent by virtue of one's youth, or whether they are stripped away as a result of an intense barrage of criticism or contrived caring, an individual so characterized is extremely susceptible to influence from the outside. Almost literally, he or she becomes what others want. Like putty or clay, the human being under such circumstances is infinitely malleable.

Student Activity Option 1.5
Brainwashing

INSTRUCTIONS

Learn all you can about brainwashing and mind-control and report back to your instructor and the class. You may wish to focus on topics such as these: (1) brainwashing during the Korean War; (2) characteristics of brainwashing; (3) F. Lee Bailey's defense of Patty Hearst; (4) brainwashing in contemporary religious cults; (5) controversy surrounding deprogramming of excult members.

SUGGESTED READINGS

In addition to the authors and titles already mentioned, consider the following:

Koestler, Arthur (1941) *Darkness at Noon.* New York: Macmillan. Fiction, extremely well done.
Orwell, George (1949) *1984.* New York: Harcourt, Brace, & World. A classic work of fiction.
Patrick, Ted and Tom Dulak (1976) *Let Our Children Go.* New York: E. P. Dutton.

THE ETHICS OF INFLUENCE

We have thus far examined the influence exerted on you by individuals and by groups. Before turning to the influence exerted by organizations, it is important to comment on the ethical issues raised up to this point. One of the important lessons implied in our discussion of brainwashing and other forms of influence is that it is virtually impossible to consider the question of influencing others without simultaneously considering the ethical questions raised by such attempts. Who, after all, has the right to influence another? What are the limitations on such rights? Upon whom does responsibility lie for changes in behavior induced as a result of persuasive messages or other forms of influence? How far does this responsibility go? (Can Patty Hearst, for example, genuinely be considered responsible for her actions as Tanya?) What constraints might legitimately be imposed on persuaders? Are there limits to ethical persuasion? Is primary influence, as we have defined it, more bound by ethical constraints than secondary influence?

There are no easy answers to these questions. The cults claim their rights to recruit new members, to solicit funds, and to influence believers are protected by the Constitution. Their claims are endorsed by members who insist that their rights to religious freedom are infringed upon when distraught parents seek them out and hire people to deprogram them. (Some parents have even gone so far as to kidnap their own children, in order that the cultists can be brought into the hands of a person skilled in deprogramming.) Yet excult members who have been successfully deprogrammed state unflinchingly that the Constitution should provide no safeguard whatsoever for the activities of these groups. They claim, from experience, that their fellows have been rendered incapable of sound judgment. Hence, they say, a typical cult member's most earnest appeals to be left alone to practice his or her religion in peace should *not* be heeded; almost literally, such cultists are "not in their right minds." Again, who has the right to influence whom? Under what circumstances? With what limitations?

Student Activity Option 1.6
Ethics and Influence

INSTRUCTIONS
Engage in a discussion of the ethics of influencing others. What are your answers to the questions raised in the preceding paragraphs? If possible, one or more of the following options can be utilized as part of your class discussion:

1. Conduct a role-play or debate in which you and one of your classmates act as spokespersons for and against the right of cults to recruit members and to exert influence on them. You might wish to research this topic by utilizing the readings mentioned in the discussion on brainwashing and in Student Activity Option 1.5. For up-to-the-minute data, consult current newspapers and periodicals. For guidance on finding current source materials, consult your instructor.

2. Invite to your class one or more cult members or excult members. Discuss their experiences and raise your questions about the ethics of influence.

3. Perhaps a member of your college's teaching staff has done research in this subject area. Invite him or her to class for a free-flowing discussion.

THE INFLUENCE OF ORGANIZATIONS

The influence exerted by organizations can be approached from two angles: (1) the influence exerted on the organizational membership and (2) the influence exerted by organizations on nonmembers. The former has been the subject of intensive study, and some rather startling conclusions have been reported in the research. Chief among these is that your membership in an organization profoundly affects your beliefs, attitudes, values, perceptions, and behavior (Meyer et al., 1979). We have all had the unfortunate experience of encountering the person we dub the "typical bureaucrat." You may have encountered this person in the registrar's office, in the local department of motor vehicles, or in the medical clinic. He or she is curt, even rude. This typical bureaucrat insists that all forms required by the organization be completed exactly as specified in the instructions. This person is insensitive to the human factor in dealings with the people he or she serves; instead, priority is placed on the rules, on adhering to fixed procedures, and on making decisions exactly in accord with existing policies.

The adoption of rigid and unfeeling attitudes and the narrowing of one's perspective seems to be an occupational hazard of work in a formal organization. Membership itself, in other words, exerts persuasive influence on an individual. More narrowly, a person's place in the bureaucratic structure shapes one's views and molds one's behavior. So subtle and pervasive is this influence that it is hardly recognized. It is like living in a particular culture or society. We recognize its molding effects only when we step outside of it and see it objectively, perhaps as a result of prolonged travel. Under such circumstances, the return home can be an enlightening experience, for we see afresh, with the eyes of a child.

A second sort of organizational influence is that exerted on nonmembers. There are two varieties of such influence. The first is exerted without conscious planning; it simply happens to a nonmember who comes into contact with the organization. For example, your behavior as a patient in a hospital is shaped by the role expectations associated with being a patient. You are expected to play the "sick role," and to manifest behaviors associated with that role. You are expected, for instance, to assume a dependent position; you are supposed to do what you are told (like a "good patient"); you are supposed to trust blindly in the medical staff. To the extent that you conform to these role expectations, you are treated well by staff personnel. The pressures they exert on you serve to reward desired behaviors and to discourage undesired ones. The same dynamics operate in schools, where you are expected to listen, to take notes, to do what you are told.

Organizations can also attempt to exert influence on nonmembers consciously. Carefully planned attempts to shape the attitudes and behaviors of nonmembers is the stock in trade of the public relations and advertising industries. It is estimated that forty million dollars is spent each year by advertisers intent on influencing consumers. They engage personnel whose task it is to plan and implement elaborate campaigns, using a variety of media, with the sole purpose of affecting your preferences as a consumer. The investment of time, talent, and money that go into attempts to exert influence is almost beyond comprehension. And all this armamentarium is aimed, ultimately, at you, the individual consumer. Persuasion in such circumstances is as sophisticated and scientific as it can be made. An in-depth knowledge of persuasion is essential to persons whose careers revolve around mass persuasion. Can you and I afford to be less concerned and aware if we are to function as alert and sophisticated consumers?

Student Activity Option 1.7
The Ins and Outs of Advertising

INSTRUCTIONS
Working alone or in a small group, find out all you can about some aspect of advertising. Your goal is to report your findings to your instructor and your classmates. Consider such topics as these:

1. How much money is spent on advertising by a major corporation during any given calendar year? How much is spent on a particular product? How is money budgeted and allocated? (For example, how much of the advertising budget for a particular product goes toward market research? how much into planning advertising campaigns? how much into the production of ads? How much is spent on radio? TV? print media? Why is one medium favored over another in some cases but not in others?)

2. What are the most difficult problems advertisers face? Do particular products pose special problems? Are some markets harder to reach than others? What goals have advertisers set for themselves over the next decade?

3. How has advertising changed over the past decade? What new problems have confronted advertisers, and how have they dealt with them? What's new in advertising, and what's out of date?

4. Is there such a thing as a philosophy of advertising? Do different companies have different philosophies? Describe an advertising philosophy.

5. How is responsibility for advertising divided up within a company or corporation? What is the job of the product manager? What is the job of the advertising manager? Who decides what ads are run? How is the decision made?

6. How are advertisements tested for effectiveness?

SUGGESTIONS
1. Read and research using library source materials, for example, the following:
    a. Books
Backman, Jules (1967) *Advertising and Competition.* New York: New York University Press.
McGinnis, Joe (1969) *The Selling of the President.* New York: Trident Press.
Packard, Vance (1957) *The Hidden Persuaders.* New York: David McKay.
    b. Newspapers
        The New York Times (business section)
        The Wall Street Journal
    c. Periodicals
        Advertising Age   *Broadcasting*
        Incentive Marketing   *Printer's Ink*
        Forbes   *Advertising Agency*
        Business Week   *Tide*
        Sales Management: the Marketing Magazine

2. Use interviews (and prepare for them carefully). You might wish to interview a faculty member in your school's business division, or a corporate executive in a local company. Contact your local newspaper, radio, or television station and schedule an interview with the person in charge of the advertising department.

The following activity, also designed to increase your knowledge of the strategy that goes into planning advertising, may be of special interest to television addicts.

Student Activity Option 1.8
Television Log

INSTRUCTIONS

The goal of this activity is to heighten your awareness of the planning that goes into the production and airing of TV commercials. Why, for example, are paper towels advertised on one type of program but not on another? Why are long-playing record collections of hits of the 1950s advertised in the late afternoon but not during prime time? Why is a docile and bland housewife portrayed in one type of commercial, while an assertive and authoritative female corporate executive is shown in another?

To complete this assignment, you will need to set aside a few time periods (say, 2:30–3:00 P.M.; 5:30–6:00 P.M.; 7:30–8:00 P.M.; and 11:30 P.M.–12:00 midnight). For a period of several days, keep an accurate log of the kinds of ads that appear on TV during those times. Try different stations on different days. You might find it useful to organize a log book following the format suggested below, or use a format more complete or suitable to you. Consult with your instructor as to the particular form of log you use. For each ad, answer questions such as these:

1. What is the product or service being advertised?
2. What time of day does the ad appear?
3. On what sort of program?
4. How long is the ad?
5. How would you characterize the ad—musical, humorous, hard-sell, serious, fast-talking?
6. Who is portrayed in the ad—men only, women only, mixed group? Are there children, families, friendship groups?
7. How are characters portrayed in the ad? How are they dressed? What are they doing? Do members of each sex conform to sex-role stereotypes?
8. What persuasive appeals are used? Do you get the impression that the product or service being sold is linked to monetary gains? social rewards? sexual rewards? Why?
9. Try turning off the sound and watching the action alone. What overriding impressions remain? Are the sights exciting? What use is made of contrasting visual images in the ad?

After gathering your data, analyze the results quantitatively. Do certain products appear only during certain programs? With what frequency? How are women portrayed in the commercials you observed? Are they portrayed differently in one sort of commercial (say, home products) rather than another (such as pharmaceuticals)? With what degree of frequency are they portrayed in one way or another? Do ads aimed at different age groups utilize different appeals? Review the discussion of Maslow's hierarchy of needs (see Figure 1.1) to see whether certain needs are appealed to in a commercial aimed at one audience, while other needs are appealed to in ads aimed at other audiences. What do your data tell you about the planning and strategy that lie behind the roughly twenty thousand hours of commercial advertising that is aired on TV each week?

SUGGESTED READINGS
An interesting, and some say definitive book on the influence of television is

Comstock, George; Steven Chaffee, Nathan Katzman, Maxwell McCombs, and Donald Roberts (1978) *Television and Human Behavior.* New York: Columbia University Press.

Thus far in this chapter I have addressed the question of why to study persuasion from the point of view of the individual. As a sender of persuasive messages, you have seen how training in persuasion and persuasive speaking can help you meet your individual needs. You have been introduced to the importance of planning and strategy in persuasion. As a recipient of persuasive messages, you have begun see the many varieties of influence exerted on you by individuals, groups, and organizations.

Now we will broaden our purview to include not only the individual but society as well. What is the place of persuasion in the functioning of a society? What methods are used by different societies to make decisions and to resolve conflicts? Why does persuasion occupy a central place in democratic societies? What is required for a democratic society to succeed? In seeking answers to these questions, you will gain an appreciation of the importance of persuasion to the society in which you live.

II. *Persuasion and Democratic Society*

To survive, societies must fulfill certain prerequisites. They must provide a medium of communication. They must allow for the satisfaction of members' needs. They must possess or create unifying threads—symbols, myths, a core of common values, beliefs, and assumptions—all of which serve to bind the social group together. In addition, societies must possess a method for resolving conflicts and making decisions. For it is inevitable that in human intercourse, disagreements and problems will arise. How a society chooses to deal with conflict simultaneously reflects and determines its essential character. Here we will examine three methods for societal conflict resolution and decision-making: the method of authority, the method of reflection, and the method of democracy.* Each possesses unique features, and each has

---

*I am indebted to Wayne Minnick, *The Art of Persuasion,* 2nd ed.; Boston: Houghton Mifflin (1967) for these categories and the general thrust of the discussion.

strengths and weaknesses. We shall see that of the three, the method of democracy relies most heavily on persuasion.

THE METHOD OF AUTHORITY

The method of authority operates when one person or a small group makes the decisions. It is the method used by totalitarian states and fascist dictatorships. In such a society, the common person is held in contempt and thought incapable of making sound decisions. The masses, despised, are only of interest to the extent that they can be led. Hitler, for instance, characteristically referred to the masses as naive, juvenile, and eager to submit to overwhelming force (Waite, 1977, p. 53). Indeed, force is a key element in states and societies run by the method of authority; for upon force and threats of force the entire society turns.

Next to force, propaganda and demagoguery seem to be the chief tools of autocratic leaders to secure the support they desire. Who has not seen the huge propaganda posters plastered around public places in communist countries? Grotesque likenesses of the leader stare down at the common people from billboards and buildings, reminders of an ever-present big brother. Not all propaganda is of the silent pictorial sort. In Nazi Germany propaganda often took the form of huge, theatrically staged meetings. Held typically at night, lit eerily by live flames, and orchestrated to a frenzy by the mesmerizing orations of the Führer, such gatherings were punctuated by symbols, banners, and other tools of mob psychology. *"Ziegheil!"* thundered the excited masses at the conclusions of the meetings. And when the huge crowds dispersed, they carried with them an overwhelming sense of unity and mission.

History has shown that the method of authority works, at least for a time. It is capable of uniting a people. Decision-making is fast and efficient, for responsibility lies with one ruler or a very few. So long as the leader is not assassinated (succession crises are common in states run by the method of authority), so long as opposition is silenced, so long as news can be censored and the perceptions and beliefs of the people controlled by the government, the method can succeed. But it is precisely these stringent requirements that represent the Achilles heel of the method of authority. For even if we lay aside the ethical issue that necessarily arises in discussing oppression, practical disadvantages lead relentlessly to the demise of the method of authority. In societies of this sort, there invariably emerges a group of dissidents dedicated to the overthrow of the oppressive regime. Like an active volcano whose destructive potential lies not far below the surface, the force of this dissident minority is ready to erupt at any moment.

Because of the ever-present threat of radical uprisings, dictatorial rulers must invest huge amounts of time and energy to keep the opposition in check. This is particularly true in contemporary societies where the people are only oppressed by virtue of their being kept in ignorance, but where media and outside information can readily stir discontentment. It may further be speculated that the longer the oppressive regime remains in power, the more resources must be expended to maintain order. Eventually, the oppressive society fails, either because the weight of its own repressive structures bring it down, or because repressive policies have prevented the infusion of new ideas, or simply because it runs counter to the nature of human beings. We saw earlier that it is a natural tendency of humankind to grow and to realize itself. The method of authority can only succeed if the members of society can be stifled and checked. To succeed, it requires that a people remain perpetually ignorant, impoverished, and complaint.

Student Activity Option 1.9
Propaganda

INSTRUCTIONS
Learn all you can about propaganda. You may work independently or in a group. Consult with your instructor about the desirability of presenting your findings to the class. Consider such topics as these:
1. What is the relationship between persuasion and propaganda?
2. Is propaganda only used by authoritarian governments?
3. What is meant by the following terms: name calling, glittering generality, the big lie, transfer, testimonial, plain folks, card stacking, bandwagon?
4. What was the Institute for Propaganda Analysis? Why was it formed? What happened to it?

SUGGESTED READINGS

Primary
Hitler, Adolf (1933) *Mein Kampf*, Trans. E. T. S. Dugdale. Cambridge, Massachusetts: Riverside.
Machiavelli (1950/1531) *The Prince*, in *Discourse*, 2 vols. New York: Humanities.

Secondary
Brown, Roger (1958) *Words and Things*, New York: Free Press. See especially Chapter Nine, "Persuasion, Expression, and Propaganda." Brown raises some interesting questions about the relationship between propaganda and persuasion.
Kecskemeti, Paul (1973) "Propaganda," pp. 844–70 in Ithiel de Sola Pool, Frederick W. Frey, Wilbur Schramm, Nathan Maccoby, and Edwin B. Parker, eds. *Handbook of Communication*. Chicago: Rand McNally College Publishing Company.
Miller, Clyde R. (1959) "How to Detect Propaganda," pp. 33–38 in Harry Shaw, ed. *A Collection of Readings for Writers*, 5th ed. New York: Harper and Brothers. This essay originally appeared in a journal called *Propaganda Analysis* in November, 1937. Miller founded the Institute for Propaganda Analysis in that year.
Qualter, T. H. (1962) *Propaganda and Psychological Warfare*. New York: Random House.
Waite, Robert G. L. (1977) *The Psychopathic God: Adolf Hitler*. New York: Basic Books. Contains valuable information on Hitler's use of propaganda techniques. See especially Chapter Two, "The Intellectual World of Adolf Hitler." Check the index for sporadic references elsewhere in the volume.

ENRICHMENT MATERIALS

Discuss with your instructor the possibility of viewing the classic film, *The Triumph of the Will,* which deals with Hitler's propaganda techniques.

THE METHOD OF REFLECTION

The method of reflection is a form of idealistic democracy. It operates when conflicts are resolved and decisions are arrived at by careful investigation, full, objective discussion, and sober thought. Argument per se is avoided; the emphasis, rather, is on the search for an answer with which everyone concerned can be content. Consensus is the goal sought. The method of reflection involves neither negotiation nor arbitration, for in each of these self-interest and conflicts of interest are openly acknowledged. In the method of reflection, conflicted situations are viewed as mutual problems. Success of the method depends on the selflessness of the participants. The common good is paramount. Rationality prevails. Control of one's emotional involvements is of critical import. Often, the method is used by small groups (it becomes unwieldy and impractical in large groups) in conjunction with contemplative or prayerful pauses that sometimes permit appeals to a higher authority such as God. Hence, reflective methods of decision-making are typically found in sheltered religious groups, communelike social arrangements, and similar organizations. The Society of Friends (or Quakers), for example, uses this method to arrive at decisions.

The method of reflection is perhaps the prototype of conflict-resolution techniques that will be used in the future, when the human race will have matured to the point that rationality and cooperation can replace emotional involvements and self-interest. For the present, however, under most circumstances the method of reflection is too inefficient and time consuming to be used in isolation as the primary decision-making tool by the majority of contemporary groups and societies. It should be noted that modified forms of the relfective method are often used in conjunction with more conventional decision-making strategies. For example, when the Senate appoints a committee to investigate a problem, that committee might be said to be seeking an answer; once they have arrived at a decision, however, they report back to the full Senate. At that point, more conventional decision-making strategies are employed, with persuasive speeches given on both sides, followed usually by a vote that serves to resolve the matter.

Student Activity Option 1.10
Conflict and Consensus

INSTRUCTIONS

Learn about the different approaches to resolving conflicts used by religious organizations, communes, residential and sheltered treatment organizations, and other social groupings. Your instructor may be interested in having you present your findings to the class.

SUGGESTED READINGS

Boulding, Elise (1953) *My Part in the Quaker Adventure*. Philadelphia: Friends Central Bureau, Religious Education Committee.

Chase, Stuart (1951) *Roads to Agreement*. New York: Harper and Brothers.

Cooke, Morris L. (1951) "The Quaker Way Wins New Adherents," *New York Times Magazine* (July 17), 21ff.

Murphy, Richard (1944) "The Forensic Mind," pp. 451–71 in Donald C. Bryant, ed. *Studies in Speech and Drama in Honor of Alexander M. Drummond*. Ithaca: Cornell University Press. A classic discussion of the pros and cons of conflict resolution via debate and discussion. Murphy raises still-pertinent questions about the desirability of training in forensics and he answers them thoughtfully. The book in which this essay appears may not be readily available. See your instructor if you have a problem finding it.

SUGGESTIONS

1. Call a local congregation of the Society of Friends and ask whether you can observe a meeting of the Society. Write up your observations and impressions.

2. If you live in a commune or know someone who does, gather and report data on how decisions are made and conflicts are resolved. Are any unusual practices used? How conventional or unconventional are the methods used to solve problems within the group?

3. Consider contacting or perhaps visiting a local residential drug-abuse treatment program. How are conflicts resolved there? Who makes the decisions? How?

4. If you have an interest in parliamentary procedure, study this very sophisticated tool for managing conflicts and facilitating decision-making and problem-solving in groups. Consider looking at and reporting on one or more of the following readings.

Bosmajian, Haig A., ed. (1968) *Readings in Parliamentary Procedure*. New York: Harper and Row. This anthology contains many interesting primary and secondary source materials, among them Thomas Jefferson's *Manual of Parliamentary Practice,* compiled while Jefferson served as Vice President of the United States and president of the Senate (1797–1801).

Hellman, Hugo E. (1966) *Parliamentary Procedure*. New York: The Macmillan Company. Written for participating members in parliamentary organizations, this basic introduction, written by a professor of speech with over thirty years of experience as a parliamentarian, contains much that is of general interest and practical value.

Robert, Gen. Henry M. (1967 and many other dates) *Robert's Rules of Order*. Glenview, Illinois: Scott Foresman and Co. The classic guide used in organizations run according to the rules of parliamentary procedure. Contains all rules and regulations. The introduction provides some background and definitions.

THE METHOD OF PERSUASION

The method of persuasion is defined by Minnick (p. 10) as the "democratic technique for resolving conflict through the expression of majority opinion after consideration of conflicting views." This method of problem-solving pre-supposes the wisdom of the people. Unlike the method of authority, which holds the people in contempt, the method of persuasion rests on a democratic faith in the people. If they have access to all the necessary information and opinion, say the advocates of the method of persuasion, the people will make the best possible choice. It is this faith in the people that is written into the Constitution, where it is made clear that responsibility resides, ultimately, in the citizens who are governed. Their elected representatives are just that— paid servants of the people, who are selected to do their bidding. Though this basic truth is often lost sight of (indeed, this is one of the dangers in demo-cratic societies), it is a basic building block of all democracy.

Prerequisites for the method of persuasion

To work, the method of persuasion requires four things. First, basic free-doms such as the freedom of speech and of the press must be guaranteed. If they are not, how can the people have access to the information and opinions they need to make the best possible choices? It is a cherished tradition in all democratic countries to protect the right of all involved parties to have their say. However, the issue of censorship will remain a continuing issue, for in all organizations (and political societies are organizations) there is a tendency toward homogeneity. Groups tend to discourage minority opinion and to exert pressure on members to accept the majority view. Only by aggressively safeguarding the rights of the minority is society assured of the input that can only be provided by the person who sees things differently.

A second key requirement in the method of persuasion is the willingness on everyone's part to be bound by majority rule. For, unlike the method of reflection, which seeks unanimous agreement, the method of persuasion rec-ognizes that consensus is often impossible. Sometimes the issues are too complex to allow for easy answers. On other occasions, self-interest cannot be put aside for the good of the group. Nevertheless, it is a principle of demo-cratically run societies that once a decision has been made all members of the society are bound. The minority retains the right to argue against the deci-sion. We see this, for example, with the protestors who let their views be known on such issues as nuclear power, disarmament, and abortion. Despite their activities, however, the law binds all.

A third requirement of the method of persuasion is that all views must be presented by advocates of approximately equal skill. Have you ever witnessed a baseball game in which the two sides were unevenly matched? Perhaps the final score was 22–3 or something equally ludicrous. Games like that suggest the importance of equal skill in cooperative-competitive efforts. Unless people are addressed by speakers of approximately equal skill, those who ultimately decide an issue are deprived of an opportunity to make a sound judgment. They are subjected to grossly uneven oratory; the very unevenness of what they heard clouds their judgment. What does this imply? In my mind it means that a basic level of speech-making ability is an entitlement of citizens of democratically run nations, like social security benefits and unemployment insurance. It is not a privilege, it is a right to which you and I are entitled. Guaranteeing the right not only enriches the life of the person, it helps ensure that this nation and others like it will continue to make effective use of the method of persuasion.

The fourth requirement is that all parties be willing to admit and to take into account all the sound arguments on both sides of an issue. This means that citizens must remain sufficiently objective at least to hear out those who disagree with them. There is an element of trust here: Democratic societies run on the principle that if you hear the arguments for and against a given issue, you will weigh them, consider their relative worth, and consider what you have heard in arriving at a decision. This is not always easy. Some people are too closed to do this. "I've already made up my mind," they say. "Don't confuse me with the facts." Such persons live by a set of attitudes that run counter to the spirit of democracy. For the democratic method requires that citizens allow themselves to be exposed to a variety of opinions and facts; only then are the people in the position of making the best possible choice.

The method of persuasion avoids the pitfalls of the methods of authority and of reflection. It does not rely on a dictatorial leader or small group; as a result, continuity of rule is ensured. It does not rely on propaganda and demagoguery to influence public opinion, for faith in free and open deliberation eliminates the need to mislead. It is not so inefficient as the method of reflection. Provision is made in democratic society for the majority to bind the minority. The method of persuasion does not place unrealistic demands on people; it does not require that all self-interest be put aside or that extraordinary analytical and critical abilities be employed. It lends itself to decision-making under time pressure, performed by a large group. It allows for unified action without requiring that everyone agree.

Weaknesses of the method of persuasion

Despite these advantages, the method of persuasion has flaws. Despite its efficiency compared with that of the method of reflection, democratic decision-making is not terribly efficient. The minority, after all, must be heard. In the long run, however, allowing dissent and criticism yields greater gains than the short-term advantages that follow when dissenting minorities are silenced. Another flaw already noted is that democratic societies can easily lose sight of the fact that elected officials are the servants of the people rather than their rulers.

Democratic societies also depend on the willingness of the people to become involved in the decision-making process. When the people consider themselves powerless, or unable to influence decisions effectively, or simply too ignorant to make good decisions, they hand over to their representatives the right to make decisions for them. They forfeit their right to rule themselves. In a complex world, with information expanding at incredible rates of speed, the burden of being a citizen in a democratic society becomes heavier almost daily. Along with the rights you possess by virtue of your citizenship in a democracy, there are responsibilities: to inform yourself, to vote, to prepare yourself to influence others in the best and most ethical way you know. This course is quite literally an important training ground for life in a democracy.

The method of persuasion has other weaknesses. Merton and Nisbet (1976) talk about mediated perception, the phenomenon whereby highly visible problems that receive extensive media coverage—a plane crash that kills three hundred people, for example—attract our attention although more serious problems of lower visibility go unacknowledged. Our attention is diverted to an immediate problem of high visibility and away from more serious problems. In 1976, for example, 50,000 people died in individual auto accidents—very few of which secured the attention of the national media—while only 1,300 people died in airplane accidents, though these were usually widely covered. My point is not to play down the importance of the 1,300 deaths, but only to illustrate that our awareness of the seriousness of the problem is disproportionate to its actual severity and scope, because of mediated perception.

Merton and Nisbet also mention dangers to democratic decision-making that arise from a too-narrow perspective on social and political problems. Because we tend to be self-centered, we remain oblivious to the existence of problems that do not affect us. We may even support a policy that works to our advantage despite the fact that many people suffer as a result. I don't know too many rich people who argue for an end to tax loopholes, do you? So long as you and I are employed, are we likely to become really concerned about rising unemployment?

Another problem with democratic approaches to societal management is that we tend not to recognize as problems circumstances and crises-in-the-making that don't have real or immediate consequences for us. Nuclear contamination, for example, is something we cannot taste, see, or feel. Its effects are not experienced, in most cases, for many years. The same is true for the current energy crisis. How many people had the foresight ten or twenty years ago to recognize the folly of wasting resources as though there were no end to them?

It would be possible to extend for many pages a discussion of the imperfections of the method of democracy. But despite its flaws, there is no doubt in my mind that it is the best of the methods for resolving conflicts and making decisions. In an imperfect world, it is as close as the human race has yet come to arriving at an adequate tool for societal management. And despite the growth of totalitarianism, there can be no doubt that the trend toward democracy will continue.

The persuasive speaker will retain a central place in fashioning the world to come. In fact, I can see no circumstances in which the speaker will fade into oblivion. Quite the contrary, persuasion and the tools of persuasive discourse will exert increasing influence in the decades and centuries ahead.

Student Activity Option 1.11
Persuasion and Democracy

INSTRUCTIONS
Working alone or with a partner or group, examine one or more facets of the relationship between persuasion and democracy. Consult with your instructor on the form of a report to be made in writing or to the class.

1. Investigate the areas of free speech, freedom of the press, and minority rights. Should the Nazi party be allowed to conduct marches on the streets of U.S. cities? Should allegedly obscene books and periodicals be banned? Do parents have the right to forbid their children to read books that the parents consider obscene but that have been approved for use in the schools by the local school board? Do the courts have the right to jail reporters who refuse to give the names of their sources for news stories? Consult recent periodical and newspaper indices and read the pros and cons on these or similar issues. Consider a classroom debate on these topics. Deliver a persuasive speech that is responsive to one or more of these issues.

With the consent of your instructor, interview or invite to class a local lawyer, legislator, judge, or government official. Engage this person in a discussion of the issues of freedom of speech and democracy.

SUGGESTED READINGS
Mill, John Stuart (1873) *On Liberty, Representative Government, The Subjection of Women,* with an introduction by Millicent G. Fawcett. London: Oxford University Press. See especially Chapter Two, "On the Liberty of Thought and Discussion."

FREE SPEECH, a newsletter published three times a year by the Commission of Freedom of Speech, Speech Communication Association, 5205 Leesburg Pike, Falls Church, Virginia 22041. This newsletter contains interesting essays and reports on current issues of freedom of speech.

2. Research the historical perspective on persuasion and democracy. Examine the historical relationship between democratic institutions and persuasive communication. From ancient to modern times (or during a specific time period upon which you and your instructor agree), how have the two been related?

SUGGESTED READINGS
Barbu, Zevedei (1956) *Democracy and Dictatorship: Their Psychology and Patterns of Life.* New York: Grove Press.

Kennedy, George (1963) *The Art of Persuasion in Greece.* Princeton, New Jersey: Princeton University Press.

SUMMARY

This chapter was designed to answer the question "Why study persuasion?" and to respond to two of the most frequently voiced objections to its study. In the first part of the chapter, I showed that persuasion is part of your everyday life. As a sender and as a recipient of persuasive messages, your familiarity with the principles of persuasion can be extremely helpful. It can increase your sophistication in planning and delivering persuasive messages; it can heighten your critical capacities as a consumer of persuasive messages. I also showed how skill in persuasion is essential to meeting your individual needs— for belonging, esteem, or self-actualization. You were invited to begin the process of strategic planning in persuasion.

The last section of the first part dealt with the many ways in which others attempt to influence you, in a range of settings from interpersonal relationships to mass communication. I discussed the influence of individuals, the role of group influence in shaping attitudes and behavior, and the influence exerted by formal organizations on members and nonmembers. I distinguished between primary and secondary influence and raised the question of ethics in persuasive communication. You were encouraged to participate in the process by which you become aware of the influence exerted on you by others.

In the second part of the chapter, I indicated the place of persuasion in a free society. Persuasion was shown to be a major decision-making tool in a democratic society. The superiority of the method of persuasion to other social tools, such as the method of authority and the method of reflection, was shown. I discussed the prerequisites to effective use of the democratic method in resolving conflicts and showed the value of training in persuasion for participation in democratic decision-making.

In the next chapter, we turn to consideration of these questions: How do you learn skills such as persuasive speaking? What process is followed in learning a skill? You will see that there is a predictable learning sequence followed in the life of the individual as well as in the life of the human species. You will be introduced to the most beneficial kind of learning: the analytical and theoretical approach.

Chapter 2

How Do You Learn to Speak Persuasively?

How do you learn skills? Chances are excellent that you know how to ride a bike, roller skate, drive a car. You can read, speak, and write English. There are a thousand other skills you take for granted in your day-to-day living. Only when illness or accident strikes do you realize the complexity and difficulty of the behaviors you engage in so unself-consciously. Then you begin thinking carefully about how you acquire, and reacquire, skills.

This chapter is intended to offer some thoughts on learning in general and on skills learning in particular. I present an original model of skills acquisition in which I focus on persuasive speaking. The model gives you the chance to learn some important facts about the history of training in persuasion while gaining an appreciation of the value of the contemporary analytical and theoretical approach to training in persuasive speaking. You will be introduced to key elements in the theories of persuasion, covered in greater depth in Chapter Four. And you will see the close relationship between theory, practice, and criticism.

LEARNING

Ask a child you know how he or she learned to read. My daughter replied to this query, "Mommy taught me, and my teacher in the first grade." Is the answer satisfactory? To an eight-year-old, perhaps; but you and I ought to pause a moment and reflect. What exactly is involved in the process of learning? What part is played by the learner? by the learner's environment? What internal changes occur as learning takes place? It is not yet possible to give a detailed answer to these questions, but I wish to suggest approaches to answering them. My intent is to help you recognize that in learning to speak persuasively, you are engaged in a process, a little understood one, and that there are qualitative differences in different approaches to learning persuasive skills.

Different fields study the way people learn. Philosophers study it from their own perspective. Epistemologists (students of the branch of philosophy that studies the origin, nature, and methods of human knowing), for example, see learning as involving the input of raw data through the senses; the raw data are then worked upon by the intellect. As a result of such operations as conceptualization and abstraction, the unknown becomes known.

Psycholinguists and students of cognitive development study learning from the vantage point of concept-acquisition and the development of rules for assimilating, processing, storing, organizing, and expressing information. Jean Piaget, for example, is known the world over for his in-depth studies of the cognitive development of children. He has sought to determine how the child's capacities develop for intelligence, language, reasoning, and other functions. While his detailed and meticulous observations are fascinating, and his careful explanations are complex and worthy of your closer scrutiny, here I will suggest only that according to Piaget, the child's capacities develop as the youngster assimilates new experiences. This assimilation results in the expansion of prior capacities.

According to Piaget, the child is continually adapting to the world. These adaptations grow increasingly complex as the youngster's behavioral repertory expands. For example, an infant sees an object, grasps at it, and tries to mouth it. As the weeks and months pass, however, the child learns to isolate and to refine these functions. The infant learns as a result of unsuccessful attempts to suck that all things are not suckable. The youngster no longer clutches at objects but learns simply to touch them. He or she explores with hands, eyes, and mouth. The child comes to perceive reality more accurately, to make important distinctions. Over time, even more sophisticated perceptions are made. He or she learns to recognize some objects. The dual process of assimilation and accommodation operate. An attempt is made to assimilate all new events into preexisting cognitive structures (for example, "objects are suckable"); when they cannot be assimilated, accommodation occurs. The inner organizational structures expand ("unsuckable objects exist"). As a result of continued adaptations, the child's repertory of concepts, capacities, and skills grows. With that growth come increasingly successful attempts to cope with the world adequately. The process of growth is cyclical: Experiences lead to refined capacities that, in turn, make new experiences possible.

The process briefly described here is true of adult living as well. Each of us is always growing and expanding. You are constantly increasing your repertory of coping mechanisms. As you enter the worlds of school, work, and marriage, you will necessarily continue learning. Like the infant, you will engage in the reciprocal processes of assimilation and accommodation. Although the process by which you learn remains largely unself-conscious and little understood, work by researchers like Piaget is helping to unlock the mysteries of learning.

American psychology has placed great emphasis on learning. One of the cornerstones of contemporary psychology is called learning theory. This theory emphasizes the importance of the environment in shaping behavior. Because learning theory undergirds a number of theories of attitude change, let us spend a moment reviewing its two main varieties: operant conditioning and classical conditioning.

Operant conditioning

In a brilliant experiment conducted four decades ago, B. F. Skinner showed that a rat could learn to perform a specific behavior as a result of reinforcement received from the environment. A hungry rat was placed in a box that contained a lever. When pressed, the lever allowed a pellet of food to fall into the box. At first, the rat ran aimlessly around the box. By accident, however, it soon touched the lever and the food fell in. This served to reinforce the behavior of pressing on the lever. After many such happenings, the rat learned to press the lever to get food. The random behavior (running aimlessly around the box) was replaced by a specific behavior. Specific behavior like this Skinner has called "operant" behavior because it operates on the environment so as to produce a reinforcing result. Note that at no point does Skinner speak of the rat's behaving *purposefully* or *intentionally*. Such concepts Skinner would call prescientific. He says we need not impute purposefulness to the rat in order to explain the behavior; we need only report what we can observe—namely, that the specific operant behavior is engaged in because it produces a reinforcing event from the environment.

The principles of operant conditioning have won considerable popularity. For example, in child-rearing, parents are advised to reinforce desirable behaviors and not to reinforce others. "Ignore it," says the husband to the wife when the child utters an objectionable word. By their ignoring—i.e., not reinforcing—it, the child is not encouraged to repeat the behavior. Chances are your instructor too uses principles of operant conditioning in the classroom. If a student answers a question incorrectly, for example, it is likely that the instructor will comment briefly and either make the correction, ask someone else to do so, or call on another student. Such a response is designed not to reinforce behavior the instructor wishes to extinguish. When you give your speeches, the instructor will most likely reinforce behavior he or she considers desirable—praising a particularly effective introduction or complimenting you on a fine bit of research if your speech shows that you really did your homework. By such responses, your teacher will employ the principles of operant conditioning in order to increase the frequency of certain behaviors and decrease the frequency of others.

Classical conditioning

In classical conditioning, learning is said to occur when a particular stimulus comes to elicit a given response as a result of its having been linked up with another stimulus that automatically elicits the response. Assume an unconditioned stimulus (UCS) that elicits an unconditioned response (UCR) without prior learning. For example, a loud noise (UCS) elicits a startle response (UCR)—you hear a crash and you jump, blink your eyes, experience increased heartbeat and other reactions. Now assume a neutral stimulus, one that does not produce a startle response; it may be pleasant or it may have no special meaning for you. For argument's sake, assume a soft romantic tune that you find pleasing. Now if I were an experimenter who wished to condition you to jump each time you heard the pleasant melody, I would pair this neutral stimulus with the unconditioned stimulus (UCS), namely, the crash. I would subject you to a number of experiences in which the crash and the pleasant melody were linked together. Over time, you would come to associate the two, so that each time you heard the melody you would expect to hear the crash. When that link-up is made, the neutral stimulus becomes a conditioned stimulus (CS), and it begins to elicit the unconditioned response by itself. That is, each time you hear the melody, you begin to grow anxious, expecting the crash. You experience increased heartbeat, you blink your eyes, you may even jump. At this point, learning may be said to have occurred. The conditioned stimulus (CS) produces the unconditioned response (UCR). Diagrammatically, this can be portrayed as shown in Figure 2.1:

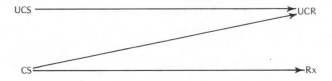

UCS = unconditioned stimulus (crash)
UCR = unconditioned response (startle response)
CS   = conditioned stimulus (pretty melody)
Rx   = response(s) elicited by the neutral stimulus prior to its becoming a conditioned stimulus (e.g., enjoyment at hearing a pretty melody)

Figure 2.1. Classical Conditioning

Learning theory is far more sophisticated and complex than I have implied here; however, my intent was simply to introduce you to the rudiments while laying the groundwork for later discussions of attitude change theories that find their roots in learning theory (see Chapter Three). It was also my purpose to show one way in which the process of learning is explained. We will now look more closely at the process by which skills are learned.

Student Activity Option 2.1
Learning

INSTRUCTIONS
If you are interested in the process of learning as approached by different disciplines, consider these alternative activities:

1. For a philosophical view of learning, read one or more of the following works, each of which grapples with the problem of how humankind learns:

Primary Sources
Descartes, Rene (1946) *A Discourse on Method,* translated by J. Veitch. Chicago: Open Court Publishing Company.
——— (1946) *The Meditations,* translated by J. Veitch. Chicago: Open Court Publishing Company.
James, William (1914) *Pragmatism.* New York: Longmans, Green and Company.
Kant, Emmanuel (1950) *Critique of Pure Reason,* translated by Norma K. Smith. New York: Humanities Press.
Leibnitz, Gottfried (1957) *Discourse on Metaphysics and Monadology,* translated by G. Montgomery. Chicago: Open Court Publishing Company.
Spinoza, Benedict de, "On the Improvement of Understanding," in Benedict deSpinoza, *Philosophy of Benedict deSpinoza,* translated by R. Elwes. New York: Tudor Publishing Company.

Secondary Sources
Collins, James (1954) *A History of Modern European Philosophy.* Milwaukee: The Bruce Publishing Company.
Durant, Will and Ariel Durant (1933) *The Story of Philosophy.* New York: Delta Books, Time Inc.
Maritain, Jacques (1952) *The Range of Reason.* New York: Charles Scribner's Sons.
Russell, Bertrand (1945) *A History of Western Philosophy.* New York: Simon and Schuster.

2. If the work of Jean Piaget intrigues you, consider one or more of the following:

Piaget, Jean (1963) *The Origins of Intelligence in Children,* translated by Margaret Cook. New York: W. W. Norton.
——— (1954) *The Construction of Reality in the Child,* translated by Margaret Cook. New York: Basic Books.
——— (1960) *The Psychology of Intelligence,* translated by Malcoln Piercy and D. E. Berlyne. Totowa, New Jersey: Littlefield, Adams and Company.

3. If you are interested in learning theory and contemporary psychology, see, for example:

Chomsky, Noam (1965) "A Review of B. F. Skinner's *Verbal Behavior,*" pp. 547–578 in Fodor, Jerry and Jerrold Katz, eds. *The Structure of Language.* Englewood Cliffs, New Jersey: Prentice-Hall. Chomsky's critical review is a classic critique of behavior theory. Basic essential reading for the student of linguistics.
Mowrer, O. H. (1960) *Learning Theory and Behavior.* New York: John Wiley and Sons.
Skinner, B. F. (1938) *The Behavior of Organisms.* New York: Appleton-Century-Crofts.
Skinner, B. F. (1971) *Beyond Freedom and Dignity.* New York: Alfred A. Knopf.
——— (1957) *Verbal Behavior.* New York: Appleton-Century-Crofts.
Thorndike, E. L. (1911) *Animal Intelligence: Experimental Studies.* New York: Macmillan.

Below is a Student Activity Option that has direct pertinence for this class. Its focus is learning as it will occur in your classroom. I recommend that you take a moment to complete the option.

Student Activity Option 2.2 _____
Learning Persuasive Speaking

INSTRUCTIONS
Read and answer the questions below. It is important to be as specific as possible. For example, in answer to the first question, "Why are you taking this course?" a response such as "to learn" would be too general to be useful for the purposes of this activity. You need to state specifically what you want to learn, for example, "I want to be able to convince my sorority sisters to elect me their president." The more concrete and specific your answers are, the more helpful they will be to you and the better they will serve the purposes of this exercise. A word of caution: This activity requires careful thought and self-scrutiny. Flippant answers and superficial responses have no place here.

1. Why are you taking this course? (Please limit your answer to no more than four reasons.)

_____
_____
_____
_____

2. What do you want to get out of this course? (Please be specific.)

_____
_____
_____

3. What do you see your instructor's role as being? How will he or she help you get what you want out of this course?

_____
_____
_____

4. Does your instructor share your perceptions of his or her role? If not, where do the two of you disagree in perceptions and expectations?

_____
_____
_____

5. What do you see your role as being? What can you do to help yourself get out of this course what you want?

_____
_____
_____

6. What can your classmates do to help you get out of this course what you want? What are your expectations of them?

_____

_____

_____

7. Does your class agree on the role of classmates in helping students get out of this class what they want? If not, where do you disagree?

_____

_____

8. How can this book help you get out of this class what you want? What purposes do you see the book serving?

_____

_____

_____

SUGGESTIONS

An open discussion of the class's answers will probably be scheduled by your instructor. If not, I recommend you meet informally with a number of students to discuss your answers.

Your answers may vary sharply. Some students may openly declare that they are taking the course because it fits into their schedule of classes. Others may be enrolled to satisfy a prerequisite for another more interesting course. Still others may be enrolled because friends have told them it's a good course. Such answers are perfectly acceptable. What matters most, aside from honesty, is that you make the best possible use of the time you are going to spend here. Hence, question two is a request for more specific goals. In effect, it says, "Now that you are here—perhaps by chance—what will you seek to make of the experience?"

The questions divide themselves into two categories. The first group (questions one, two, and eight) has to do with your own goals and motivations. These will be our special concern on the pages to follow. The second group of questions (numbers three through seven) is included to make it possible for you, your instructor, and your classmates to come to some basic agreements regarding allocation of responsibility, mutual expectations and shared purposes. This kind of learning, called contract learning, is based on the premise that the most productive educational experiences occur when all parties know what they are setting out to accomplish and what is—and is not—expected of each of them.

Chances are that when you formulated your personal objectives for this course, you indicated that you wanted to learn how to do certain things—how to talk your roommate into cleaning up, how to persuade your boss to give you a raise, how to convince your parents that young women aren't failures if they aren't engaged by the time they leave college. If you were consistent in your thinking, you likely indicated that this textbook, and your instructor as well, ought to provide you with prescriptive advice on how to achieve your goals. Asked to complete this one of my students wrote, "I want you to teach me persuasive techniques and methods." Her request is not unreasonable. Like yours, her comment reflects a fairly sophisticated view of how people learn things. Nevertheless, it is important to examine just how beneficial it would be for your instructor or this text to provide you with prescriptions.

Let's examine the way people learn skills, and let's take as our main focus persuasive speaking skills; for the question of how to teach them has occupied scholars, philosophers, and educators for literally thousands of years.

LEARNING SKILLS

Psychologists have unearthed several principles that apply to the learning skills. I will briefly summarize them here and show their applicability to learning to speak persuasively. Following our brief discussion, we will turn to the model of skills learning about which I spoke earlier. As you read the discussion here, I recommend that you recall your own experiences in learning basic skills. Do the principles discussed here jibe with your own experiences? How accurately do these principles reflect your own thinking about skills training? Consider, too, the specific applications of these principles to your individual learning in this class.

Principle One: Skills acquisition involves what is called multiple response learning. We proceed from simple responses that appear singly, to patterns or sequences of responses. For example, in learning to read, you begin with recognizing letters. Only after you know letters can you recognize words, and later phrases, sentences, and paragraphs. One of the distinguishing features of the early reader is that he or she reads word by word, rather than in phrases, thought groups, or sentences. To consider another example, learning to drive involves many varities of responses, all of which must be coordinated. The experienced driver acts automatically, but think about how many sophisticated skills are involved in driving: the visual and motor skills of exerting just enough pressure on the steering wheel to turn the car neither too much nor too little; the skills of responding to a red light or stop sign by removing your foot from the accelerator, placing it on the brake, and exerting the proper amount of pressure for a smooth stop; the elaborate set of skills involved in shifting gears. The list could go on. However, I think you can already appreciate the extent to which many skills must be coordinated in the act of driving.

Multiple response learning only works when the single, isolated skills are mastered before proceeding to more sophisticated and interconnected sets of skills. In learning to speak persuasively, therefore, you will likely begin—indeed, you have already begun—by mastering the more basic skills of language usage, grammar, and such. Once you are able to put a message together, the basic skills of speaking before an audience have to be learned. You learn to stand in front of a group, to speak loudly, slowly, and clearly. You learn to maintain eye contact with your audience. Chances are that each of these skills came to you only at great cost. You were probably tongue-tied at the outset and could not look at your audience. Your voice was too soft and you spoke rapidly out of nervousness. Many, many other basic competencies had to be acquired before you could conceive of actually influencing your audience as a result of the words you utter.

In this course, these basic competencies are assumed. The responses you will learn to coordinate here are more sophisticated ones; for example, the preparation of arguments on a controversial topic to be given to an audience opposed to your position (see Chapter Six). The same building-block approach will be used, however: You will proceed methodically from lower-level skills developed in isolation to more sophisticated sets of skills used in sequence.

Principle Two: More efficient learning occurs when several short practice sessions, spaced fairly widely apart, are substituted for a very few long sessions cramped together. The human brain and musculature system seem to require respite from the tasks imposed on them by skills learning. A bit of downtime is needed to rest up from the exertions involved in forming new response patterns and new habits. During this downtime the body has a chance to assimilate new learnings and to confirm new ways of thinking and behaving.

This is the reason why cramming for tests is an inefficient way of learning. To *really* learn, it is important to study regularly. In this class especially, cramming does not work. Perhaps you can commit to memory a number of historical names and dates; however, just as you cannot cram for a driving test, you cannot cram for a speech. For most people, several regular, brief rehearsal sessions are more beneficial than one or two hours of intense rehearsal.

Principle Three: More efficient learning of complex skills is aided by partialization. The complex process must be broken down into component parts and each component practiced separately. Only then can most benefit be derived from combining the parts.

As a novice student speaker, you were given the chance to partialize the complex tasks in speech-making. Rather than being asked to produce a finished product on your initial try, you likely learned first how to research a speech, how to construct an outline, how to prepare introductions, transitions, and conclusions, and so on. To the extent that it was possible, your instructor partialized the skills involved in learning to give speeches.

Principle Four: Imitation of experts is a valuable way of learning skills. "Here! Watch the way I do it!" is a directive you've probably heard, whether you were learning to paint or to cook. It's valuable to learn from the experience and expertise of others. While I have some reservations about the value of imitation (it can stifle creativity and produce carbon copies rather than original creations), there is no doubt that judicious imitation has value.

Principle Five: Actual performance is vital to learning. It has been observed that there are two kinds of people in the world—those who *do*, and those who

talk about those who do. In other words, there is an enormous distinction between performing a task and commenting on others' performance. Another
way of putting this is to say that learning by *doing* is superior to learning by
talking about. Needless to say, in this book and in this course, performance
is built in. Your instructor and I recognize that you can learn the skills of
persuasive speaking best by actually preparing and delivering persuasive
speeches.

Principle Six: Immediate feedback is superior to delayed feedback. After taking a test, don't you talk about it to other students? "What'd you get for
number three?" you ask in a hushed whisper after you've left the classroom.
"How'd you do?" is a question on everyone's lips. It is human to desire feedback and confirmation. In acquiring skills, there is value in securing commentary on the quality of your performance as soon as possible after it is completed. Hence, in this course, opportunities will be provided for you to get
feedback from your instructor and classmates. In most cases, this commentary
will follow your speech immediately. By listening as your instructor and classmates identify areas of strength and weakness in your performance, you will
be better able to build on identified strengths and to make needed corrections
next time.

I always emphasize in my classes that comments on student speeches are
designed to facilitate learning. They are not intended to belittle or to stigma-
tize. The classroom, in my opinion, is a learning laboratory. There, experiments in behaving can be conducted, new ways of acting can be tried out. In-
novation and risk-taking are encouraged, for without them, a person never
changes or grows. School is actually a sheltered environment; the stakes are
relatively low, compared with the possible results of risks taken in life on the
outside. For instance, getting a C in a course, while certainly not a cause for
celebration, is far less tragic than losing a job at 45. My point is that I hope
you will use this class an an opportunity to try new things, to take risks. The
feedback you get will help you determine the success or failure of the experiments you try. However, far better to experiment here and perhaps not
succeed than to stand pat and never grow or learn.

*Principle Seven: It is easier to learn something when you experience it as
meaningful.* Did you ever wonder why learning some tasks goes smoothly and
seems almost effortless, while learning others is a slow, painstaking affair? Do
you play baseball? tennis? Can you drive? Such skills as these, while requiring
effort to acquire, were doubtless fun to learn because you wanted to learn
them. Other skills, while no more difficult, likely posed far greater problems.
Were you forced to take music lessons as a child? Did an unenlightened gym
teacher make learning to play basketball a chore? Can you type well? Chances
are you experienced certain skills as less desirable. Consequently, it was an
effort to acquire them, if you did at all.

Your learning to speak persuasively will be influenced in no small measure
by your intrinsic motivation. Do you want to learn? What is the place of persuasive speaking in the future you project for yourself? How important is it to

you that you learn to speak persuasively? Your answers to these questions will have an enormous impact on the quality of your experiences in this class. There is also another angle to the question of meaningfulness and self-motivation—the topics about which you choose to speak. For your speeches to have maximum impact, it is important that you talk about subjects that have meaning to you. You will learn best how to reach an audience when you genuinely feel a need to get across to them. (For more on the subject of topic choice, see Chapter Six.)

Principle Eight: Rewards teach more quickly than punishments. Researchers have found that positive reinforcement is more effective in shaping behavior than is negative reinforcement. Punishment for example, may serve to confuse the learner more than it serves to facilitate the learning process. For one thing, the learner may fail to see the connection between the physical or psychological pain inflicted and the behavior that prompted it. Further, the learner may come to dislike the skill to be learned if he or she associates it with punishment.

This principle has very clear implications for this class. I hope your instructor agrees with me that you should not be penalized for less-than-outstanding work. Grading of speeches, if it is done at all, is best done tactfully. Terms for grading should be worked out by you, your instructor, and the class. To the extent that it is humanly possible, grades ought not to serve as punishment. Far more valuable for your learning is precise praise about clearly identified elements in your performance. What you do well should be the central theme of commentaries referring to your speech.

Principle Nine: To learn best, a person must be ready. Readiness refers to a variety of component elements: physical and intellectual maturity, coordination, and psychomotor skills, to name a few. It can also refer to psychological preparedness. You have probably had the experience of advising someone in response to a request for help, only to have the person become angry or hurt and say, "You know I didn't want to hear that!" Such a response indicates that people must be ready to hear before they can listen.

In this class, the principle of readiness refers not only to course prerequisites but to your attitude toward being here. Are you ready to learn? Are you receptive to your instructor's comments and to those of your classmates? Are you willing to hear what people tell you about your effectiveness as a persuader? If not, it is unlikely that this course will do you much good.

Student Activity Option 2.3
Grading

INSTRUCTIONS

Engage in a discussion with your instructor and classmates about the matter of grading in this class. If possible, arrive at a class contract, in which criteria for grades are spelled out precisely. Your instructor may wish to distribute contract forms and negotiate individual contracts. An open and freewheeling discussion can do much to clear the air at the outset. Here are some questions to consider in your discussion:

Course Grade
1. How will your course grade be determined?
2. How much will speeches count in computing the final grade? speech outlines? written assignments? class participation? Student Activity Options?
3. What criteria will be applied in arriving at grades for written work?
4. How will speech grades be arrived at?
5. Who, if anyone, will grade speeches?
6. Who will provide the criteria for grading written and oral work? (I have successfully conducted class discussions aimed at arriving at criteria to be applied. Is that possible to do in your class?)
7. To what degree will self-evaluation contribute to the determination of course grade?
8. Will you meet with your instructor periodically to discuss your progress in the course?
9. Will a final grading conference be held?
10. What will be the effect of peer evaluation in arriving at speech and course grades?

Speech Commentaries
1. What is your instructor's responsibility so far as commenting on speeches is concerned?
2. What is the resonsibility of your classmates?
3. How will commentaries be conducted?
4. What are the ground rules for speech commentaries?
5. Will students have the right to request or forbid certain kinds of comments? Which ones would you like to request? forbid?

A MODEL OF SKILLS LEARNING

The sequence that is typically followed in the learning of skills is discoverable not only as an historical progression but is repeated in the life experience of every individual as well. Biologists say that ontogeny (the developmental course of each individual organism) recapitulates phylogeny (the developmental course of the species); I am suggesting that the same statement can be made about how we learn skills. Historically, evidence for my contention can be gleaned from even a casual reading of the primary sources in the history of persuasive speaking. Individually, your own experience provides evidence. Thus the model I present in Figure 2.2 represents both an historical and an individual perspective on attitudes toward skills learning. The model lists three cognitive tools: mysticism, imitation/prescription, and analysis/theory-building. I think these follow roughly in sequence. Study the model before we look more closely at each of these tools.

Cognitive Tool	Assumptions About Learnability	Attempt to Understand Reasons for Observed Effects	Position of Learner	Typical Explanations of		Historical Documentation
				Successful Practice	Observed Outcome	
Mysticism	the skill cannot be learned	primitive, nonexistent, minimal	extremely dependent, weak	a gift from the gods	gods' will, fate (pre-determination)	*Iliad:* Phoenix tells Achilles that the latter is "a speaker of words and a doer of deeds."
Imitation/ Prescription	learning can come from watching what others do and following their lead or taking their advice	very little	moderately dependent (follower, advice-taker)	a talent, a knack, a gift, though not necessarily from the gods	inspiration: coupled with talent, knack, or skill brought about the result	Rhetorical handbooks contained prescriptions, model speeches; recommended emulation of masters
Analysis/ Theory-building	by the application of reason and the tools of reason (observation, plus deduction, inference-drawing) the skill can be learned	high to very high. Stress is placed on accounting for observed effects; observable or quantifiable factors account for observed effects	an inquirer, a searcher; relatively autonomous	speaker may have a talent, but the talent can be broken down, understood, partialized	certain things the speaker does (independent variables) have certain effects (dependent variables)	*Classical:* Plato, Aristotle *Traditional:* Bacon, Campbell *Modern:* Winans and current authors

Figure 2.2.

The cognitive tool of mysticism

We usually describe as primitive a society lacking tools for careful measurement and observation, or unsophisticated in its understanding of the natural order. In such societies, a skillful practitioner of any art is believed to be the recipient of a gift from the gods. Lacking any other basis on which to explain successful performance of an art, primitive peoples look outside the natural order for the rationale. The witch doctor, for instance, is thought to possess magical powers.

Evidence that this orientation influenced early attempts to understand the power of persuasion is provided by ancient Greek history. The Greeks envisioned a goddess of persuasion, Peitho, who was always portrayed as a companion of Aphrodite, the goddess of love, for the effective persuader was considered a seducer of the audience. In the *Iliad,* the warrior Achilles is described by the god Phoenix as being "a speaker of words and a doer of deeds." Heroic stature was revealed both in deeds of physical courage and in deeds of consummate intellectual and rhetorical skill. The great orator, in other words, was both a fine intellect and a brave warrior.

The concept *logos,* from which the word logic derives, was a mystical one in ancient Greek culture. It meant more than logic in its present-day sense. *Logos* referred to the power of reason, strength of mind, and intellectual capacity. Together with these qualities went confidence, independence of thought, sound judgment, leadership ability, and wisdom. To this day, we tend to associate physical and military prowess with intellectual and leadership ability. (Consider Eisenhower, a World War II general of great stature who was elected overwhelmingly to the Presidency shortly after the end of the war. Think of John F. Kennedy, former Coast Guard officer, scholar, and charismatic speaker whose able oratory helped vault him to the Presidency.)

According to the ancients, the power of *logos* was unexplainable in human terms. The power of the word was thought to be divine. So seriously was this taken that many Greek orators actually set themselves up as minor gods. The sophist Gorgias (circa 483–375 B.C.), typically dressed the part of a god in lavish robes resplendent with jewels. Revered by followers who listened adoringly to his words, he turned fine phrases and delivered them with much pomp and ceremony.

Supernatural explanations are not wholly unfamiliar in the modern world. For example, until fairly recently mentally ill persons were considered to be possessed by demons. In contemporary education we have secularized the concept somewhat, but we still speak of people as having a gift, or being gifted.

It may be speculated that the more powerless and lacking in understanding a society (or an individual), the more likely it is to rely on supernatural explanations. Recall when you were a child, watching your parents perform seemingly impossible tasks. They were able to read, they could compute math problems—all manner of incredible feats were within their ken. So completely beyond your reach or understanding were these tasks that you likely explained your parents' ability to perform them in magical terms.

The cognitive tool of mysticism carries with it a basic assumption about the learnability of the skill. It places the learner in a very definite psychological position. It provides a basis for explaining outcomes that are observed. And it reveals little interest in determining the natural reasons for observed effects. Let's consider each of these statements.

To the adherents of a mystical view, skills are not learnable. If the gods are the givers of gifts, then one really does not learn a skill; it is simply given. Psychologically, the learner assumes an extremely dependent position. He or she can try to persuade the gods to grant the gifts, but that's a Catch-22 situation—it is precisely the ability to persuade that is being sought. The learner can offer sacrifices, do things that the gods will find pleasing, and in other ways attempt to cajole them into granting the gift. I am being only half serious; however, the point is that since successful practice is utterly beyond the control of humankind, the student has no choice but to assume an extremely passive and dependent position.

Observed outcomes are explained in terms of the will of the gods. Successful practice is the result of the deployment of gifts given the practitioner by the gods.

I want to emphasize further that in attributing persuasive success to the fact that the speaker has a gift, the mystics do not reveal any serious interest in determining the natural reasons for observed effects. Nor do they make it possible to talk meaningfully about the speaker or the skill. Because the speaker has a direct hookup with the gods, there is little that a person lacking such a connection can do. The gift cannot go beyond the speaker. It cannot be passed on, except by magic.

The cognitive tool of imitation/prescription

Over time, as a society or an individual attains a firmer grasp of the world, the cognitive tool of mysticism is gradually replaced by that of imitation/prescription. From this more sophisticated perspective, it is believed that the learning of skills *can* occur and that skills *can* be communicated and passed on. However, because there is still little understanding of those factors accounting for successful practice, it is believed that others hold the key to success. Blind faith is placed in imitation and prescription.

The history of rhetorical training is rich in examples of the use of imitation/prescription in teaching persuasive speaking skills. The earliest Greek handbooks on rhetoric are a good instance. Written in response to a popular need, much like today's psychological self-help books, these handbooks provided basic instruction in rhetoric.

Toward the end of the fifth century B.C., a popular uprising occurred on the islands that made up the Greek state. One of the results was that land titles were called into question and conflicting claims of ownership made. Decades of litigation followed as claimants sued for ownership. Because there did not exist the equivalent of today's lawyers, people generally argued their own cases in court. Needless to say, the ability to persuade became highly prized. In response to the need and desire to be able to speak persuasively, handbooks on rhetoric were written and a class of teachers emerged, called sophists.

In addition, Athens possessed a growing middle class of wealthy merchants who exerted considerable influence on the affairs of state. Instead of electing representatives to stand in for the citizenry, Greek citizens themselves constituted the popular assembly. An effective persuader could influence public policy in ways that suited his practical desires or idealistic concerns; moreover, the doors to power, prestige, and even government office were open to any assembly member eloquent enough to impress his fellows.

Thus the two principal threads of litigation and a spreading popular democracy combined to produce a keen interest in training in persuasion.

The sophists offered not only training in court oratory but in political oratory and statesmanship as well. Our inheritance from the sophists is very significant. From Gorgias, for example, comes an appreciation of the role of a beautiful prose style in effective persuasion. From Isocrates come the virtues of simplicity and directness, insistence on the value of a broad education, and genuine concern for the welfare of society. From Protagoras, called the Father of Debate, comes the idea that comprehensive preparation for argument includes learning to debate both sides of an issue.

In short, the sophists represent an intellectual counterpart of the movement away from the mystical tradition in ancient Greece. They tended toward the practical, the pragmatic, and the earth-bound.

The rhetorical handbooks used by the sophists were of two types. In one type, emphasizing a prescriptive approach to learning persuasion, the authors stressed the parts of a speech and the functions of each part, as well as advice on how to convince listeners by means of arguments from probability. The second type of rhetorical handbook utilized model speeches to be studied, sometimes memorized, and emulated by students.

The imitation/prescription method of instruction is still used, though hopefully contemporary students are not encouraged simply to copy. As in the method of mysticism, this method also places the learner in a very passive and dependent position. It represents an improvement over the cognitive tool of mysticism inasmuch as it places skill in rhetoric within the reach of the mortal or the layman. Nevertheless, the student remains a mere recipient of knowledge. The imitation/prescription method involves little attempt to understand why a persuader succeeds or fails. Success is "explained" in terms of the presence of a knack or talent, but the explanation fails to account for the presence of the knack or to demonstrate why it succeeded.

Student Activity Option 2.4 _____
The Gods and the Sophists

INSTRUCTIONS
If you are interested in classical Greek history and the early origins of rhetoric, you might find the following books and articles challenging. You are also invited to read these sources with an eye to supporting or refuting the model of skills learning that appears in Figure 2.2. Do you think the historical progression argued for in this chapter holds up under careful scrutiny? What evidence can be gleaned to support or to refute it? Here are some sources that might help you answer these questions while gaining a more complete appreciation of ancient Greek history and the origins of rhetoric:

Clark, Donald L. (1957) *Rhetoric in Greco-Roman Education.* New York: Columbia University Press.
Kennedy, George (1963) *The Art of Persuasion in Greece.* Princeton, New Jersey: Princeton University Press.
Stone, I. F. (1979) "I. F." Stone Breaks the Socrates Story," The *New York Times Magazine* (April 8), 22ff.
Thonnsen, Lester, A. Craig Baird, and Waldo W. Braden (1970) *Speech Criticism,* 2nd ed.; New York: Ronald Press. See especially Part II, The Development of Rhetorical Theory, pp. 33–156. Note that an excellent bibliography of additional source material appears on pages 153–156.
Note that primary source materials appear in Student Activity Option 2.5.

_____

The cognitive tool of analysis/theory-building

This approach to learning emerges when people begin seriously to ask the question why in their attempts to explain successful practice. "Why did Demosthenes succeed in persuading the assembly?" "Why couldn't President Carter convince the American people that the gasoline shortage was real?" "Why is one candidate for office successful and another unsuccessful?" By the time the question of why is asked seriously, people are no longer satisfied with mystical explanations, nor are they satisfied with slavish imitation and empty prescription. A "what works" mentality is replaced by a "howcum?" mentality, an analytical orientation. People are seeking reasons, causes, and explanations (see Chapter Four).

Only when the cognitive tool is analysis/theory-building does the learner assume a relatively independent position. The learner is an enquirer, a searcher who seeks explanations. He or she wants to know why. The learner is no longer content to sit idly by, waiting for the muses to strike or for someone else to point out what to do and how to do it. Instead, he or she observes, makes connections, and experiments.

From the perspective of this cognitive tool, successful practice is the result of certain behaviors that can be partialized and understood. Any outcome can be explained by identifying and isolating pertinent variables and particular behaviors engaged in by the speaker. The speaker manipulates certain speaker and speech variables in order to bring about changes in the audience.

Historically, the earliest attempts to construct a theory of rhetoric were made by Plato and Aristotle, whose rudimentary theories are described below.

CLASSICAL THEORIES OF RHETORIC

Plato (c. 427–347 B.C.)

What follows is not meant to be a comprehensive discussion of Plato's criticism of rhetoric nor of his suggestions for an ideal philosophical art of persuasion. Rather, my intent is to highlight his chief criticisms and to show his major contributions to the analytical-theoretical approach to the study of persuasion. If you are interested in Plato's thought on the subject, I strongly recommend that you read his two dialogues that most clearly deal with rhetoric specifically, the *Gorgias* and the *Phaedrus*. Comments on rhetoric and criticism of the sophists, to whom Plato was strenuously opposed, appear throughout most of his dialogues, including the classic, *The Republic*. (See Student Activity Option 2.5 for complete references to these works and for additional reading material.) Many of the comments that follow are drawn from the *Gorgias* and the *Phaedrus*.

Plato's contribution to persuasion theory was twofold. On one hand, he offered important criticisms of the sophistic conception of rhetoric and of the sophists' methods of teaching. On the other hand, Plato offered suggestions on those criteria an adequate rhetoric would have to meet. It is his discussion of these requirements that represents a rudimentary theory, although Plato's "theory" hardly conforms to the strict scientific use of the term.

Plato's central criticism of rhetoric was that it provided skill in achieving a result, but without explaining why the effect was achieved. The student of a sophist could utter the right words and succeed in persuading his listeners. But at no point did he learn *why* his listeners were persuaded. The sophist, in short, taught "whyless" proficiency. Thus, Plato disparagingly referred to rhetoric as a "knack" or a "routine." He saw the sophist as producing a low-level skill. There was no true art in that, Plato maintained: the sophist was guilty of pandering and flattery.

This criticism cuts to the core of the weakness of the sophists. It was precisely their failure to be interested in anything more than "what works" that constituted their chief weakness as theorists. Plato insisted that a true art of rhetoric would require a comprehensive and genuine theory, one that explained results as well as conveying a competence. He sought instead a body of organized and universally valid principles. For him, it was not enough simply to be able to persuade; the true rhetorician would know how and why his results are achieved. Consider the following passage, 463–64,* from the *Gorgias* (1952: 25), which is a reasonably succinct statement of Plato's point of view:

> Cookery has smuggled herself into the guise of medicine . . . so that if a cook and a physician had to dispute their claims before a group of boys, or before men as silly as boys, as to which of the two completely understood which foods are beneficial and which are harmful, the physician would starve to death. Now I call this flattery, and I say that such a proceeding is foul . . . because it aims at pleasure without consideration of what is best; and I say that it is not an art, but a knack, because it is unable to render any account of the nature of the methods it applies and so cannot tell the cause of each of them.

In light of this criticism, what sort of rhetoric could rightfully claim the title of art? Plato set down the requirement that an adequate rhetoric would be based on a knowledge of the kinds of souls there are, and of why each kind of soul responds to a particular argument. In modern dress, Plato was calling for a rhetoric that had its roots in psychology, a knowledge of psyches or souls. More particularly, he stressed the importance of recognizing and adapting to audience variables (see Chapter Six). He advocated a theory of rhetoric that would enable the speaker scientifically to plan a persuasive strategy based on the audience to whom he was talking. Rhetoric, which Plato criticized as having no subject matter of its own, ought to claim as its subject matter a knowledge of souls and how to reach them. Only then could the rhetorician claim with any validity that he could account for the results he got.

Plato's second major criticism, closely related to the first, was that rhetoric was suited to the mob. It produced belief but no genuine knowledge. Here again, Plato's abhorrence of probabilities as the basis for persuasion comes

---

*These numbers refer to points in Plato's dialogues. They remain standard regardless of which translation or edition you use.

through. In his eyes, knowledge was absolute; the sophists' emphasis on probabilities appalled him. They dealt in illusion—what most people thought to be true—rather than in actual truth. In his own words (*Phaedrus* 1956: 46), 260:

> I have heard it said that it's not necessary for the man who plans to be an orator to learn what is really just and true, but only what seems so to the crowd who will pass judgment; and in the same way he may neglect what is really good or beautiful and concentrate on what will seem so; for it is from what seems to be true that persuasion comes, not from real truth.

I think you will agree that many of Plato's criticisms have a contemporary ring to them. For example, haven't you ever heard a present-day politician criticized for telling people what they want to hear rather than what's really true? This is exactly what Plato had in mind when he faulted the sophists for pandering and flattery. The very word *sophistry* bears testimony to the timeless effect of Plato's criticism. In the jumble of conflicting attitudes most people hold, two are inconsistent: an idealism that borders on absolutism (Plato would have been pleased to know that such idealism still survives), and pragmatism. Thus, we can admire a person for being practical, even for being pragmatic. But when the person bases all choices on what is expedient, we lose respect. This was precisely the way Plato saw the sophists; they were oriented toward the expedient, not toward the noble.

A true rhetoric would be different in several respects. First, it would aim at genuine improvement of the audience. The rhetorician would need to do more than seek to please his hearers; he would have to be concerned with ennobling them. In a sense, then, the rhetorician would be a sort of teacher-philosopher. Rather than basing his arguments on what people believed to be true, the rhetorician would know Truth. He would be schooled in philosophy, particularly dialectic, the art of analysis. This background, coupled with a strong commitment to ethics, would allow the orator to improve his audience rather than simply flatter them.

A dialectician would also know how to divide a subject according to its natural points of division. Recall that one variety of rhetorical handbook placed emphasis on the four parts of a speech—introduction, background, proof, and conclusion. An oration was said to be divided arbitrarily into these several parts, and the student of rhetoric was urged to learn to organize his material in accordance with these arbitrary divisions. Plato strongly objected, maintaining that a true rhetorician, as a student of dialectic, would know how to divide his subject at its natural dividing points. He would not need to rely on stereotyped organizational patterns, nor would he simply impose a preestablished organizational scheme over his subject matter.

In the following passage (*Phaedrus*, 1956: 72), 277, Plato's views on the ideal rhetorician are summarized. Note that he makes reference to the importance of the rhetorician's knowing the truth of his subject matter. He refers to the speaker's knowledge of how to divide a subject. And he returns once again to the importance of knowing the various kinds of souls, and of adapting speeches to the hearers for whom the messages are intended.

> A man must first know the truth about every single subject on which he speaks or writes. He must be able to define each in terms of a universal class that stands by itself. When he has successfully defined his subjects according to their specific classes, he must know how to continue the division until he reaches the point of indivisibility. He must make the same sort of distinction with reference to the nature of the soul. He must then discover the kind of speech that matches each type of nature. When that is accomplished, he must arrange and adorn each speech in such a way as to present complicated and unstable souls with complex speeches, speeches exactly attuned to every changing mood of the complicated soul—while the simple soul must be presented with a simple speech. Not until a man acquires this capacity will it be possible to produce speech in a scientific way, in so far as its nature permits such treatment, either for purposes of instruction or of persuasion.

Plato's "theory" of rhetoric is extremely sketchy at best. Yet it does represent the first significant attempt to move rhetoric beyond the realm of "what works" and into that of "howcum?" Plato's emphasis on understanding the interaction effect of audience and speech variables is amazingly contemporary. He and his student, Aristotle, lacked the tools and techniques available to current-day researchers. Nevertheless, they performed the valuable service of formulating the correct questions and pointing the way to the future. Let us look more closely now at Aristotle's contribution to the theory of persuasion.

Aristotle (c. 384–322 B.C.)

To Plato, the sophists and rhetoric were of primary interest as negative examples: both were to be abhorred; each represented a facet of societal decay; neither was worthy of serious study. His pupil, Aristotle, felt otherwise. Though he was generally critical of the sophists, he saw in their writings and teachings much that was of merit. Further, Aristotle devoted an entire work to rhetoric. His *Rhetoric* is a classic that many students of persuasion still see as the definitive work in the field. Although I disagree with this contention, since many important theoretical advances have been made since Aristotle's time, there is much in the work that is of interest to the contemporary student. And, from our perspective in this chapter, the work is noteworthy for its scientific orientation.

While you and I might think of Aristotle primarily as a philosopher, he was in fact a student of biology and may even have been a physician. What is fascinating about these facts is that, due to his training, Aristotle was primarily an observer. Not surprisingly, Aristotle's starting point for the study of rhetoric was his keen powers of observation, which give his treatment of rhetoric its essentially scientific character. (In Chapter Three, we shall see that observation is the first step in the scientific method.)

In addition to using observation as a point of departure in his study of rhetoric, Aristotle did three other things that place his work clearly within the realm of science. First, he sought cause-and-effect connections. While the notion of cause and effect is considered an oversimplification today (it is rare that a single cause corresponds to a particular effect on a one-to-one basis), for centuries it was at the heart of scientific inquiry. And in all but the most sophisticated scientific circles, causes and effects are still spoken about without awareness of the oversimplifications implied by the terms. Not only in his thinking but in his writing as well, Aristotle was concerned with the effects of certain behavior. The *Rhetoric* is replete with references to the effects of certain speaker behaviors. Emotions such as anger, for example, are described as capable of being produced by certain rather specific things speakers do. For instance, Aristotle writes (1379a 27–29) that "the persons with whom we get angry are those who laugh, mock, or jeer at us, for such conduct is insolent" (*Rhetoric*, 1954, p. 95). Later (1380a 1–5) he suggests that "the orator will have to speak so as to bring his hearers into a frame of mind that will dispose them to anger, and to represent his adversaries as . . . possessed of such qualities as do make people angry (*Rhetoric*, 1954, p. 97).

Aristotle also revealed a scientific orientation in his tendency to prefer description to prescription. Although there are points in the *Rhetoric* at which prescriptive advice is offered, for the most part Aristotle was far more interested in describing. He classified and he categorized, he showed connections and relationships. His *Rhetoric* is not a handbook in the same sense as the sophists' writings since it is philosophical in spirit and scientific in orientation.

Finally, as Cronkhite, observes (1969, p. 20) many of Aristotle's thoughts can easily be translated into testable predictions. Implied in much of Aristotle's writing are many predictive statements that lend themselves to scientific testing, and prediction is at the heart of the scientific method (see Chapter Three). Of course, Aristotle did not design his propositions for research purposes; nevertheless, a few alterations in his phraseology would make them perfectly suitable for scientific testing. For example, consider the remarks cited about the excitation of anger. Aristotle's remarks might be rephrased roughly as follows: "A speaker who portrays his adversaries as persons who laugh, mock, or jeer at his audience will create anger at his adversaries." While this hypothesis is loosely phrased for scientific testing purposes, it does lend itself to testing. Many such testable propositions can be formulated from Aristotle's writing; his keen interest in and appreciation of the scientific method—as primitive as it was in his day—is revealed in the ease with which his thoughts can be recast to fit a contemporary scientific mold.

Plato and Aristotle: Some differences

How did Aristotle's treatment of rhetoric differ from Plato's? Like his teacher, Aristotle believed that the speaker must know the different kinds of souls so that messages may be specifically adapted to them. Unlike Plato, Aristotle discussed this subject in some depth, providing guidance on constructing arguments and emotional appeals to touch different kinds of audiences. Many of Aristotle's descriptions hold true today. For example, he describes older men as timid, younger ones as brash. The former have been humbled by life; the latter, not yet humbled, are proud and overly confident.*

Both Plato and Aristotle objected to the contrived and ineffective "all-purpose" organizational schemes proposed by the sophists. But unlike his teacher, Aristotle proposed an alternative. In Book Three of the *Rhetoric*, he offered a flexible organizational pattern, adaptable to the demands of a speaker's topic, his audience, and the occasion of the talk. Aristotle always advocated the application of common sense in deciding on what should be included in a speech.

Like Plato, Aristotle cared about the ethics of rhetoric. But here he and his teacher parted company, for Aristotle was less idealistic than his mentor. Aristotle considered ethics to be a matter to be worked out privately by the speaker.

In other areas, Aristotle veered even more sharply from the course set by his instructor. Perhaps the most significant departure occurred around the issue of probabilities in rhetoric. Plato, you recall, despised them. He faulted the sophists for dealing with appearance and illusion, or what seemed true to the mob. Aristotle did not despise the use of probabilities. In fact, he stated openly throughout the *Rhetoric* that they constitute the substance of an orator's arguments. The orator's stock in trade, according to Aristotle, is probabilities. The phrase "proof or apparent proof" appears throughout Book One of the *Rhetoric*.

Probabilities are the stuff of rhetorical syllogisms, or enthymemes. An enthymeme is a deductive chain of reasoning that has as one premise a widely held belief, or probability. Usually the premise is not stated, since the audience already accepts it. It thus constitutes a sort of given building block of argument. Here is an illustration of the relationship between syllogism and enthymeme. Item One is a syllogism, Item Two an enthymeme. The enthymeme is recast as a syllogism in Item Three, and the probable premise is placed in parentheses.

Item One (syllogism):
　　All men are mortal.
　　Henry is a man.
　　Henry is mortal.

*I think you will find Aristotle's descriptions of people in different age groups thoroughly fascinating. I recommend enthusiastically that you read them in the *Rhetoric*, Book Two, Chapters 12–14, 1389b, 12 to 1390b, 31.

Item Two (enthymeme)
 Henry, a student, probably enjoys learning.

Item Three:
 (All students probably enjoy learning.)
 Henry is a student.
 Henry probably enjoys learning.

Note that the word "probably" in the conclusion of the syllogism indicates that the conclusion, drawn from a probable premise, is itself probable.

It would be impossible to summarize here Aristotle's discussion of rhetoric. The interested reader should consult the *Rhetoric* for firsthand knowledge of what it contains. For its breadth, comprehensiveness, and scientific orientation, the *Rhetoric* is noteworthy. That it has survived for over two thousand years and that it still speaks to the reader today with much that is interesting and thought-provoking—these facts bear testimony to the quality of the intellect that gave it birth. Cronkhite wrote of Aristotle's influence as a theorist that "the study of rhetoric of persuasion until at least the eighteenth century is not much more than a study of the ways in which succeeding writers rearranged and rephrased essentially the same material" (Cronkhite, 1969, p. 22). It is generally agreed that not until publication in 1776 of George Campbell's *Philosophy of Rhetoric* was there a work that represented in any sense a theoretical depth or perspective equivalent to the one of Plato and Aristotle.

Of course many people wrote about rhetoric between the fourth century B.C. and 1776. Cicero (106–43 B.C.), for example, in his *De Oratore* provided much practical advice, written from the perspective of a successful, practicing politician. Another work attributed to him, *Rhetorica Ad Herennium,* is noteworthy for its discussion of the five classical canons of rheoric: (1) *invention* (the art of constructing proofs), (2) *disposition* (the art of organizing material), (3) *elocution* (language style), (4) *delivery,* and (5) *memory.* These canons are still used as organizational rubrics for current textbooks on public speaking.

Quintilian (c. A.D. 35–95) wrote the monumental *Institutes of Oratory,* which revealed a deep appreciation of Greek and Latin oratory, and which set forth the timeless definition of the perfect orator: "the good man speaking well."

Rhetoric, like almost everything else developed by the Romans, was turned to the purposes of the Church following the decline and fall of Rome. For thousands of years following the death of Christ, much of what was written on rhetoric was penned by and for priests. The Church father Augustine (A.D. 354–430), for example, wrote extensively on oratory. His *On Christian Doctrine* (written toward the end of the fourth century and beginning of the fifth century A.D.) contains valuable advice on speech preparation and presentation.

In the following Student Activity Option, you are invited to read and to report upon primary source materials. By taking advantage of this opportunity, you can gain greater appreciation of the historical roots and contemporary import of rhetoric.

Student Activity Option 2.5
Plato, Aristotle, and the Classical Tradition

INSTRUCTIONS
You may wish to read and report on one or more of the following source materials. With your instructor's consent, you might find it informative to structure a class activity around your readings.

SUGGESTIONS
1. With a few of your classmates, conduct an oral reading of an excerpt from one of the two Platonic dialogues listed below. For example, you might wish to play the role of Gorgias while a classmate might see himself as Socrates and a third person might assume the role of say, Polus. You might even conduct the reading in costumes appropriate to the period. This activity can be fun, but it should also be instructive. To do an adequate job, you and your partners will need to steep yourselves in the dialogue in order to convey a real understanding of the points of view expressed by the various characters.
Note that many of the translations listed contain additional reading material that may be valuable to you in your preparation for this activity.

2. With a few of your classmates, conduct a discussion of rhetoric. Each discussant should play the role of one major theorist and writer whose work is listed here or who is mentioned in the works cited. Again, costumes are appropriate. You might wish to prepare a list of questions to be discussed. If well-phrased, they will point up the disagreements among the participants. You might have a mock newspaper reporter in contemporary dress interview the panel members. Once again, this activity can be pleasant as well as educational, but you will need to be thoroughly familiar with the viewpoint of the character you are portraying to do an adequate job.

PRIMARY SOURCE MATERIALS
Aristotle (1954/c. 330 B.C.), translated by W. Rhys Roberts *Rhetoric*, in *Aristotle's Rhetoric and Poetics*. New York: The Modern Library.
Augustine (1960/c. A.D. 426) *The Confessions of St. Augustine*, translated by John K. Ryan. Garden City, New York: Image Books, a division of Doubleday and Co. (Note that comments on rhetoric are scattered throughout this work.)
———— (1958/c. A.D. 426), *On Christian Doctrine*, translated and with an Introduction by D. W. Robertson, Jr. Indianapolis: The Bobbs-Merrill Co.
Cicero (1959/55 B.C.) *De Oratore* (Vol. I), translated by E. W. Sutton and H. Rackham. Cambridge, Massachusetts: Harvard University Press.
———— (1960/55 B.C.) *De Oratore* (Vol. II), translated by H. Rackham. Cambridge, Massachusetts: Harvard University Press.
———— (1964/82 B.C.) *Rhetorica Ad C. Herennium*, translated by Harry Caplan. Cambridge, Massachusetts: Harvard University Press.
Plato (1952/c. 387 B.C.) *Gorgias*, translated by W. C. Helmbold. Indianapolis, Indiana: The Bobbs-Merrill Co.

———— (1956/c. 380 B.C.) *Phaedrus*, translated by W. C. Helmbold and W. G. Rabinowitz. Indianapolis, Indiana: The Bobbs-Merrill Co.
Quintilian (1920/c. A.D. 80) *Institutes of Oratory*, translated by H.E. Butler. Cambridge, Massachusetts: Harvard University Press, 4 vols.

SIX CONTRIBUTORS TO THE THEORY OF RHETORIC

By and large, with the passing of the classical period, rhetoric declined in importance and utility. Though relatively little is known about rhetoric as written about and practiced during the so-called Dark Ages, its reemergence in the twelfth century shows it to have lost much of its depth and scope. For many, rhetoric meant—and continues to mean to this day—empty ornament. The word rhetoric as commonly used today refers to empty verbiage. To refer to a politician's speech as rhetoric is roughly equivalent to referring to the talk as a lot of hot air. The charge against rhetoric as a subject of study is perhaps unfair; as we have seen, the subject has a long and proud history. Nevertheless, many of the works of the recent past—up until the end of the nineteenth century, in fact—have been concerned almost exclusively with language ornaments and with rather hackneyed delivery styles. They reflect the shallowness into which rhetoric sank over the centuries; and they account for the poor image the subject has in the contemporary world.

There were exceptions, however. Several works written over the last several hundred years warrant careful study, for they represent steady progress toward an analytical-theoretical approach to the study of persuasion, and because each made a significant contribution to contemporary theories of rhetoric and persuasion. In the following paragraphs I wish to summarize briefly the contributions of Francis Bacon, George Campbell, Richard Whately, James Winans, Kenneth Burke, and Stephen Toulmin. No attempt will be made to detail the work of these people; I want only to present the major thrusts of the contributions each has made.

Francis Bacon (1561–1626)

Born in 1561, in the third year of Queen Elizabeth's reign, Francis Bacon lived at a time that witnessed the flowering of Elizabethan culture. He was a highly successful politician during his life, a man of letters and influence. Though in the end he fell from power—not an unusual occurrence for men of might during those volatile times—he exerted considerable influence on the affairs of his day. One commentator has observed that Bacon rose to an office roughly equivalent to that of chief justice of the United States Supreme Court (Patrick, 1948, p. vi). Not accidentally, Bacon's interest in rhetoric was tied to the opening up of political opportunities in his day.

Bacon did not write an entire treatise on rhetoric. Instead, he devoted sections of his major work, *The Advancement of Learning*, and of other works, to the subject. His special interests were the preparation of logical proofs, and the interaction of logic and emotion that occurs when a person is motivated or when attempts are made to motivate others. Though primitive, his way of conceiving of this interaction was based on the premise that the persuasive process cannot be understood without an awareness of how the psyche works. His writings on rhetoric were tied to the psychology of his day, faculty psychology. According to this simplistic view, the human being possesses a number of faculties, each of which serves a discrete function, though at times the various faculties work in consonance. For example, one faculty is *reason;* its function is to weigh and to evaluate. The rational functions of thought and judgment are housed in the faculty of reason. *Imagination* serves other functions, chief among them to direct and drive the *will* by representing to it (in the mind's eye) the object to be attained.

Bacon's conception of the purpose of rhetoric ties together these three faculties of reason, imagination, and will. That purpose, he wrote is, "to apply reason to the imagination for the better moving of the will." In other words, the speaker's task is to combine the influence of the two faculties of reason and imagination so as to bring about a desire to act in ways the speaker wants. The human being is not always rational, according to Bacon, and so appeals directed solely to reason cannot succeed. On the other hand, to appeal solely to the passions or to the imagination is insufficient too. The special skill of the orator is to structure appeals that bring together the influence of both reason and the imagination. Audience adaptation was thus a central theme in Bacon's writings.

Francis Bacon's treatment of rhetoric can hardly be called scientific in the strict meaning of the term. Nor can it compare in comprehensiveness to the treatment accorded the subject by Aristotle. Nevertheless, it is considered by some as "the first important new analysis of persuasion to appear after the classical period" (Cronkhite, 1969, p. 28).

George Campbell (1719–1796)

For comprehensiveness, George Campbell's *Philosophy of Rhetoric,* which appeared in 1776, is noteworthy. Generally recognized as the forerunner of contemporary rhetorical theory, the *Philosophy of Rhetoric* updates and expands upon classical doctrine. Campbell's discussion covers the main topics considered by Aristotle, including the nature of rhetoric (of which the primary end, Campbell observes, is persuasion), logical proof—including reasoning, evidence, and probabilities—emotional proof, personal proof, and style. Interestingly, Campbell's treatment of personal proof is in most respects a forerunner of contemporary research in *Ethos.* Without using the words, he talks about a speaker's credibility and expertise, and about the audience's perceptions of the speaker's character. He further recognizes that the group affiliations of the audience can affect the listeners' judgments and perceptions of the speaker.

Chief among Campbell's many contributions is his emphasis on the intended effect of the speech. In his own words, "in speaking there is always some end proposed, or some effect which the speaker intends to produce in the hearer. The word *eloquence*, in its greatest latitude, denotes 'that art or talent by which the discourse is adapted to its end' " (Campbell, 1963/1776, p. 34). Note that Cambell's emphasis on intended effects is a remarkably contemporary idea, for it is always by comparing intended effects with actual ones that the success of a speech or any other change effort is measured (see Chapter Four). Campbell saw speeches as having one of four possible intended effects: to "enlighten the understanding, please the imagination, move the passions, or influence the will" (1963/1776, pp. 1–2). Any one of these effects predominates in a particular speech, according to Campbell, and other intended effects assume places of lesser importance in a well-planned speech.

Richard Whately (1787–1863)

Fifty-two years after the appearance of the *Philosophy of Rhetoric*, an Anglican bishop by the name of Richard Whately published *Elements of Rhetoric*. Popular at the time of its publication, the book continues to exert far-reaching influence. Whately's name is usually associated with two key terms in the arena of logical argument: presumption and burden of proof. Both are borrowed from the courts and applied by Whately to nonjudicial oratory. *Presumption* refers to the prevailing sympathy toward existing institutions, policies, or traditions. Just as in court a person is presumed innocent until proven guilty, Whately maintains that in everyday argumentative encounters, any existing institution has a presumption in its favor. What *is*, in other words, is presumed to be adequate, desirable, or good until proven otherwise. Logic is in favor of that which is familiar. Only after logical arguments shake familiar institutions down from their position of security can they be reasonably questioned.

The counterpart of presumption is *burden of proof*. If you choose to argue against an existing instituion, policy, or tradition, you assume the burden of proof. For example, suppose your family traditionally visits a bachelor uncle on holidays, despite the fact that all of you absolutely hate to visit him. If one year you were to argue against the annual visit, you would take on yourself the burden of proof. It would be up to you to convince your family that the traditional visit is unnecessary, undesirable, unpleasant, or otherwise inadvisable. The presumption would be in favor of the visit, if only through the sheer force of momentum. In fact, you could assume that you'd create quite a stir merely by suggesting that your family break with tradition, so strong is the impetus created by existing traditions and institutions.

While these two doctrines do not go unchallenged in contemporary rhetorical theory, and while my presentation of Whately's point of view has been brief, the concepts of presumption and burden of proof should provide useful direction for you as you prepare your speeches.

James Winans (1872–1956)

Nearly a century after the publication of *Elements of Rhetoric*, at the very birthpoint of the field of speech communication, a scholar named James Winans, professor of public speaking at Cornell University, heralded the contemporary approach to the study of persuasive speaking with his *Public Speaking*. Published in 1915 and again in 1917, Winans's popular and influential text is noteworthy for its adherence to the established tradition of tying together psychology and rhetoric. Like the work of Campbell, *Public Speaking* draws on the psychology of its day. The work's chief emphasis is on attention, since Winans believed that "whatever holds attention determines action" (1917 ed., p. 24). Hence, he sees the speaker's task as controlling the attention and thoughts of the listener. In his own words (1917 ed., p. 24):

> To persuade a man, there seems to be nothing more or less than to win his undivided attention to the desired conduct, to make him think of that and stop thinking of other courses, or of any inhibiting ideas . . . . Persuasion is the process of inducing others to give fair, favorable, or undivided attention to propositions.

If you noted a similarity between Winans' notion of thought control and the contemporary phenomena of psychological manipulation as discussed in Chapter One, you can perhaps sense the contemporariness of Winans' view of persuasion. I'm not implying that Winans was aware of brainwashing, only that his way of conceiving of the process of persuasion predates the concept and is not inharmonious with it.

Despite its popularity and its merit, Winans' *Public Speaking* was not without its detractors. It was published at about the time the infant science of psychology began to challenge time-honored ways of conceiving of human behavior. For example, from Aristotle's time, it was considered pedagogically convenient and psychologically sound to distinguish between logical and emotional proofs. Similarly, in the early twentieth century, it was customary to distinguish between speeches designed to convince (i.e., those addressed to the faculty of the understanding) and those designed to persuade (i.e., those addressed to the will). Winans, influenced by tradition and immersed in the psychological conceptualizations current in his day, made such distinctions. As a result, he was taken to task by more sophisticated students of human behavior and *Public Speaking* was roundly attacked. There is no real distinction between logical and emotional proofs, Winans' critics contended. Psychologically, the human being cannot accurately be so compartmentalized. Conviction and persuasion are, in fact, two components of the same process. Traditional distinctions like these, Winans' critics contended, are both inaccurate and misleading, as well as pedagogically unsound.

Many of the criticisms to which Winans' work was subjected are valid. Despite that fact, most contemporary books—this book among them—still rely on some traditional concepts in discussing the process of persuasion. In spite of their psychological inaccuracies, many classical concepts remain valuable as teaching tools. They provide starting points for speech preparation. To refuse to rely on them, in the absence of equally useful intellectual handles provided by contemporary psychology, seems short-sighted and self-defeating. Rejecting them is akin to a drowning person's obstinate refusal to grab onto a red life preserver because of an aversion to the color red.

Kenneth Burke (1897–)

Burke, a philosopher with an interest in language, a keen social observer and critic, and a student of Freudian psychoanalysis, conceives of rhetoric broadly. Rhetoric he says, operates whenever individuals and groups interact. We are continually influencing one another. The very social order could not continue to exist if its members were not persuaded to believe in the rightness of that order. Status differences, for example, must be accepted by those of all social ranks. Hence, considerable effort is spent—consciously or otherwise—in ensuring social cooperation by using symbols and other rhetorical strategies in such a way as to induce cooperation. While many attempts to persuade are, according to Burke, quite unspeechlike, others are more deliberate and are structured as persuasive speeches. In the preparation of these, Burke offers suggestions that are clearly classical in main thrust; his approach is strongly influenced by the classical theories of Aristotle. For an excellent discussion of Burke's contribution to rhetorical theory, see Marie Hocmuth (1952), "Kenneth Burke and the 'New Rhetoric,' " *Quarterly Journal of Speech* (April) 38: 133–44.

Stephen Toulmin (1922–)

In the tradition of Richard Whately, the English logician Stephen Toulmin is of interest to the contemporary student of persuasive speaking primarily because he provides insightful comments on logical proof. Toulmin has offered an innovative way of representing the structure of logical arguments. Traditional Aristotelian logic emphasizes deduction and induction. The former is a reasoning pattern that proceeds from general premises to specific conclusions. The syllogism is a deductive argument. For example, consider the syllogism below:

> Americans are friendly. (general principle)
> Estelle is an American.
> Estelle is friendly. (particular "truth")

Induction, conversely, proceeds from one or more specific truths to a general conclusion. Reasoning from example is a form of inductive reasoning. Here is an instance:

John, an American, is friendly.
  (one particular instance)
Pamela, an American, is friendly.
  (another particular instance)
June, an American, is friendly.
  (another particular instance)
Therefore, Americans are friendly.
  (general conclusion)

Students of logic use many sophisticated concepts to test the accuracy of conclusions drawn inductively and deductively—concepts like formal validity, moods and figures of syllogisms, and copulative propositions.* These ways of conceiving of the logic of an argument remain useful, though cumbersome. In addition, many contend that traditional logic is not of much use when it comes to analyzing and constructing rhetorical proofs. One major flaw is that without elaborate and careful study of the inner workings of the processes of induction and deduction, a person is simply unprepared to recognize the flaws in an argument. Nor does the syllogistic form explicate the many qualifying and intervening factors that operate in the reasoning process.

Toulmin has constructed a model that explicitly points to these intervening and qualifying factors and makes it possible for a layperson to scrutinize and test logical processes used in everyday argument. There are three critical components in his scheme: (1) *data* or *support* (that evidence upon the basis of which the advocate's claim is based); (2) *claim* or *conclusion* (the advocate's main point in this particular chain of reasoning; the claim, it should be noted, may constitute an intermediate point in a more elaborate chain of logic); and (3) *warrant* (a statement of principle that certifies the relationship between the data and the claim; the warrant is the intellectual bridge along which the advocate and the hearer move from the data to the claim). Consider Figure 2.3, which shows how data, warrant, and claim are related.

Three other elements Toulmin includes in his model deserve mention. One of these is the *backing,* or support for the warrant. If the warrant is not obvious and noncontroversial to the listener, then the argument usually includes supporting material. In Figure 2.3, for instance, historical data may be required to establish the inverse relationship between interest rates and stock prices proposed in the warrant.

The second element is the *rebuttal,* or reservation. This component of a proof unit spells out the exceptional circumstances under which the data and the warrant (plus the warrant's support, if any) might not yield the claim advanced. The reservation is usually preceded by the word *unless,* which implies that it represents limitations or exceptions under which the claim could not logically be maintained.

---

*For an application of the syllogistic model to speech preparation (together with evaluative commentary), see Chapter Five, "Logical Proof: Inference," pp. 57–81 in Erwin P. Bettinghaus (1966) Message Preparation: The Nature of Proof. Indianapolis, Indiana: The Bobbs-Merrill Co.

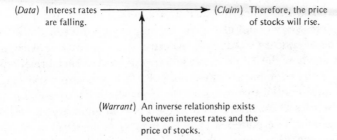

Figure 2.3. The Toulmin Model, I

The *qualifier* specifies the strength of the claim. It is included in a proof unit when the claim is less than wholly certain. The qualifier may be required because of evidence that is less than complete, or because the rebuttal, if true, would undermine the validity of the claim. Consider again Figure 2.3, which I now present with the addition of the support, the rebuttal, and the qualifier (see Figure 2.4).

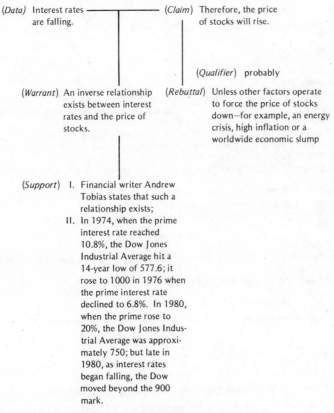

Figure 2.4. The Toulmin Model, II

Compared to the syllogistic model, Toulmin's scheme is far more detailed and complete; yet without elaborate machinations, it reveals the key elements likely to be of concern in the vast majority of argumentative encounters. You can easily see how the Toulmin model represents the crucial relationships that exist among the components of a proof unit. As a persuasive speaker, you may find it useful to outline your arguments along the lines specified by Toulmin.

As in the case of Whately's contribution to contemporary rhetorical theory, Toulmin cannot be credited with enlarging our understanding of the psychological processes that operate in persuasion. It is a limited contribution that focuses on the logical aspects of argument. Nevertheless, it is a valuable addition to your fund of knowledge about the logic of persuasive discourse.

Student Activity Option 2.6
Traditional and Modern Theorists

INSTRUCTIONS
Read one or more of the following items and report back to your class and/or instructor in a manner agreed upon in advance. See Student Activity Options 2.4 and 2.5 for ideas on how to present the results of your readings.

SUGGESTED READINGS

Primary Source Materials
Bacon, Francis (1605/1955) *The Advancement of Learning,* pp. 157–220 in Francis Bacon (1955/many dates) *Selected Writings of Francis Bacon,* with an Introduction and notes by Hugh G. Dick. New York: The Modern Library.
Burke, Kenneth (1950) *A Rhetoric of Motives.* Englewood-Cliffs, New Jersey: Prentice-Hall.
Campbell, George (1963/1776) *The Philosophy of Rhetoric,* ed. Lloyd Bitzer. Carbondale, Illinois: Southern Illinois University Press.
Toulmin, Stephen (1959) *The Uses of Argument.* Cambridge, England: Cambridge University Press.
Whately, Richard (1963/1828) *Elements of Rhetoric,* ed. Douglas Ehninger. Carbondale, Illinois: Southern Illinois University Press.
Winans, James A. (1915, rev. 1917) *Public Speaking.* New York: Century.

Secondary Sources
Wallace, Karl R. (1943) *Francis Bacon on Communication and Rhetoric.* Chapel Hill: University of North Carolina Press.
Hochmuth, Marie (1952) "Kenneth Burke and the 'New Rhetoric,' " *Quarterly Journal of Speech,* vol. 38, 133–44.

SUMMARY

In this chapter I discussed learning in general and skills learning in particular. The subject of learning can be examined from a variety of perspectives, among them, philosophical, psycholinguistic or developmental, and psychological. American psychology has placed a great deal of emphasis on learning theory, the essence of which was presented here. You saw the difference between operant and classical conditioning, and how behavior is shaped by environmental reinforcement. Also discussed were nine principles whose application can expedite the learning of skills.

A model of skills learning that traces the historical trends characteristic of the process was applied specifically to the acquisition of persuasive speaking skills. The earliest writings on rhetoric reveal a reliance on the primitive cognitive tool of mysticism. Since users of this tool assume that a skill is a gift from the gods and that one cannot learn in any natural way to perform competently, there is little attempt to account for persuasive effects. The learner is placed in an extremely passive and dependent position and successful practice is explained in terms of the gods' will or their gifts.

At a later stage in the evolution of thinking about skills learning, the cognitive tool of imitation/prescription replaces that of mysticism. Users of this tool assume that by listening to the advice of successful practitioners and by imitating their work a person can learn a skill. Little attempt is made to understand the reasons for success: A "what works" mentality characterizes this cognitive tool. Successful practice is explained in terms of a knack or talent. While the learner is not extremely dependent or passive (one *can* learn by imitating others), he or she is nevertheless deprived of any real understanding of why one technique works and another fails. Resting on imitation/prescription, the earliest popular textbooks on rhetoric contained rules that students were supposed to follow and model speeches that students were directed to emulate.

Only when the cognitive tool of analysis/theory-building emerges is there any attempt to understand the reasons for observed outcomes. Users of this cognitive tool reject the ideas that competent performance is the result of a gift from the gods or that imitating others and following prescriptions represents an adequate way to learn a skill. In place of these tools, analysis/theory-building relies on observation, inquiry, and investigation by which tactics it is possible to understand why a speaker succeeds or fails. By understanding how variables operate in a persuasive speaking situation, it is possible to formulate an adequate theory of persuasion. Among the ancient Greeks, Plato and Aristotle were the first to give a truly scientific cast to their study of persuasion. Though they differed along many lines, their emphasis on knowing how and why persuasive speakers affect various audiences represents a crucial common element.

This chapter also showed the major links in the chain that binds rhetorical practice today to that of the ancients. Such thinkers as Cicero, Augustine, Francis Bacon, George Campbell, and Richard Whately all made important contributions to rhetorical theory; in our own century, substantial contributions have been made by James Winans, Kenneth Burke, and Stephen Toulmin.

We are still at a relatively early stage in the development of rhetorical theory. Although many conflicting and even inferior theories of attitude change exist, I provide you here with the best that the field of persuasive speaking has to offer. I have attempted whenever possible to integrate contemporary perspectives and valuable, traditional ones. With effort on your part, with a willingness to experiment, you can take the materials presented here and use them to become an effective persuasive speaker as well as a knowledgeable student of attitude change.

PART TWO

The Science
of Persuasion

Chapter 3

Thinking Like a Scientist

The purpose of this chapter is to familiarize you with the rudiments of the learning approach characteristic of the sciences. As you should know by now, the way scientists study things is quite different from the way other people do. Some people know things intuitively; they feel certain things to be true, and this is all the evidence they need. Some people believe blindly in the opinions of others; they know something is so because someone told them. Others know mystically, through visions and other supernatural messages. But these kinds of knowing are distinctly unscientific. The scientist has an approach to learning that is based on objective evidence. The scientist insists on hard facts rather than on intuition, evidence rather than authority, data rather than mystical visions. In this chapter I will spell out the requirements for what may be called scientific knowing.

My intent is to help you learn to think like a scientist and to form the habit of thinking scientifically about persuasion. I also want to prepare you for the discussion of persuasion theories that appears in Chapter Five, by defining key terms and concepts. Here I will answer such questions as: What is a theory? an hypothesis? a model? What are the tests of a theory? of an hypothesis? I will further introduce you to the scientific method, pointing out the sequence of steps roughly followed when the answer to a problem is sought scientifically. I want to show you that the scientific method is not a strange, esoteric thing, but an entirely reasonable approach to learning. The scientific method is something into which you and I fall almost automatically, by virtue of our rationality. I will show, too, the applicability of the scientific method to the study of persuasion, and particularly to the study of persuasive speaking.

In Chapter Two you saw that of the three learning tools applicable to the study of persuasion—mysticism, imitation/prescription, and analysis/theory-building—the latter seems to hold the most promise for you as a student. The analytical/theoretical approach to the study of persuasion puts competence within the reach of everyone. While innate talent cannot be discounted, you need not rely exclusively on gifts from the gods or on inspiration in learning to speak persuasively. Nor are you bound to imitate others or to follow blindly the prescriptions they set down. Even more important, the analytical approach to the study of persuasion leads to understanding the origins of successful practice. Armed with a basic grasp of why and how persuasion operates, you can, within that broad framework, find your own style. You can be you, and succeed as a persuasive speaker.

In fairness, however, I must remind you that the analytical/theoretical approach to the study of persuasion may seem to have drawbacks. It tends to be more descriptive than prescriptive. If you want specific techniques, if you want to know "how to do it," then the analytical approach may disappoint you. The scientific orientation is geared toward understanding first, applications second. Unlike the sophists of fifth-century B.C. Greece, the scientifically inclined student is more interested in comprehending why something seems to work under a certain set of circumstances than in applications.

Learning to persuade is an indirect outcome of learning about persuasion. This truth may seem curious to you, yet there is no disputing it. When you study persuasion theory, you learn about persuasion. The application of the principles you learn is what makes you an effective persuader.

UNDERSTANDING AND PRESCRIPTION

To see the need for understanding as a prerequisite to prescription and effective practice, consider the following example. Suppose you know a bit about how automobiles run. And suppose a friend came to you with car trouble. The dialogue might go something like this:

> *Friend:* My car won't run. What should I do?
> *You:* What's the matter with it?
> *Friend:* It just won't run. It doesn't start.
> *You:* What happens? I mean, when you turn the key, what goes on? Do you hear a noise?
> *Friend:* Yes, a clicking sound.
> *You:* And that's all?
> *Friend:* Yes.

Before you could give advice to your friend, you needed to determine what was going on. Hence, your earliest efforts were geared to understanding the problem. In fact, in the dialogue you did nothing but ask questions. You needed information before you could prescribe anything. Inquiry geared to understanding always precedes responsible prescription. In the example, you questioned your friend so that you could find out what you needed to know. By answering your questions, he or she made it possible for you to address the situation. Only after assessment could you begin suggesting courses of action.

The problem itself was relatively simple. The clicking sound your friend described suggests a dead battery or a faulty battery cable. A boost or some inspection of and tampering with the battery cable might do the trick. If your friend had said, "It turns over, but it doesn't start," you might have suspected something else. Perhaps gas wasn't getting to the carburetor; perhaps the carburetor was flooded; perhaps the spark plugs were badly fouled. Further questioning would have been required to reduce uncertainty in order to make it possible for you to provide a proper assessment.

The phrase "reduce uncertainty" implies a great deal. It is meant to suggest that reasoned inquiry proceeds systematically through a series of choice points. This is the way a computer works; a program is a set of instructions designed to reduce uncertainty by guiding the mental machine through a maze of choice points. As each is passed, more uncertainty is reduced and it becomes possible to arrive at a conclusion. Let's analyze the dialogue with your friend from this vantage point.

> *Friend: My car won't run. What should I do?* (This comment reduces little uncertainty. It tells you your friend has a car, which you probably knew, and it tells you the car won't run. This is a sort of choice point, since the comment indicates that of the two categories into which cars fall—those that run and those that don't run—your friend's falls into the latter group. Thus it would be utterly inappropriate for you to respond to the comment with the words, "Can I have a ride?")
>
> *You: What's the matter with it?* (Your comment is designed to reduce uncertainty. You want your friend to identify the nature of the problem. But your question is vague, so it doesn't serve your intended purpose very well.)
>
> *Friend: It just won't run. It doesn't start.* (Ah ha! Now you're getting somewhere. It doesn't start. This reduces uncertainty somewhat. It tells you, for example, that the car doesn't start up and then stall out.)
>
> *You: What happens? I mean, when you turn the key, what goes on? Do you hear a noise?* (Here you are again probing for more information to reduce still more uncertainty. Your first question was vague, but your second and third probe for more specific data. You recognize that the more you know about the problem, the better able you'll be to solve it.)
>
> *Friend: Yes, a clicking sound.* (Now you're really getting somewhere. If this is the only sound your friend's car makes, then a great deal of uncertainty is reduced. So you check.)
>
> *You: And that's all?*
>
> *Friend: Yes.* (Now you've reduced a great deal of uncertainty. You may reasonably conclude that the problem originates in the electrical system—perhaps the battery is very weak, or a battery cable is fouled. Further investigation would serve to reduce the remaining uncertainty still further. In the meantime, you've identified the problem as one involving the electrical system. So

at least for now you can rule out other potential problems, such as carburetor flooding. Later these problems may be found to exist, too; if so, they will be discovered and assessed just as this one was.)

The preceding analysis indicates the function of inquiry and investigation in formulating strategies for problem-solving. In a sense, a situation in which you are called on to persuade is a problematical one. You must bring your listeners from one point to another. If you are a salesperson, you have a product and your customer has money. Your goal is to convince your customer to take out the money and exchange it for the product you have to offer. Before you do that, you must inquire and investigate: How can I make this man want to buy my item? What sort of person is he? How can I reach him? Such questions are among those asked by persuasion theorists: What sort of persuasive strategies exist? What are their effects? What sort of auditor are you addressing? Scientific inquiry and systematic investigation lead to tentative conclusions that can be applied to solve persuasive problems. As you can see, the "investigation-prior-to-application" approach makes a great deal of sense.

THEORIES OF ASSESSMENT AND INTERVENTION

In addition to the fact that the scientific approach to the study of persuasion places a premium on understanding, there is a related fact of which you should be aware. Though the distinction is rarely made in the persuasion literature, in reality there are two classes of persuasion theories: *theories of assessment* and *theories of intervention*. *Theories of assessment* are made up of theoretical perspectives on what people are like and how their inner mechanisms operate: theories of personality, for example, and theories of attitude change. *Theories of intervention* are an entirely different, though closely related, set of theories. They have to do with the ways in which people may be changed: for example, how does a persuader bring about changes in an audience's beliefs, attitudes and behavior? Theories that answer these questions are theories of intervention. They are dependent upon an understanding of how people work, but they are apart from such theories, being more closely tied to interventive strategies and techniques for inducing and altering certain attitudes.

In persuasion theory, we are at the very beginning of formulating adequate theories of assessment. This, therefore, is the category into which the vast majority of research studies done to date fall. There is relatively little information available on precisely how to intervene in order to bring about the changes you desire.

Where does this leave you? It leaves you spending a great deal of time learning theories of attitude change, none of which say very much about *how* to go about changing attitudes. What they do tell you is why, when, and under what circumstances attitudes are changed. It will be up to you (with my help) to deduce from that information as many interventive principles as you can.

THE NATURE OF A THEORY

A theory can be defined as a scientific explanation of observed phenomena. The two key words in this definition are *explanation* and *scientific*. Each has a quite specific meaning.

A theory is an explanation in the sense that it accounts for something. Suppose you are driving along a highway. On the right shoulder, you see a late-model sedan. It is jacked up at the rear and a young man is changing the left rear tire. As he works, a young woman stands watching, glancing nervously at the passing cars. Ten or so yards in front of the jacked-up car is a small sports car that looks as though it had been pulled rather hurriedly off to the side. You take in the entire scene as you drive by. What do you make of it? Perhaps you speculate that the young woman driving the sedan got a flat. As she stood on the side of the road, looking desparingly at her tire, the young gallant in the sports car pulled over to lend a hand.

This explanation is a sort of theory to account for what you've observed. You should be especially aware of the fact that theories involve inference. To account for something, you must go beyond the data; you must make a mental connection among the phenomena you've observed.

Viewed from this perspective, theories are not at all foreign to you. They are part of your everyday experience. You make inferences to account for things all the time. For example, in answer to the question of why you always see Shirley when you see Richard is the theory that perhaps they are dating. Why do people who smoke a great deal tend to get lung cancer? Perhaps the two are related. Why do certain speakers seem to convince larger segments of their audience than others? Perhaps there is a tie between speaker behavior and audience responses.

Inference-drawing is central to theorizing. But inferences can be critical or uncritical. Often, it takes a trained mind to piece together the facts of a case. It is typically the untrained mind that arrives at snap judgments and instant explanations of what has been observed. The danger of uncritical inference-drawing is pointed out colorfully by Villers (1962, p. 4): "It would be wrong," he comments, "to conclude from finding that Scotch and soda, bourbon and soda, and rye and soda all produce intoxication, that soda is the only factor in common and therefore the cause of the intoxication!" Going beyond the facts, which is at the heart of theory-formulation, is a delicate business. It requires patience and highly polished observational skills.

Criteria for a scientific explanation

What makes an explanation scientific? Why, for example, are meteorologists considered scientists while devotees of rain gods are called primitives?

Each can explain or account for changes in the weather. What makes one explanation scientific and another nonscientific?

According to Boyce Rensberger (1977), science reporter for *The New York Times*, our age seems to have some difficulty making the distinction between scientific and nonscientific. For example, Rensenberger reports that according to a recent Gallup pole, thirty-two million Americans believe in astrology. Countless books and articles are written purporting to prove that humankind was planted here by beings from outer space; others testify to the magical qualities of the so-called Bermuda Triangle. Recent fads include biorhythms, parapsychology, and psychic surgery. The "explanations" provided by these pseudosciences are perhaps remotely plausible, but they are hardly scientific.

Strictly speaking, a scientific explanation must meet four criteria: (1) it must be tentative, (2) it must be provisional, (3) it must be testable, and (4) it must be based on observation. The first two criteria imply that a truly scientific explanation is never absolute. It is always subject to revision and qualification in light of new facts and evidence. The truth it embodies is invariably based on certain contingencies and circumstances. There can be no scientific dogma, no official or absolute truth in science. Rather, in the realm of science, there are tentative conclusions and plausible explanations. Science is—or ought to be—open-ended. The door is never quite closed on scientific inquiry.

Recently, much criticism has been aimed at science on the grounds that its methods and findings are beginning to take on a dogmatic and absolutist quality. Modern science has been compared to theology during the Middle Ages—it is considered the only source of true knowledge. The scientific method is believed by many to be the sole source of valid information. Whether you agree with this criticism or not, science does run the risk of becoming absolutist. Scientific dogmatism, which occurs when the door to inquiry is closed, lurks not far beneath the facade of objectivity.

The third critierion a truly scientific explanation must meet is testability. It must be based on more than authority or popular belief; evidence must be provided. Here again the pseudoscientists present an illusory form of evidence. One typical strategy is to bombard the skeptic with reams of data so overwhelming as to preclude careful examination. "How could this person be wrong?" the skeptic may ask. "This person seems so sure, so bolstered by evidence . . ." But careful examination of the evidence provided invariably reveals more puff than substance. Flimsily worded statements conceal a dearth of hard data. Speculation masquerades as fact.

Evidence for a claim may be of two sorts: direct and indirect. Both are gleaned from a careful test of the claim. Direct evidence points to the claim without any intermediate steps. For example, if you were to formulate an hypothesis that a speaker's credentials affect audience judgment of the speaker's credibility, you might test your hypothesis by having the same speaker introduced to two separate audiences. In one case, the speaker would be described as possessing a long list of impressive credentials that would be recognized and esteemed by the audience. In the other case, the speaker would be introduced without any credentials given. Immediately after the introduction, you would ask the members of the audience for their estimates of the speaker's credibility. Your prediction would be that the audience would find the same speaker more credible with a long list of impressive credentials. If they did (and it is very likely that they would), then your claim would be supported directly.

Indirect evidence includes an intermediary step. Schematically, indirect evidence for a claim might look like this: "If proposition X is true, then Y should follow; hence Z will occur." To use the example above, you might proceed as before; but rather than predicting directly that the audience would consider the same speaker more credible with an impressive list of credentials, you would predict more attitude change *after* the speaker had given the speech. This difference in degree of attitude change would be due only to the difference in audience judgments of speaker credibility. For example, the same speaker would present the same speech before the two audiences; the only difference between the events would be in the way the speaker was introduced. If you found—as you probably would—that the speaker with impressive credentials induced more attitude change than the speaker without credentials, then you might reasonably conclude that the difference was due to the credentials, rather than (for example) to the speech delivered. Thus you would have gleaned indirect evidence for your claim that a speaker's credentials affect audience judgment of the speaker's credibility. Put into schematic form, this line of thought would look like the representation in Figure 3.1.

The fourth criterion for a scientific explanation is that it must be based on observation. The difference between the mystic and the scientist is that the former relies on an internal sense of the truth of a thing; the latter eschews the intuitive and the subjective and seeks instead objectively verifiable truth. Hence, science has been described as a public undertaking; studies are conducted in the open and are subject to evaluation and scrutiny. In fact, it is a tradition in reporting scientific experiments to include sufficient information—on the subjects used, the techniques, measuring instruments, and methodology—to make it possible for someone interested in verifying the

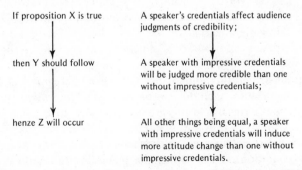

Figure 3.1. Schematic Illustration of Indirect Evidence for a Claim

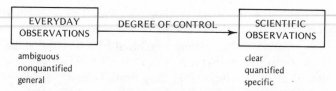

Figure 3.2. Difference Between Everyday and Scientific Observations

findings to replicate the study, to see if the same results are obtained as those reported. This is very much unlike the "truth" reported by the visionary, which is unverifiable. A person may feel something to be true on the gut level, but that knowledge is hardly scientific, although it may nevertheless be true.

It is important to emphasize that observations may vary from uncontrolled to very tightly controlled. Those upon which scientific truths are based are invariably tightly controlled. They differ from casual, everyday observations very sharply. As depicted in Figure 3.2, everyday observations are ambiguous, nonquantified, and general. Scientific observations are clear, quantified, and specific. Hence the scientist's fascination with reducing observations to quantifiable form. The scientist prefers a numerical rating to a general description. For example, to say that a person is depressed is a general description that conveys an impression but is not specific. It is quite another thing to say that a person has scored 68 on a depression inventory on which a score of 65 indicates need of immediate hospitalization. Scientists favor verifiable, objective data. They base their preference on the view that the more objective knowledge you and I possess, the more likely we are to make an accurate assessment of a situation.

Hypotheses, generalizations, and theories

Here I want to introduce the term hypothesis and show the relationship among hypotheses, generalizations, and theories. Simply put, a theory is a set of generalizations, which are hypotheses that have been proved valid. An hypothesis, in other words, is a single statement having bearing on one tiny piece of reality. When an hypothesis is tested and found to be true, it becomes a scientific generalization.

Note that there are different kinds of generalizations. In the social sciences, most generalizations are normative and contingent. By normative is meant that they establish central tendencies, not exact mathematical formulas. A normative generalization includes words like *most, typically*, and *characteristically*. Because the social sciences are inexact, normative generalizations are often the best principles they can generate. The second characteristic of generalizations in the social sciences is contingency. A contingent generalization specifies the conditions under which the generalization applies. Key words that imply contingency include *under these certain conditions* (usually the conditions are specified in the generalization) and *given these circumstances.* Regardless of whether generalizations are normative and contingent, however, a theory consists of an interrelated set of generalizations.

A theory, in other words, consists of a system of coordinated, validated hypotheses, which when taken together constitute a complete explanation. The hallmark of a good theory is that a few general propositions can account for a large number of particular facts.

The social sciences generally, and persuasion researchers in particular, have been criticized for trying to formulate theories too early, that is, before basic research has generated a sufficient number of valid findings to make possible the construction of useful general principles (Cronkhite, 1969, p. 21). Whether you agree with this criticism or not, it rests on the distinction I have made here between hypotheses (the testing of which constitutes basic research) and theories.

What, exactly, is an hypothesis? Formally defined, it is a tentative statement of a relationship between two variables. Usually, an hypothesis implies a causal relationship: when even *A* occurs, even *B* follows. For example, when a strong fear appeal* is used by a highly credible source (event *A*), then the likelihood of audience behavior that runs counter to the appeal is diminished (event *B*). Note that an hypothesis is the result of inference and creative thought. As you saw earlier, inference-drawing means making connections between things you see. Before explaining the term *variable,* and before distinguishing between dependent and independent variables, I want to present the following timely activity.

Student Activity Option 3.1
Person Perception

INSTRUCTIONS
An hypothesis is a tentative statement of a relationship between two variables. When you and I formulate hypotheses, we infer on the basis of one thing that another is true. According to one point of view, our perceptions of people are influenced by the hypotheses we formulate about them. When we meet someone for the first time, we tend to go beyond the data (those personal attributes we actually see) and infer the presence of other personal qualities (Hastorf, Schneider, and Polefka, 1970). This is the process by which audiences form first impressions of speakers as well.

The following exercise is designed to help you become aware of some of your own internal hypotheses about people. Please read each of the following statements, then fill in the blank with an appropriate word or phrase that describes a personal trait. It is important that the words you choose refer to a personal attribute or characteristic. Thus, words like "shy," "happy," or "extroverted" would

---

*A fear appeal is a line of thought which plays upon an audience's fears. For example, "If you don't brush your teeth regularly, they will rot and fall out."

be appropriate; but words like "from big cities" or "film makers" would be inappropriate. After you have filled in each blank, consult with your instructor and classmates regarding their word choices.

Fill in the blank spaces in each of the sentences below:

1. People who are educated are generally _____.
2. People who are artistic are often _____ .
3. People who are aggressive are seldom _____.
4. People who are soft-spoken are usually _____.
5. People who are ambitious are generally _____.

Did you and your classmates choose the same words to fill in the blanks? How much variation is present in your class? Chances are that a considerable range of responses is present because each of us tends to carry around internally an individual set of hunches about what people are like. Based on our past experience, we tend to infer that a person with one particular personality trait is likely to possess another. For example, you may have known a number of artistic people. On the basis of certain qualities they displayed, you have formulated a private and internal hypothesis about artistic people, perhaps that they are impulsive or unreliable. Your stereotype is uniquely your own. Others in your class may have had quite different experiences with artistic people. Consequently, their private hypotheses may be very different from yours.

Interestingly, people tend to vary in their willingness to discard their hypotheses. Although it is possible to form an erroneous first impression, a person might be utterly unwilling to revise it. (This unwillingness to revise a first impression is at the heart of prejudice.) Unable to revise stereotypes, the person for whom first impressions are permanent likely possesses a very low tolerance for ambiguity and a strong tendency toward authoritarianism. On the other hand, the more open you are to experience, the more you are willing to admit that your first impressions may be in need of revising. Thus, you may say to yourself, "He seemed like a stuffed shirt when I first met him, but he turned out to be a regular guy!"

This sort of statement implies a revision of your initial hypothesis about what the individual was like. Technically speaking, what you did first was to form an impression on the basis of your private view of people. Then, in light of new data you gathered, you revised your hypothesis to construct one that more accurately conformed to reality. Once you have formulated this revised hypothesis, you operate on the basis of it until it is validated (in which case you feel that you really "know" the person) or once again revised.

SUGGESTED READINGS

If you are interested in this view of interpersonal perception, you will find either of the following fascinating:

Hastorf, Albert H., David J. Schneider, and Judith Polefka (1970) *Person Perception*. Reading, Massachusetts: Addison-Wesley Publishing Company.
Wiggins, Nancy P., P. Hoffman, and T. Taber (1969) "Types of Judges and Cue Utilization in Judgements of Intelligence," *Journal of Personality and Social Psychology*, 12: 52–59.

Dependent and independent variables

Hypotheses tie together variables. A variable is anything that can vary. For example, you can vary the amount of sugar in a cake recipe and come up with a more sweet or a less sweet cake. You can vary your style of delivery in a speech and come up with a speech that is more effective or less effective. If you examine the two preceding statements carefully, you will probably note that in each there is one variable that is manipulated (i.e., the amount of sugar in sentence one, the style of delivery in sentence two) and another variable that is changed as a result of the manipulations (i.e., the sweetness of the cake, the effectiveness of the speech).

There are two kinds of variables that are of special interest for the scientist who formulates and tests hypotheses and for the consumer of scientific research. The first kind are *independent variables;* these are the variables the experimenter manipulates—the amount of sugar and the style of delivery. The second are called *dependent variables*, since changes in them are dependent on the experimenter's manipulations. Since the testing of hypotheses involves making one or more predictions, the researcher speculates that if changes in variable *A* (the independent variable) occur, changes in variable *B* (the dependent variable) will follow. Here are some examples of hypotheses that have been tested in persuasion research:

1. A study of male and female speech patterns tested the hypothesis that strongly assertive grammatical forms (for example, "please don't," "you mustn't," "I want") would be attributed relatively more often to males, while less assertive forms (for example, "if it wouldn't be too much trouble," "I'm sorry to bother you, but") would be attributed relatively more often to females. (Siegler and Siegler, 1976). In this case, the grammatical forms constitute the independent variable; judgments of who said them are the dependent variable. The hypothesis was confirmed.
2. Initial favorability toward a message's position is positively related to amount of recall of that message (Burgoon, 1975). In this case, initial favorability is the independent variable; amount of recall is the dependent variable. The hypothesis was validated.
3. Varying the number of arguments presented to support an advocated opinion should influence the effectiveness of an expert source more than an attractive source (Norman, 1976). In this case, the number of arguments presented is the independent variable; the effectiveness of the speaker is the dependent variable. The hypothesis was not validated.

I think you can see that in each of these cases there is a clear prediction made. The prediction says that as a result of manipulations of an identified independent variable, changes will occur in a dependent variable. Thus the definition of an hypothesis as a tentative statement of a relationship between two variables can serve to orient you to the method of science.

Three additional important points need to be made about hypotheses. First, like observations, hypotheses can vary in the care with which they are made. Intuitive and loose hypotheses, like those discussed in Student Activity Option 3.1, are not really testable. They are not truly scientific, although they do serve as one basis upon which we behave. A truly scientific hypothesis is always precise, rigorous, and testable by reference to specific numbers. Whether an audience is inclined toward a message's position is something that can be put in quantitative terms: audience A rated 3.6 on initial favorability toward the message's position; audience B rated 9.8 on the same scale. It is important to keep this principle in mind, because in Chapter Seven you will have the opportunity to formulate hypotheses for testing. When you do so, you should avoid intuitive and nontestable hypotheses and prefer rigorous, testable ones.

The second point is that the language of hypotheses can vary in operational specificity. Intuitive and nonscientific hypotheses typically contain loose and vague language, words that cannot be defined operationally. Scientific hypotheses, on the other hand, are invariably precise; the concepts they contain can always be defined operationally. A scientist does not merely say that the subjects in the experiment were intelligent; a scientist defines the concept operationally by saying that the subjects scored between 120 and 145 on a particular IQ exam. Operational definitions demand objectification and quantification; hence the scientist is characteristically referred to as "hard-headed" because of insistence on precise arithmetic data; the nonscientist is usually referred to as "soft-headed" because of acceptance of such loose terms as *love, understanding,* and *brotherhood,* each of which is rather difficult to define operationally.

The third point I wish to make is that in persuasion research a number of variables are tested. It is convenient to organize them into three categories—speaker variables, message variables, and audience variables. Hypotheses that predict changes in audience response on the basis of who the speaker is, what the speaker is like, and how the audience perceives the speaker, focus on the impact of speaker variables. The independent variables manipulated by the experimenter have to do with the speaker. In these studies the experimenter manipulates the audience's beliefs about or perceptions of the speaker.

Hypotheses in which message variables are the independent variables concern themselves with characteristics of the speech itself; for example, message organization, evidence, or speech length. A third set of hypotheses focuses on audience variables as the independent variable. In these, the speaker and speech remain constant, but certain audience traits vary from one speech situation to another. For example, an hypothesis might include a prediction that a more intelligent audience will be less influenced by emotional appeals than will a less intelligent one. (Remember that such concepts as "more intelligent" would have to be defined operationally!) Other audience variables include age, sex, level of authoritarianism, and group affiliations. It is not the purpose of this book to present more than a rudimentary knowledge of statistical methods; however, you should know that certain statistical procedures make it possible for an experimenter to study the effects of alterations in more than one variable at a time. For example, as an experimenter, you might manipulate both speech variables (for example, message organization) and audience variables (for example, listeners' sex).

The number of variables an experimenter might manipulate is infinite. This is a mixed blessing, for it permits virtually unlimited testing of propositions about persuasive speaking. However, there has been a tendency over the years to have research go off in several directions at once, with little order or system to the investigations undertaken. This results in a piecemeal approach to theory-building that is unsystematic and often redundant. The most brilliant researchers, those who make a real contribution to a field, think carefully before they conduct studies. They ask themselves provocative questions: What study would prove or disprove a central tenet of a particular theory of persuasion? What question in the field is yet to be resolved? What kind of study would answer it once and for all? The challenge of research is not merely to generate study after study, but to create critical studies, investigations that answer real questions and that help to advance the task of theory-building.

Student Activity Option 3.2
Theory and Research

INSTRUCTIONS
If you want to read a more detailed discussion of the relationship between theory and research, you will find the following essays interesting:

SUGGESTED READINGS
Becker, Samuel (1965) "Methodological Analysis in Communication Research," *Quarterly Journal of Speech* 51: 382–91.
Simon, Clarence (1951) "Speech as a Science," *Quarterly Journal of Speech* 37: 281–98.
Thayer, Lee (1963) "On Theory-building in Communication: Some Conceptual Problems," *Journal of Communication* 13: 217–35.
Webb, Eugene J. and Donald T. Campbell (1973) "Experiments on Communication Effects," pp. 938–52 in Ithiel de Sola Pool, Frederick W. Frey, Wilbur Schramm, Nathan Maccoby, and Edwin B. Parker, eds. *Handbook of Communication*. Chicago: Rand McNally College Publishing Company.

TESTS OF A THEORY OR AN HYPOTHESIS

Earlier in the chapter, I asked you to picture a scene on the shoulder of a road. There was a jacked-up sedan and a sports car. A young man was changing the left rear tire of the sedan; while he worked, an attractive young woman stood by glancing nervously at the passing traffic. When I asked what you made of the scene, we agreed that most likely the woman had gotten a flat and that young Sir Galahad had stopped to lend a hand. That theory seems plausible enough.

However, think again. How certain are you that what you hypothesized in fact occurred? Did you have any evidence that the sports car was his and the sedan hers? How do you know the two of them weren't traveling together in the sedan? Perhaps the sports car was totally unrelated and was present quite by accident. The answer to these questions is that you don't know, you cannot be certain. As a matter of fact, the little scene you witnessed can be explained in any number of ways. My personal favorite is that the two individuals are spies who met at a prearranged site. As he fixed the tire, he slipped into the hubcap a microfilm of some top-secret document. Once he had hidden the film, the female spy had instructions to drive to a lonely street corner and . . . . Well, you get the picture! Silly, isn't it? Perhaps so, but you still can't be sure, on the basis of what you saw, that my hypothesis is incorrect.

My point is that while the same phenomenon can often be explained in more than one way, there must be some way to estimate the plausibility and quality of an explanation. That two theories can account for the same thing is not subject to question. Light, for example, can be explained by wave theory and by quantum theory. Each is plausible; each provides a satisfactory explanation of what you and I experience as light. In the same way, attitude change can be explained by several different theories.

What makes one theory or hypothesis better than another? How are qualitative distinctions made? Fortunately, a set of rather clear criteria can be applied to answer the question. Some of these criteria you have already encountered. For example, you know that a scientific explanation is tentative, provisional, testable, and based on observation. In addition to these familiar criteria, however, there are additional ones. Let's look briefly at these.

A satisfactory scientific explanation must account for all known data. It cannot leave unexplained any observed bit of information. For example, a theory of the Earth's origins that failed to explain the presence of oceans would be unsatisfactory. A theory of persuasion that failed to account for the presence of resistance to counterpersuasion would be inadequate. Believe it or not, through the ages many widely accepted theories have failed to account for obvious facts; only when those deficits were pointed out and a new, more comprehensive theory formulated was scientific advancement possible. Thus, for example, William Harvey's theory that blood circulates through the body explained the fact that arteries pulsate rhythmically; before Harvey demonstrated the validity of this viewpoint, this fact was simply not accounted for adequately.

A second criterion for evaluating a theory or an hypothesis is that it must be consistent with all known facts. Put another way, an adequate explanation must not contradict any known facts. Some agnostics, for example, are fond of arguing that Jesus did not exist, that he was a figment of someone's imagination. This skeptical viewpoint fails to account for the fact that evidence of his existence can be found not only in the Bible, but also in completely independent secular sources—in the writings of Josephus, Pliny the Younger, and the historians Tacitus and Suetonius, for example.

Still another criterion has been implied in much that I have said so far: An adequate scientific explanation must predict. This is another way of saying that it must be testable. The accuracy of the predictions it generates is a measure of the worth of the explanation. Thus, for example, Einstein's theory of relativity postulated that under certain conditions the gulf between matter and energy could be bridged, resulting in an unleashing of a tremendous force. That force is called atomic power. Einstein's theory proved to be correct.

Medical diagnostics relies heavily on prediction. To confirm a diagnosis, a doctor will often go beyond the data observed and predict that if the patient is suffering from a particular illness, certain consequences will follow. For example, if someone has strep throat, a throat culture will reveal the presence of the streptococcal bacteria. Hence a culture is taken, the appropriate chemicals are applied, and the consequences observed. If the diagnosis is accurate, the prediction—that the patient has strep throat—will prove to be true.

In the same way, theorists of attitude change make predictions. If it is true, for example, that a speaker with impressive credentials will be more effective in inducing attitude change than will a speaker without credentials, then if everything else is held constant except the audience's beliefs about the speaker's credentials, it follows that a well-credentialed speaker will induce more attitude change than a speaker without credentials.

A closely related criterion is that a scientific explanation must be disconfirmable—it must be capable of being disproved. An explanation is flawed when it is so broad and general that it can't be disproved. This criticism has been leveled at the dissonance theory of attitude change (see Chapter Four). Critics contend that the theory is so vague and general that just about any eventuality can be accounted for within its framework (Chapanis and Chapanis, 1964); hence, it is not disconfirmable. To be accepted as scientifically verified, an explanation must be subject to critical experimentation that can test basic components of the theory. If those basic components are so general that they can't be tested empirically, then there is something wrong with the theory.

An adequate explanation must be internally consistent, that is, it cannot contradict itself. To say at one point that the major factor contributing to attitude change is the organization of the message, and at another point that organization seems to exert the least influence of all message variables, is to issue two statements that are contradictory. Any theory that says something is both true and untrue is internally inconsistent.

An additional criterion that many writers set down is that an adequate explanation must be consistent with previously confirmed explanations. A theory of attitude change would be subject to criticism if it were inconsistent with the previously well-established principle in social psychology that individuals act so as to maintain cognitive balance. In other words, you and I resist changes in our attitudinal sets; any theory of attitude change that runs counter to that well-established principle would be subject to serious doubt. This is not to say that an unconventional or original theory is invariably wrong; rather, this criterion implies that a theory that requires substantial revision in the accepted view of things ought to have an impressive preponderance of evidence in its favor. Recall my discussion of burden of proof (Chapter Two).

Finally, an adequate scientific explanation must be brief and concise, yet general and complete. The best theories are those that explain a great deal by means of a very few general principles. In the physical sciences, there are many such elegant explanations. Einstein's $E = MC^2$ (which roughly translated means that energy equals mass times the speed of light multiplied by itself) is noteworthy because it is simple, stark, and profound. Bernoulli's theorem (that the faster a fluid moves past an object, the less sideways pressure is exerted on the body by the fluid) explains a wide variety of phenomena, from the operation of a carburetor to why a curved ball curves. It is also the basis of all wing design and explains in a rudimentary way why airplanes fly. The wide range of phenomena accounted for by Bernoulli's theorem is testimony to its explanatory power.

In the social sciences, there are relatively few simple propositions with such wide-ranging explanatory power. In part, that is because the phenomena with which the social sciences deal are so complex. Further, serious study in the social sciences is of relatively recent origin, and the sciences simply aren't sufficiently developed to generate such principles. However, if I had to state three representative principles of the social sciences, I would choose these: (1) the frequency of behavior that is postively reinforced is greater than that of behavior that is not reinforced; (2) as a result of social learning, people generalize beyond their experience to new but similar or related situations; and (3) progress toward the attainment of a desired goal is experienced as pleasant, whereas frustration and failure are experienced as unpleasant.

A great deal more can be said about evaluating alternative explanations of the same phenomenon. The following Student Activity Option is designed to deepen your understanding of this topic; it also includes a list of strongly recommended readings, carefully selected for interest value and substance.

Student Activity Option 3.3 _____
Evaluating Explanations

INSTRUCTIONS
For this activity, read the brief articles indicated and prepare a written or oral report. With your instructor's consent, present your findings to the class. Another possibility is to engage in a debate with a classmate on the subject of evolutionary theory. The readings listed after the activity are more general in scope. They are well worth your time.

Debate Over Evolutionary Theory

Almost from its promulgation, the theory of evolution has encountered stiff opposition from religious fundamentalists who view it as a threat to their basic beliefs. In 1925, a young biology teacher in Tennessee ran afoul of the law by teaching evolutionary theory. The famous Scopes trial (also called the "monkey trial") was the result. Resistance to evolutionary theory continues to this day. In California in 1972, the state Board of Education was taken to task by fundamentalists for adopting elementary and junior high school books that considered only evolutionary theory. Critics maintained that their religious rights were being infringed upon because the God theory of creation was not included in the texts. How does the God theory of creation compare with evolutionary theory? What are the strengths and weaknesses of each? Were the California educators guilty of scientific dogmatism when they chose to adopt texts that did not include an alternative to evolutionary theory? Note that a similar controversy erupted in Iowa in 1979, resulting in emotionally charged protests at Iowa State University and on the statehouse steps. The following readings deal with the Tennessee, California, and Iowa controversies.

Tennessee
Scopes, J. T. (1971/1925) World's Most Famous Court Trial: State of Tennessee V. John T. Scopes. New York: Da Capo.
Sprague de Camp, L. (1968) *The Great Monkey Trial*. Garden City: Doubleday

California
Hechinger, Fred M. (1972) "Should God Have Equal Time?" *The New York Times* (Sunday, December 17) Section E, p. 7.

Iowa
"Iowa Takes a Breather in Dispute Over Theories of Human Origins," *The New York Times* (Sunday, June 3, 1979), Section A. p. 49 (United Press International).

Suggested Readings
Boring E. G. (1953) "The Role of Theory in Experimental Psychology," *American Journal of Pscyhology*, 2: 71–75.
Copi, Irving M. (1953) *Introduction to Logic*. New York: Macmillan. See especially Chapter Thirteen, pp. 384–428.
Kleiman, Dena (1980) "Foes of Evolution Theory Ask Equal School Time" *The New York Times* (April 7), p. 1.
Rensberger, Boyce (1977) "The Invasion of the Pseudoscientists," *The New York Times* (November 20), Section E, p. 16.
Skinner, B. F. (1971) *Beyond Freedom and Dignity*. New York: Bantam Books. See especially Chapter One, pp. 1–23.
Standen, Anthony (1950) *Science Is a Sacred Cow*. New York: E. P. Dutton.
The Zetetic. This periodical published by the Committee for the Scientific Investigation of Claims of the Paranormal, includes detailed criticisms of the claims of pseudoscientists.

THE SCIENTIFIC METHOD

One of the ways scientists ensure the validity of the explanations they generate is by following a set of principles collectively known as the scientific method. This approach to problem-solving is used in two types of studies and in the investigation of two problems that have pertinence to you as a student of persuasive speaking.

To provide you with an overview, I want first to present the steps in the scientific method: (1) recognition and statement of the problem, (2) formulation of a tentative hypothesis, (3) testing the hypothesis, (4) analysis of the data, (5) formulation of the conclusion, and (6) application of the conclusion to the problem. Let's look at each of these in turn.

Recognition and statement of the problem

The first step in all scientific investigation is inquiry. You notice that each time you eat chocolate you get a headache. "Why does that occur with such regularity?" you ask yourself. In doing so, you have begun to operate according to the scientific method.

Suppose you are a male who's gotten a job as a salesperson in an auto dealership. At about the same time, a young woman named Sue was hired. She is about your age and has a college degree from the same institution from which you are about to earn yours. In fact, you introduced yourself because you thought she looked familiar. Sure enough, the two of you were in the same classes a few semesters back; she was a speech-communication major just as you are! On the job, you notice that Sue sells much more consistently than you. She is closing deals and earning money while your sales are few and far between. "Why is Sue so successful?" you ask yourself.

The problem consists of a group of facts looking for an acceptable and satisfactory explanation of Sue's success. How do you define the problem? Problem formulation involves narrowing down, focusing in on factors that seem to be able to account for what you see. The way you formulate the problem is critically important, because your definition of a problem dictates the terms of the solution.

Before defining the problem properly, let's quickly look at two inadequate definitions and examine the erroneous "solutions" to which they point. You might, for example, conclude that Sue's success is due to a gift from the gods (the same factor to which some ancient Greek rhetoricians attributed success in persuasion). If that were the case, you might try to succeed by praying, offering sacrifices, or otherwise attempting to persuade the gods to give you the same gifts they gave Sue. More plausible is the view that Sue's success is due to some ill-defined quality called luck. Maybe Sue carries a rabbit's foot or has a red ribbon tied to the steering column of her car. If this were the case, you might seek to emulate her success by purchasing a rabbit's foot or tying a red ribbon to the steering column of your car.

As you can see from these examples, improperly defined problems lead to inadequate solutions. For this reason, it is especially important to state your problem clearly, simply, and directly, together with the assumptions upon which you are basing your investigation. For example, you might state explicitly that you assume that Sue's success is due to natural causes. The problem statement should include your ultimate objective in researching the problem ("to increase my sales success"). It should also specify any limiting conditions that may operate in your study (are there limitations to the amount of trouble you're willing to go through to answer the question?). Finally, an adequate statement of the problem should include an indication of your proposed method of attacking the problem, perhaps by observing Sue's behavior and studying any other observable factors that may contribute to her high success rate.

To focus more sharply on the problem of increasing your sales success, you spend time eliminating all those factors that don't seem to be able to explain what you have observed. Sue is selling the same product as you, so it can't be that. She is working in the same showroom, has an office equivalent to yours, and puts in no more hours than you do. Her education? sales training? prior experience? All these are equivalent to yours; hence these can't account for her higher success rate. She sells to the same sort of prospects you confront, walk-ins and phone-ins primarily, and the number of customers she deals with is about the same as you do. You discreetly inquire and learn that Sue does not cut her commissions, nor does she have any other cozy arrangement with the boss that makes it possible for the dealership to make less money per car and thereby increase Sue's sales volume.

Having eliminated a good many factors that might have accounted for what you observed, you focus in still more clearly, working with what's left—since these factors may operate to produce the observed effect. Let's suppose for good reasons you eliminate things like personality, age, hair color, and ethnicity, and that you are left with the factor of sex as a primary distinguishing feature between Sue and you. You mull this over in your head: Perhaps Sue's sex is a factor. You decide to begin compiling data on the sex of Sue's successful prospects. Does she sell to more men than you do? to more women? In what proportion does she sell to members of both sexes? Then a number of other questions arise: What percentage of serious prospects who enter auto dealerships are male? What percent are female? Who actually buys cars, and in what proportions?

At this point, you have prepared the way for some refined observations. You might study statistical data on auto purchasers, on the clientele of your dealership, and on the success rate of female salespersons in other dealerships. You might want to limit your survey to dealers who sell the same cars as you do or to those who sell cars in the same price range.

Your approach to the problem up to this point has tended to be descriptive rather than experimental. This distinction is important. Descriptive research has as its end the accumulation and interpretation of data. But it does not involve the manipulation of variables in the sense about which I spoke earlier. When an experimenter deliberately manipulates an independent variable to see the effects on a dependent variable, he or she is doing an experiment. For purposes of illustration, I will continue with the problem of accounting for

Sue's sales success by means of a descriptive study. Later, I will show the operation of the scientific method in an experimental study.

Whether you decide to conduct descriptive or experimental research, you will need to formulate an hypothesis. That is the next step in the scientific method.

Formulation of a tentative hypothesis

Once you've formulated a problem, your next task is to make an educated guess that can serve to explain what you have observed. Speculating that Sue's sex has something to do with her success record, you decide to begin gathering data. Your informed guess is that saleswomen of Sue's age and background complete a higher percentage of sales than do salesmen of equivalent age and background. This statement serves as a guide for research. Notice that it contains a prediction; you are forecasting that the data you compile will support this view. Thus, the hypothesis provides you with a structure. To validate it or to prove it untrue, you will need to collect data on the number of deals initiated by male and female salespersons of Sue's age and background, and on the number of deals consummated by both males and females. Should you find that a larger percentage of deals are consummated by females, your hypothesis would have some support. You might even conclude tentatively that Sue's success is due to her sex. Of course, other factors could be operating, and a careful researcher would look more deeply into the matter for a more satisfactory answer. Perhaps, for example, it is not one's sex *per se* that makes the difference, but certain ways of thinking and acting that females tend to learn while males do not. In fact, the matter is likely far more complex than has been suggested here, but I think you can see nevertheless that an ordered and systematic approach to problem-solving is characteristic of the scientific method.

Testing the hypothesis

As I have said, there is no manipulation of variables in a descriptive study in the same sense as there is in an experimental study. In this instance, therefore, the test of your hypothesis would consist of gathering data on the incidence of deals initiated and consummated by male and female salespersons. Note that in descriptive as in other forms of research, as data are gathered, it may be necessary to abandon or to refine your hypothesis. You may find that the data available do not allow you to establish or to disprove your hypothesis. For example, perhaps dealerships do not keep statistics on the sex of the salespersons involved in closing deals. Or perhaps saleswomen have not worked in auto dealerships long enough to make possible a meaningful across-sex comparison. In these cases, your hypothesis would have to be abandoned. (This does not mean you could not attack the problem differently, however.) Another possibility is that dealerships may keep records that include information on the sex of salespersons but not on their background. This situation would also require a revision of your hypothesis.

What I am suggesting is that the scientific approach to problem-solving is often circular: A hypothesis provides a direction for research, but data sometimes result in changes in the hypothesis. This sort of mutuality of influence is required in order to ensure that a researcher says neither more nor less than the data allow.

Analysis of the data

Once you have compiled your statistics, you would need to interpret them. This involves looking for their meaning. A comparison would be done between statistics for male salespersons and those for females. Then it would be necessary to crosscheck the results of this comparison with the differences you might expect to find if chance alone operated. Statistical significance occurs when the findings you get are very, very unlikely to have occurred by mere chance. (The old saw about the likelihood of a monkey's writing the Bible if you set enough monkeys down in front of enough typewriters gets at the notion of the likelihood of chance occurrence of an event.)

All data analysis involves making sense of the statistics you've gathered. Your concern at this stage of the problem-solving process is to see whether the information at hand points to the fact that sex alone accounts for Sue's success as a salesperson.

Formulation of the conclusion

What has your analysis of the data allowed you to conclude? To what conclusion do your findings point? Perhaps your data indicate that what you suspected is true—namely, that female salespersons close more deals than their male counterparts. This interesting finding might well lead to still another study, one designed to determine what it is about the behavior of females that accounts for their remarkable success rate. But the purposes of this particular study have been realized. At this point, you are able to apply your conclusion to the original problem in the final step in the scientific method.

Application of the conclusion to the problem

Recall that this entire inquiry began with observations of an unexplained fact—Sue's success. Your intent was to begin solving the mystery by gathering and interpreting appropriate data. Your study as depicted here was a preliminary one, but it enabled you to begin isolating one factor as a major contributing cause of Sue's superior rate of sales. With more thought and more research, it might be possible to account for Sue's track record in even more detail. The ultimate aim of these studies, of course, would be to answer the question definitively. A final solution to the problem occurs when an adequate and verified hypothesis (or several hypotheses) explains the observed facts that were the spur to inquiry originally.

EXPERIMENTAL RESEARCH

As I indicated earlier, the sort of research dealt with in our hypothetical study was descriptive. Another kind of research is experimental. Let's take a moment to retrace the steps in the scientific method, this time seeing how they operate in the context of an experimental study. As a starting point, let's suppose you've noticed two speakers in your class. One of them, Marcia, succeeds consistently, while the other, Sandy, seems never to move the audience. You've thought about those features that distinguish one speaker from the other, and the one that seems most obvious is message organization. Marcia gives speeches that invariably seem well organized. Sandy's talks seem scattered and disorganized. In most other respects—delivery, quality of proofs, and so on—the speeches they give are roughly equivalent in quality. On the basis of these observations, you decide to study the effect of message organization on speech effectiveness.

Recognition and statement of the problem

At this point, you have recognized a problem and have formulated it in such a way that it is limited and specific. Your purpose is clear. In the narrowest sense, it is to account for Marcia's success as a persuader. More generally, your purpose is to determine the influence of message organization on speech effectiveness. You do a literature search to see what findings have been reported by other researchers. Let's assume you find no studies dealing with message organization. (This is, however, pure fiction. Many such studies have been conducted.) You're on your own. In your approach to the problem, you are limited to an investigation that can be undertaken by an undergraduate student. Further, let's assume you've decided that your study will utilize other undergraduates; for example, you will use an undergraduate speaker who will talk to other undergraduates.

This limitation raises the interesting question of the generalizability of your findings. When a study is conducted, care is taken to ensure that the sample utilized in the study is representative of some larger population; therefore, what is true of the subjects in the study can be generalized to the larger group that they represent. It has been said that the extensive use of undergraduate students in studies conducted by academic psychologists has led to the specious definition of psychology as the science of the behavior of the college sophomore! This definition actually conceals a real concern—namely, that the findings reported in the majority of psychological studies conducted by academics may not be valid for people as a whole. They may be limited in applicability to college sophomores (or to the college population) since the samples utilized may only be representative of *that* population rather than of people in general.

You have decided to approach the problem experimentally. You will carefully observe the effect of message organization on audience attitude change. You plan to accomplish this by keeping tight controls on other variables that may influence message effectiveness. To the extent that you are able, you will hold constant all other factors: for example, quality of proofs, language style, speaker and audience variables.

Formulation of a tentative hypothesis

You have speculated that Marcia's success is attributable to the fact that her speeches are well organized. Building on this observation, you formulate an hypothesis that specifies a relationship between message organization and speech effectiveness: All other things being equal, a speech that is well organized will be more effective than one that is not. Note that the hypothesis contains (1) an independent variable (message organization, which you will manipulate), (2) a dependent variable (speech effectiveness, defined operationally as the amount of audience attitude change), and (3) a prediction. In keeping with good scientific practice, your hypothesis is testable and includes terms that can be defined operationally. It is tentative, provisional, and based on observation rather than on faith or on authority. It is disprovable as well as being consistent with known facts and with previous validated hypotheses, which have indicated that message variables do, indeed, contribute to speech effectiveness. It is not internally inconsistent, and it appears to be neat and concise.

Testing the hypothesis

Since this is to be an experimental study, you will test the hypothesis by holding all variables constant and manipulating only your independent variable. By means of a pre- and a posttest of attitudes, you will gauge the effectiveness of the speeches given.*

These requirements pose several interesting questions. Who will make up

---

*The example given here is intended to be introductory in nature. If this were a more advanced course, I would spend more time on various research designs, their advantages and disadvantages. It is only fair to tell you, though, that the rather simple design sketched here has been criticized along several lines. Campbell (1957), for example, has noted that the pretest can have a number of adverse effects. It can cause the subjects to think about the content with which the persuasive communication deals. This can make them amenable to persuasion or, in other cases, it can solidify their opposition. Hence, Campbell argues that the sort of design described here offers no basis for generalization to an unpretested population. If you are interested in reading more about this controversy as well as about research design in persuasion, see D. Campbell (1957) "Factors Relative to the Validity of Experiments in Social Settings," *Psychological Bulletin*, 54: 297–312, and Chester A. Insko (1967) *Theories of Attitude Change*. New York: Appleton-Century-Crofts, pp. 3–11.

your audience? How will audience variables be held constant? How will speaker variables be held constant? How will you manipulate the variable of message organization? How will the audience's attitudes be measured? Such questions as these are the critical concerns of researchers. I will not attempt to answer them in depth (it would be possible to write an entire book on the subject!); rather, I want only to suggest some of the ways in which such problems are dealt with in experimental research.

The audience presents two concerns. First, how will you ensure that the subjects of your experiment are representative of a population larger than themselves? Assuming that a basic speech course is required at your school, you might choose to solve the problem by selecting a random sample of students currently enrolled in that course. With the cooperation of your school registrar, you might randomly select students from each section of the course. This would mean that you could reasonably expect your subjects to be a representative sampling of all students currently enrolled in the course. You might even extend this line of thinking farther and say that students enrolled in this course are in fact representative of the college population as a whole, since all students are required to take the course. You might go even farther out on a limb and say that your sample is representative of the overall adult population, since college students are typical people. (You may feel this last extension is unreasonable; nevertheless, it is the working assumption on which many, many experimental studies are based.)

The second concern has to do with controlling audience variables. The simplest method is to pool all the subjects you've selected and, by a process of randomization, break that pool down into three equal-sized, smaller groups. One of these we'll call Experimental Group One; the second, Experimental Group Two; and the third, Control Group. Group One will be exposed to a disorganized speech; Group Two will be exposed to an organized speech. The Control Group will be exposed to no speech, though the members of this group will be given a pretest and a posttest of attitudes just as though they were an experimental group.

Note that other methods of controlling audience variables are available. Rather than forming experimental and control groups from a randomly selected sample, it might have been possible to select your sample purposively by the application of specific criteria. For example, you might have administered a self-concept scale, and then chosen as your pool of subjects only individuals who scored above or below a certain point on the exam. Still other approaches are possible, but for our purposes here, let's stay with the idea of choosing subjects from a pool of randomly selected individuals. You should realize that in selecting from a larger pool, you are assuming the sample represents a normal distribution—for example, that each group represents roughly the same range of intelligence, personality types, and other audience variables as does the larger pool (which, in turn, is representative of a still larger population).

At this point, you have three matched audience groups, two of which will serve as experimental groups, and one of which will serve as a control. You can safely assume that any variations in the attitudes of the experimental groups will be due to factors other than those arising within the audiences. You have controlled audience variables.

Your next problem is how to control for speaker variables: How do you hold constant all the potentially influential factors that might arise because of who the speaker is or how the speaker is perceived by the audience? This solution is relatively simple; you might simply arrange to have the same speaker give the same two speeches back to back. To hold other potentially influential factors constant, you might arrange for the speeches to be given at the same time of day, in the same room, under the same circumstances. You may think that it is impossible to control all variables in the ways suggested here. If the speech is ten minutes long, for example, then the second audience would hear it twelve or fifteen minutes after the first one. Further, the second audience would be exposed to a speaker who is perhaps a bit more tired than the one the first audience heard. Some of these features can be controlled—for example, by using a videotape machine and simultaneously telecasting two prerecorded speeches to audiences seated in matching rooms. However, such elaborate precautions would probably not be required for the simple sort of experiment I am describing here. In nature, it is always impossible to reproduce two matching situations exactly. The experimenter must do the best he or she can, taking elaborate and expensive precautions only to the extent that the demands of the work require it.

You have now controlled for audience and speaker variables. The third question is how you will manipulate the independent variables of message organization. To hold all other speech variables constant (quality of evidence, language, and so on), you would have to start off with one speech. For example, you might prepare a really excellent persuasive speech on the United Nations. You might then break the speech down into segments and arbitrarily rearrange them. The intact speech would be called the organized one; the arbitrarily arranged speech would be called the disorganized one. (For safety's sake, you might wish to pretest the speeches, perhaps delivering them to a panel of speech instructors who would be asked to judge how well organized each version is.)

An additional task remains before exposing each of your groups to the speech. In order to assess the degree of attitude change, you need a point of reference. Each group should be given a pretest of attitudes toward the United Nations. Whatever test you choose from among the variety available, however, you will wind up with a numerical rating of the attitudes of each individual in all three groups, and for each group as a whole. By comparing the results of this pretest with the results of a posttest that you will later administer after exposure to the speech, you will have a measure of attitude change. You may be wondering why the pre- and posttests are given to the control group despite the fact that the members of that group will hear no speech. You test this group to gauge the influence exerted by the mere fact that the attitude test is being given. In other words, the control group helps you know that any observed changes in the attitudes of members of the experimental groups are in fact the result of the speeches and not of the attitude tests or the conditions of the experiment.

A few other questions might be occurring to you. For example, won't the experimental groups catch on about what you're up to? Might not that affect their responses on the posttest? These are good questions. Yes, they certainly might catch on and if they did, the results of your experiment would be distorted. For this reason, you might deliberately mislead your experimental groups in a number of ways. You could disguise the questions on attitudes toward the U.N. by including them in a longer test with a broader focus. Then your audience wouldn't know which items were significant for the purposes of your study and which were not. Further, rather than merely giving the same attitude test before and after the speech, you might give two forms of the same test, which a naive subject wouldn't recognize as equivalent. You might change the order of the questions, or the wording, or use a different type of scaling technique. To further ensure that your audience does not give you what they believe you want, you might mislead them about the purposes of their participation. You might not even tell them that you are interested in their attitude change brought about by the speech. Any plausible rationale for their participation might be enough to disguise the purposes of your study, and so increase the likelihood of undistorted results.

Everything is now ready. You have controlled for audience and speaker variables. You have two speeches ready to go, both identical except for message organization. Your audience's attitudes have been pretested. The day for running the experiment has come. At a precisely designated time, Experimental Group One arrives and is given a pretest of attitudes. Following the pretest, the disorganized speech is given. When the speaker is done, a posttest of attitudes is administered. (Later you will conduct statistical analyses to determine the amount of attitude change induced by the speech.) A few minutes later, Experimental Group Two arrives. The same procedures are followed. Meanwhile, in a nearby room, the Control Group is given the pretest and, ten minutes later, the posttest. By the time all three groups leave, you will have three sets of data, one for each group. Soon you shall see whether your hypothesis has been verified or contradicted.

Before turning to the analysis of the data, I want to emphasize that the procedures described here have been vastly simplified. While essentially accurate, the description of this experimental study glosses over many subtle issues. Feel free to consult your instructor if any questions occur to you, or if any matters seem unresolved, or if any of your concerns haven't been addressed to your satisfaction.

Analaysis of the data

By applying the appropriate statistical tests, you can compare the amount of attitude change within groups and between groups. There are many ways in which you may manipulate your data and test it for significance. For instance, you can determine the amount of attitude change that occurred in Experimental Group One, which had been exposed to the disorganized speech. This is a "within-group" comparison. You can also compare the differences in the amount of attitude change between groups. Your analysis will make it possible for you to determine whether in fact the organized speech produced significantly more attitude change (as you predicted it would), no significant difference in the amount of attitude change, or significantly less attitude change. By comparing the experimental groups' scores with those of the control group, you will also be able to assess the degree to which the conditions of the experiment—the testing itself—produced attitude change. (For information on statistical procedures, see the Suggested Readings in Student Activity Option 3.4.)

For purposes of illustration, let's assume you come up with data that clearly indicate that the organized speech produced significantly more attitude change. This means that your hypothesis has been validated. Careful cross-checks indicate that no confounding factors operated in the experiment. The results are unmistakable.

Formulation of the conclusion

Your long, hard labors have yielded fruit. You have established scientifically that message organization and speech effectiveness are related. You may need to qualify your results somewhat, for a number of possible issues still remain. How sure are you that you adequately controlled for audience variables? Was the second speech perhaps more effective because the speaker was more relaxed the second time around? How about the fact that the sun came out while the second speech was under way? It had been a gloomy morning; perhaps Experimental Group One was simply out of sorts. Maybe *that* accounts for their failure to change attitudes. And remember that a few students might have guessed your purpose and given you the results they thought you wanted. Others might have misread the instructions on the attitude questionnaire. Can you be absolutely certain that the data you got accurately measured audience attitudes? Do your findings have applicability to a different population than that composed of college students? Perhaps you need to limit the applicability of your results to audiences like the one of which your groups were composed. These and other questions linger.

As I indicated earlier, scientific findings are never absolute. They are tentative, provisional, subject to qualification and contradiction. As you can see, many, many factors may have impinged on your results. For this reason, you may wish to publish the results of your study. Since you will provide sufficient detail so that another researcher could replicate your experiment, he or she might provide additional evidence that organized speeches do produce more attitude change. Or perhaps the researcher will detect a flaw in your experimental design. In the interests of good science, such criticism and replications are welcomed by responsible researchers. The ultimate aim, after all, is a more accurate accounting for reality.

Application of the conclusion to the problem

Assuming that your conclusion is valid, you now have the satisfaction of having begun to solve the riddle of why Marcia's speeches are consistently more effective than Sandy's. You cannot be certain that organization alone explains her effectiveness, but your research indicates that it may well be a factor.

Actually, your results go beyond the original query that prompted your research. You have broadened your horizons beyond Marcia and Sandy, and have arrived at a generalization about persuasive speaking. Your generalization, it should be noted, constitutes only a tiny element in a more elaborate theory of persuasion, but it is out of such generalizations that comprehensive theories are built. You have the satisfaction of having made a contribution to humankind's understanding of effective speech-making.

This illustration was designed to introduce you to the steps in the scientific method. At the same time, it served to impart a basic knowledge of experimental methodology. The following Student Activity Option includes exercises to strengthen your grasp of these concepts. It also includes readings you might find interesting.

Student Activity Option 3.4 _____
The Scientific Method

INSTRUCTIONS
Complete one or more of the exercises below. Consult with your instructor about which one(s) might be most pertinent for this class. You may wish to submit the results of your work in oral or written form.

EXERCISES
How would you go about answering each of the following problems?

1. You notice a wide variation in your classmates' major fields and academic interests. You are curious about this and would like to understand better what brings such a diverse group together for one particular course. You suspect that there is some common element that unites your class as a group. Perhaps the link is that persuasive speaking is of critical importance in the job each student hopes to get after completing college.

The Problem
a. What is the problem you are addressing?

_____

b. What is your objective in researching the problem?

_____

c. What limiting conditions operate in your study?

d. How do you plan to go about solving the problem? Why?

The Hypothesis
a. What hypothesis would you formulate? (Please state it as precisely as possible.)

b. What are the variables in your hypothesis? The independent variable? (Please define this operationally.)

The dependent variable? (Please define this operationally.)

Testing the Hypothesis
a. How would you test the hypothesis? Why?

b. What special concerns would you have as you set out to test it?

2. You notice that your classmates respond enthusiastically to speeches in which the language is emotional and the description vivid. You wonder about the effects of such language on attitude change.

The Problem
a. What is the problem you are addressing?

b. What is your objective in researching the problem?

c. What limiting conditions operate in your study?

d. How do you plan to go about solving the problem? Why?

The Hypothesis
a. What hypothesis would you formulate? (Please state it as precisely as possible.)

b. What are the variables in your hypothesis? The independent variable? (Please define this operationally.)

The dependent variable? (Please define this operationally.)

Testing the Hypothesis
a. How would you test the hypothesis? Why?

b. What special concerns would you have as you set out to test it?

c. How would you select your sample? Why?

d. How would you control for
audience variables?

speaker variables?

speech variables?

e. How would you measure changes in the independent variable?

In the dependent variable?

Analyzing the Data
In analyzing the data you get, what would be your intent? (You are not asked here to give the specific statistical tests you would apply, only a conceptualization of what such tests would get at.)

Applying the Data to the Problem
a. Speculate as to what you might find if you were to conduct such a study.

b. What might be the problems you would encounter if you were to conduct such a study?

3. You notice that some speakers in your class use profanity in their talks. Some audience members have commented on this and seem upset by hearing profane language. You wonder about the effects of the use of profanity on audience judgments of speaker credibility. Does a speaker's use of profanity influence audience judgments of his or her credibility?

The Problem
a. What is the problem you are addressing?

b. What is your objective in researching the problem?

c. What limiting conditions operate in your study?

d. How do you plan to go about solving the problem? Why?

The Hypothesis
a. What hypothesis would you formulate? (Please state it as precisely as possible.)

b. What are the variables in your hypothesis? The independent variable? (Please define this operationally.)

The dependent variable? (Please define this operationally.)

Testing the Hypothesis
a. How would you test the hypothesis? Why?

b. What special concerns would you have as you set out to test it?

c. How would you select your sample? Why?

d. How would you control for
audience variables? (if, indeed, you wanted to)

speaker variables?

speech variables?

Analyzing the Data
In analyzing the data what would be your intent? (You are not asked here to give the specific statistical tests you would apply, only a conceptualization of what such tests would get at.)

Applying the Data to the Problem
a. Speculate as to what you might find if you were to conduct such a study.

b. What might be the problems you would encounter if you were to conduct such a study?

SUGGESTED READINGS

Auer, J. Jeffrey (1959) *An Introduction to Research in Speech*. New York: Harper and Row.

Barber, T. X. and M. J. Silver (1968) "Fact, Fiction, and the Experimenter Bias Effect," *Psychological Bulletin Monograph* 70: 1–29. An excellent discussion of problems in data analysis and interpretation.

Edwards, Allen (1954) "Experiments: Their Planning and Execution," Vol. One, pp. 259–88 in Gardner Lindsey, ed. *Handbook of Social Psychology*. Two volumes. Reading, Massachusetts: Addison-Wesley.

Horowitz, Gideon (1972) *Sadistic Statistics*. Garden City, New York: Adelphi University School of Social Work. A highly recommended, readable, often funny text that presents sophisticated concepts pertaining to survey, experimental research, and data interpretation.

Lacey, Oliver (1953) *Statistical Methods in Experimentation*. New York: Macmillan.

Tripoldi, Tony, Philip Fellin, and Henry J. Meyer (1969) *Assessment of Social Research*. Itasca, Illinois: Peacock.

Webb, Eugene J. and Donald T. Campbell (1973) Experiments on Communication Effects," pp. 938–52 in Ithiel de Sola Pool, Frederick W. Frey, Wilbur Schramm, Nathan Maccoby, and Edwin B. Parker, eds. *Handbook of Communication*. Chicago: Rand McNally College Publishing Company. This is an excellent discussion of the special concerns of experimenters.

THE MODEL

Descriptive and experimental studies represent two ways in which the scientific inquiry may be conducted. The model is still another observational tool of which scientists make use, however. Though the demands placed on the creator of a scientific model are somewhat less stringent than those placed on the theorist, models do constitute an important component in learning about our world. You already have a good idea of what models are since you have probably built or even played with them. Dollhouses, for example, are models, as are the toy airplanes and automobiles so popular with youngsters. Have you a globe in your house? If so, that too is a type of model.

Most simply, a model is an analogy. It is a representation of a complex reality. Toy airplanes, dollhouses, and globes are called replica models. On a smaller scale than the complex realities they represent, they contain many of the details characteristic of the real thing. Some replica models are larger than the reality they depict—for example, a model of the structure of the atom.

There is another kind of model, called a symbolic model. This type of model is not tangible; it is not a mockup of a physical thing. A symbolic model is on a higher level of abstraction. Symbols such as arrows, lines, and boxes represent in abstract fashion the components of the reality they represent and the relationships among those components. Scientific models have been formally defined (Chapanis, 1963, p. 109) as "representations or likenesses of certain aspects of complex events, structures, or systems, made by using symbols or objects which in some way resemble the thing being modeled."

Figure 3.3 presents an example of a symbolic model.

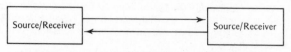

Figure 3.3. A Symbolic Model of Communication

In this model, each person in the communication system is represented by a box. He or she is designated as a source and a receiver, since both parties in the communication process send and receive messages. The two lines in the model indicate that the flow of messages goes both ways. It thus represents the possibility of feedback and adjustments in response to feedback. The model does not say a great deal, but it captures in very schematic fashion several critically important components in the communication process. The model also implies more than it says—for example, it implies the possibility of mutual influence. It implies that each source-receiver can make a difference in the efficacy of communication. It suggests that messages get from one person to the other by some medium or another. This process raises a range of questions regarding what medium is chosen and why. Are messages being sent verbally, by means of language? Are they being sent nonverbally, by a touch or a caress? It would be possible to delve even further into what the model says and implies, for the range of possibilities depicted is very large. However, before going on, it is important here to distinguish between a model and a theory.

Once it was customary to say that a model merely represented whereas a theory explained. But it has been noted (Allport, 1955, p. 10) that "explanation is description in the broader sense." While I am still partial to that old-fashioned distinction (to me, a model doesn't account for anything in quite the same way as does a theory), recent scholarship indicates that models are simply less rigorous than theories. Because models are analogies, they only approximate reality, while much more is expected of a theory. A theory must be wholly accurate and can leave out no elements in the reality to be accounted for. The facts it contains must correspond to what's out there in the real world. The theory must truthfully correspond to that which it purports to explain, while models are not expected to be as truthful as they are useful. A model can contain inaccuracies and it can fail to include parts of the reality it represents. Nevertheless, a model may be extremely useful. Despite its inaccuracies, a model enjoys considerable popularity and respect. But what exactly are the functions of models? In what sense are they useful?

Functions of scientific models

Models serve a variety of purposes. Among the most important is that models help us understand complex systems or events. For instance, there are models of the gasoline engine that can help us understand how it works, or you may have seen a model of the structure of your college. Symbolic models can do even more to represent physical and social realities since they can represent the steps in a process. Such an intangible reality as the communication process (as shown in Figure 3.3) defies representation by a replica model. But because humankind possesses the capacity for abstraction, you and I can picture an abstract process. Thus, models give concrete form to a nonconcrete but nevertheless conceptualizable reality. By identifying elements in the process, by showing the relationships among those elements, models make it possible for us to talk meaningfully about what we ordinarily take for granted. Thus models are particularly effective as teaching tools and memory aids.

In the speeches you give this semester, you would be wise to make use of models as visual aids (see Chapter Six). Nothing fascinates an audience like a working model or a mockup of the subject a speaker is talking about. Noth-

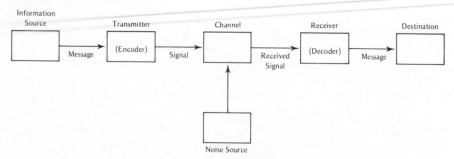

Figure 3.4. Shannon and Weaver's Model of the Communication Process

ing clarifies an audience's perceptions of a process better than a well-drawn symbolic model that depicts critical elements and relationships.

It should be noted that models can vary along a number of dimensions—in their level of sophistication, for example. Figure 3.3 represents a relatively simple model of communication. The model depicted in Figure 3.4 is considerably more complex, taking into account a good many more elements in the communication process. Models also reflect the viewpoint of their creator whose perspective dictates what the model will include and exclude. The model in Figure 3.4, for example, was constructed by two electrical engineers. It is primarily concerned with the manner, speed, and efficiency that characterize the transmission of a message from one point to another. It ignores entirely parts of the communication process that you as a student of persuasive speaking are probably very concerned with. There is no mention, for instance, of the circumstances under which or the occasion upon which the message is sent. As a student of rhetoric, you know that the circumstances of a speech can make an enormous difference in its outcome. When you construct your own model of persuasive communication in Student Activity Option 3.5, the model you create will undoubtedly reflect those things that you consider important in the persuasive speaking process.

A second important function of models is that they help us see new relationships. I noted earlier that the way a problem is defined can make a big difference in the manner in which one goes about solving it. Models can help us to redefine problems, to see them differently from the way we are accustomed to seeing them. The Shannon and Weaver model in Figure 3.4, for instance, opened up new possibilities for communication theorists. As electrical engineers, Shannon and Weaver paid special attention to the channel along which a message is sent. They were interested not only in channel capacity but in the influence of noise in the channel. Consequently, these elements are given prominent places in their model. When their creation is applied to human communication, it raises some interesting issues. For example, just as the capacity of a given channel—say, a telephone wire—is limited, might it not be that the human being's capacity to process information is also limited? Have you noticed that there are limits beyond which your capacity to process information breaks down?*

Similarly, the Shannon and Weaver model raises interesting questions about the effects of noise on information transmission. Physical noise can distort a physical sound wave—a speaker's voice can be drowned out by a passing airplane. But if you extend the analogy, you can reasonably talk about psychological noise as well. A speaker's message can be distorted because of psychological reactions triggered in listeners by the speaker. Has anyone ever told you that you reminded her of a former friend, or a cousin? Such a remark indicates that a sort of psychological noise affects that person's reactions to what you say.

Closely related to a model's ability to help us see things in new ways is its function as a spur to research. Models often provide a framework for scientific inquiry. Models can generate questions to be answered and they can predict. Often they can help us anticipate difficulties in the conduct of our affairs. For example, the Shannon and Weaver model suggests that there are many critical points at which the process of communication can go wrong. Predictable breakdown points include (1) the encoding/transmission phase (in terms of persuasive speaking, has the speaker encoded properly? Has he or she found the proper words to convey the message with just the right emotional and logical impact? Does the speaker transmit the message adequately, without faulty articulation that might distort meanings or call attention to herself?); (2) channel (Are the verbal and nonverbal messages congruent or do they contradict one another? Do messages sent along one channel—say, the visual one— support or undermine messages sent along another channel?); (3) the reception/decoding phase (Have the listeners heard what the speaker said? Do they understand the speaker's words? Do they grasp the explicit and implicit meanings? Do they talk the same language?). A number of research possibilities are suggested by these questions. As a persuasive speaker, you can see that the model alerts you to a number of important factors that you should be aware of as you go about preparing and presenting your speeches.

Student Activity Option 3.5
Communication Models

INSTRUCTIONS
Construct a symbolic model of the communication process. (Your model may also be a replica model, in which case you might wish to consult with your in-

---

*In his *Future Shock* (New York: Bantam Books, 1970), p. 354, Alvin Toffler cites a research study in which a group of subjects was asked to process information that was hurled at them at ever-increasing rates of speed. The experimenters were interested in the reactions of subjects to the stress so induced. A wide range of responses was observed—from giddiness to giving up to flaring of tempers. The study was reported in an interestingly titled piece: G. Usdansky and L. J. Chapman (1960) "Schizophrenic-like Reaction Responses in Normal Subjects Under Time Pressure," *Journal of Abnormal and Social Psychology*, 60 (January), 143–46.

structor and arrange to bring it to class for a demonstration). Your model should be appropriate to persuasive speaking and should perform at least one of the functions of models given in this chapter. In constructing your model, you might find it useful to consider some of the following suggestions and readings.

SUGGESTIONS
Your answers to these questions will provide guidelines for your model construction.

1. How do you conceive of persuasive speaking? What goes on when one person tries to persuade another? What are the central components of the persuasive process?

2. Along what channel or channels (verbal, nonverbal, vocal) are persuasive messages sent? How does the channel affect audience reactions to the message? How might messages sent along different channels interact with one another?

3. How about audience reactions to messages that contradict their beliefs or attitudes? How does resistance operate?

4. What influence is exerted by the speaker's and the listener's fields of experience? In what ways do their past experiences affect the transmission and processing of messages? What is the role of the context—psychological, social, physical, temporal—in influencing communication?

5. Feedback certainly affects the behavior of speakers. What kinds of feedback are there? What might be the effect of each?

6. What factors influence the audience's decision to pay attention or not? (For instructions on constructing a replica model of attention, see the Chapanis article cited in Suggested Readings.)

SUGGESTED READINGS
The following articles and essays provide information about the nature and functions of models. Most contain drawings of symbolic models that may be helpful as you set out to construct your model.

Berlo, David K. (1966) *The Process of Communication*. New York: Holt, Rinehart, and Winston. See especially "A Model of the Communication Process" and "The Fidelity of Communication: Determinants of Effect," pp. 23–70.

Blankenship, Jane (1966) *Public Speaking: A Rhetorical Perspective*. Englewood Cliffs, New Jersey: Prentice-Hall. See especially Chapter One, "The Nature of Communication," pp. 3–22.

Chapanis, Alphonse (1963) "Man, Machines, and Models," pp. 104–29 in Melvin H. Marx, ed. *Theories in Contemporary Psychology*. New York: Macmillan.

DeVito, Joseph A. (1976) *The Interpersonal Communication Book*. New York: Harper and Row. See especially Unit 3 (Communication Models), pp. 20–29 and Unit 4 (Forms, Functions, and Styles of Communication), pp. 30–42.

Schramm, Wilbur (1973) "How Communication Works," pp. 28–36 in C. David Mortensen, ed. *Basic Readings in Communication Theory*. New York: Harper and Row.

LAW

Only one other term—law—need concern us before we move on to the matter of testing the significance of persuasive effects. A law in science is a principle asserting a definite and virtually invariable relationship between two or more things. Examples of scientific laws are the law of gravity and the law of the conservation of energy. Less rigorous laws have been stated in the nonphysical sciences. G. W. F. Hegel's and Friedrich Engle's theories about history led to the law of dialectical materialism that states that capital and labor will interact in predictable ways that lead invariably to communism. The English economist T. R. Malthus (1766–1834) formulated a law pertaining to overpopulation that states that populations tend to increase faster than the means of subsistence. This situation results in an inadequate supply of the goods supporting life, unless war, famine, or disease reduces the population or the increase in population is checked by sexual restraint. Malthus' principle made sense in the early nineteenth century, but developments in automated agriculture and methods of food production have caused it to fall out of favor with many thinkers. The change in popular acceptance of Malthus' principle illustrates an important point: Even laws, regarded as the most definitive conclusions to which science can come, are subject to revision.

Scientific laws are not absolute. Not only in the social sciences but in the physical sciences as well, laws are open to change. Although we all learned in physics that no object can travel at a speed faster than that of light, it now appears that deep in space there are quasars and at least one galaxy that seem to be moving at a speed faster than that of light! This discovery suggests a need to revise the long-held principle that no object can travel faster than the speed of light. And closer to home, the law of energy conservation has had to be revised in light of Einstein's theory of relativity in order to allow for the possible interconversion of matter and energy.

What has all this to do with persuasive speaking? I simply want to suggest that perhaps one day research in this subject area will advance to the point where laws of communication can be set down. The best we have at present are a number of validated hypotheses and a few barely adequate starting points for theories. Some day, perhaps as a result of research conducted by you or one of your classmates, significant breakthroughs in our understanding of persuasive communication will occur. Then it might be possible to identify virtually invariable principles of communication. Even if that occurs, however, you should bear in mind that scientific laws always remain open to revision.

SUMMARY

In this chapter I have reviewed the essence of the scientific approach to knowing. You learned why adequate description—conceptualization and understanding of variables—is a necessary prerequisite to prescription. You learned, too, that the scientific approach to learning places emphasis on observation.

You learned the requirements of a truly scientific explanation—it must be tentative, provisional, testable, and based on observation. You learned as well the tests used to evaluate explanations—namely, a superior explanation accounts for all known data, is consistent with all known facts, generates testable predictions, is capable of being disproved, and is internally consistent. Further, it ought to be consistent with previously validated explanations, and it should be simple and concise, yet possess far-reaching explanatory power.

I pointed out the relationship between an hypothesis and a theory, noting that a theory is a coordinated set of validated hypotheses. An hypothesis, on the other hand, is a single tentative statement of a relationship between two variables (a dependent variable, which changes as a result of some external factor, and an independent variable, the effects of whose manipulations can be studied in an experiment).

Six steps were identified as constituting the scientific method: recognition and statement of the problem, formulation of a tentative hypothesis, testing the hypothesis, analysis of the data, formulation of the conclusion, and application of the conclusion to the original problem. I showed how these steps are applied in persuasion research, sketching briefly two simple studies that might be undertaken to answer questions about persuasion.

Scientific models were defined as abstract representations of processes, events, or structures that exist in the real world. You saw that models serve important functions in science, since they help us understand reality by showing relationships and identifying pertinent elements. They also provide a framework for scientific inquiry, often generating ideas for research.

You learned that a scientific law states a definite and invariable relationship between two things. Although open to question, scientific laws are the most complete and definite of the statements made by the scientific community. Since we know so little about how humankind functions, however, the best the social sciences can do is to generate normative generalizations, statements that point to tendencies and trends among people.

In Chapter Four I want to familiarize you with some of the techniques used to estimate persuasive effects, as well as with the concerns of scientists in selecting and applying these measuring instruments.

Chapter 4

Testing the Significance of Persuasive Effects

In Chapter Three, in an illustration of the steps in the scientific method, I outlined a simple experiment having to do with the effect of speech organization on attitude change. I mentioned that to gauge the amount of audience attitude change, it would be necessary to administer pre- and posttests of attitudes. By comparing before-and-after scores on these scales, and by comparing the scores of the group that had heard the organized speech with those of the group that had heard the disorganized speech, it would be possible to determine the impact of manipulations of the independent variable (message organization) on changes in the dependent variable (attitude change).

At this point, a number of important questions about attitude change need to be raised. For example, why use an attitude change scale as a measure of effectiveness? Wouldn't it be possible simply to observe audience behavior and thereby gauge the effect of the speech? Do audience members, for instance, voice support for the U.N. after hearing a speech designed to encourage its support? In terms of the scales themselves, how many attitude change scales exist? What are the advantages and disadvantages of each? How reliable are the scales? Do they in fact measure attitudes? What are attitudes, anyway?

The answers to these questions could fill a huge volume. It is my intent in this chapter simply to summarize the more important principles you should be aware of as a student of persuasive speaking. If you are to understand and to appreciate the research on persuasive strategies, it is important that you have an appreciation of the problems and techniques in gauging the effects of persuasive messages.

A basic assumption in measuring the effects of persuasion is that there is

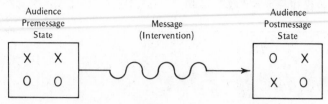

Figure 4.1. Model of the Effects of a Persuasive Communication

some sort of causal link between speaker behavior and audience response. Diagrammatically, the sequence can be depicted as shown in Figure 4.1. It is not always possible to gauge the premessage state of an audience. Sometimes a person with an interest in assessing the effects of a persuasive message can go only by the audience's postmessage or postevent state. For example, one line of research in social psychology is geared to assessing the impact of disasters on victims and witnesses. What happens to the people in a community when an earthquake occurs? a plane crash? What are the survivors' responses to a disaster or near disaster? In cases like these, researchers are limited to postdisaster effects, since no one could predict with any reliability when or where the disaster would strike. Similarly, there is ordinarily no formal assessment of the internal state of a person who joins an extremist organization or cult. Anyone interested in determining the effect of organizational membership has only the postmembership measures to go by in drawing conclusions. In fact, these measures are often supplemented by anecdotal material and by informal assessments of the individual's prior state provided by relatives, friends, and acquaintances. "He's just not himself," they might say. "He used to be so soft-spoken and polite! Now he's rude, aggressive, and insensitive!" Both informal testimonies and postevent measures are useful, but they are not equal in value to careful before-and-after measures. As you saw earlier, careful assessment of an audience's preexperience state is the standard procedure in experimental research. Only with such data can you realistically estimate the effects of the persuasive message.

In your own classroom, it is highly likely that no premessage assessment will be made of your classmates' attitudes prior to your persuasive speeches. Judgments of your speeches' effectiveness will be drawn after the speech from your classmates' responses, which will provide estimates of the strength and quality of your persuasive appeal. Your instructor as well will gauge the worth of your persuasive efforts. Although such audience feedback is valuable, it is not the same as careful pre- and postmeasures of audience attitudes and feelings. If you wish to have the benefit of such measures, consult with your instructor and see Student Activity Option 4.4. Be aware, however, that a confounding effect in such measures frequently arises when the audience knows the intent of the person who administers the test. If your classmates know that you are measuring their attitudes in order to estimate the effects of a persuasive message, they are likely to give you the results they think you want.

(Refer to the following section, Disguised Techniques. It might be possible to administer such a test in your classroom.)

FACTORS TO CONSIDER IN MEASURING PERSUASIVE EFFECTS

People from all walks of life are concerned with assessing the impact of persuasive messages. A politician, for example, would like to know which messages result in solidifying support or in winning converts from among the ranks of opponents. An advertiser certainly wants to know the effectiveness of ads run in the various media. Do the ads change consumers' preferences regarding their product? How many people who used to buy G.M. products shift over to Ford as a result of a particular ad campaign? Do any ads actually backfire and result in a decrease in sales? You may be thinking that a simple and easy way to gauge the effects of persuasive messages exists for these people—the politician is either elected or not, the advertiser can study sales statistics. You are quite right, but such results don't say very much about what precisely is being done well or badly in an electoral or ad campaign. The advertiser cannot know on the basis of sales statistics alone what is working or not working in the ad campaign. And the politician who waits till election day to determine the effects of persuasive appeals is locked into an all-or-nothing situation: Either the election is won or lost. Even if elected, can the politician know with any degree of precision exactly what it was that resulted in the victory? No, because such gross measures of effectiveness do not provide sufficiently detailed data to be of use in rational planning. For this reason, whenever possible, careful experimentation under controlled conditions is the best measure of persuasive effectiveness.

There are five general concerns shared by people interested in persuasion research. First, who is affected by the persuasive communication? For example, does the preacher's sermon result in more fervent belief among those already in the flock or does it result in the conversion of nonbelievers? If the preacher intends to do the latter and only succeeds in doing the former, can the sermon be judged effective?

A second concern of persons with an interest in persuasion has to do with the number of people who are affected. At what point does a speech succeed? Must 100 per cent of the audience be persuaded by a speech to consider it successful? Should the figure be 50 per cent? 10 per cent? The question is impossible to answer in precise mathematical terms, for context and situational factors play an enormous role. In a Presidential election, for example, when the results hinge on the "undecideds," a speech that reaches only a tiny portion of a national audience can make all the difference. In fact, many politicians, writing off their opponents and assuming the support of party loyalists, most often direct their speeches at the "undecideds" upon whom victory or defeat hinges.

A third question is, how much change is brought about by a message? It is the rare person who can bring about a radical transformation in an audience. The New Testament is replete with examples of people deeply moved by Christ's preaching. Many of the apostles were so taken by this carpenter from Nazareth that they left their wives and families. At the opposite moral extreme is a person like Hitler, who was able to command a whole nation with the power of his oratory (supplemented, of course, by the S. S. and a huge propaganda budget). The numbers of people who can achieve such sweeping persuasive effects is very, very small.

Most of us must be content to bring about only minor changes in the people we address. Maybe we can get them to see things a bit differently, or perhaps something we say makes them question a belief they have held unthinkingly for years. Unfortunately, experimental research indicates that most changes in attitude following persuasive messages are very short-term; people return to their prior ways of thinking rapidly, unless subsequent messages reinforce the persuasive effect of the first. Still, even a minor change can have major effects. The set of beliefs, attitudes, and values you hold is viewed as an interlocking network; hence a change in one part of the system has impact throughout the entire network. Each of us maintains a sort of cognitive balance. When the balance is upset by the introduction of a new belief, a change in an old one, or the elimination of another, the entire cognitive system must adjust to accommodate the change. To use an analogy, a well-decorated room cannot easily tolerate the addition of a new piece of furniture without a readjustment of the preexisting furnishings. New arrangements may be necessary—pictures may have to be relocated, perhaps the entire conception of the room may need to be altered. In the same way, your internal psychological set may change as a result of only a minor change in one of your beliefs or attitudes. Consequently, you needn't always strive for major shifts in your audience's internal set or external behavior. Even tiny changes may have enormous impact.

The fourth question is closely related: How difficult is the task faced by the persuader? With what degree of opposition must the persuader contend? How much does the audience's initial position differ from the position the speaker is advocating? How much of an emotional investment does the listener have in his or her prior position? If it is very great, then the task faced by the persuader is extremely difficult. For example, if your listener has worked as a nurse for thirty years and you want her to accept the belief that nursing is an inferior profession, you face a next-to-impossible task. Similarly, a spokesperson for Zero Population Growth is unlikely to win adherents among the parents of large families. Think about yourself for a moment. How readily do you accept messages that contradict your basic beliefs? Do you easily adopt the opinions of acquaintances who advise you against going on with your college education? If you are a junior or senior, you have invested a great deal in your education—emotionally, financially, and in other ways. Would you be inclined to accept the proposition that a college education is a waste of time? In all likelihood, you would vehemently oppose a speech with that proposition.

A final concern of persons interested in persuasion has to do with the kind of change that is brought about. As we saw in Chapter Two, there has long been a debate over whether speeches to convince are the same as speeches to persuade. The conviction/persuasion duality was at the heart of the controversy prompted by the publication of Winans' *Public Speaking* in 1914. It was considered convenient by some (and still is by a few) to distinguish between the internal and the external effects of a speech. Internal changes (alterations in beliefs, attitudes, and values) were considered different from changes in overt behavior. It is now generally recognized that such a distinction is false and invalid, for both internal and external changes represent alterations in preferences and behavior. Internal and external changes are perhaps most accurately seen as falling on a continuum of behavior that runs from "indirectly observable" (for example, attitudes, which can't be seen directly) to "directly observable" (for instance, the behavior of giving money to a charitable organization).

Nevertheless, the distinction between conviction and persuasion points the way to a number of important issues in persuasion research. Chief among these is the relationship between attitudes and behavior. When we know someone's attitudes, can we predict the behavior? How accurately? From the opposite perspective, can we infer a person's attitudes from behavior? Under what circumstances are there discrepancies between the way you act and what you believe?

THE RELATIONSHIP BETWEEN ATTITUDES AND BEHAVIOR

A classic study conducted in the 1930s forced researchers to confront these thorny questions of the relationship between attitudes and behavior. A French researcher named LaPiere traveled around the U.S. with a well-educated and attractive Chinese couple. The threesome stopped at many hotels and restaurants and were treated courteously in all but one. Roughly six months after the trip, LaPiere conducted an attitude survey. To each of the establishments at which he and the couple had been served, he sent a questionnaire in which he asked whether his respondents would accept Chinese guests. Out of the 250 establishments to which the letter was sent (only one, remember, had refused to accommodate the threesome), 128 replied. Of these 128, only one said that they would accept Chinese guests! Clearly, LaPiere's study raised interesting questions about the correlations between attitudes and behavior. Why did the attitude survey point one way when the actual behavior was exactly the opposite?

Without going into detail, I want to suggest a number of possible explanations for the discrepancy. For one thing, behavior is often strongly influenced by situational factors. Saying that you'll do something and actually doing it when the situation arises are two different things. The hotel and restaurant managers *said* they would not serve Chinese guests; but when actually confronted by an attractive and well-dressed couple, accompanied by a suave and erudite European gentleman, the question of not serving them hardly arose. LaPiere's questionnaire was rather abstract in nature and failed to capture the exact situation in which the managers found themselves. I doubt seriously that any paper-and-pencil test can capture the essence of a real situation. That is why you must actually give speeches in a class like this one and why you must take a driver's test to prove you can drive a car, and not only talk about how to drive!

Another set of constraints on behavior arises as a result of social pressures to conform. If you are with a group and everyone begins participating in a given activity, it is difficult to refuse to participate. Most people allow themselves to be swept along by the majority, thinking as they do and acting as they act. In light of this, merely observing someone's behavior may not give a true indication of attitudes.

Similarly, behavior is often influenced by matters of convenience and availability. We delude ourselves if we think that such matters fail to operate when we make choices. For example, the person you eventually decide to marry may well seem to be the only person suitable for your mate. But realistically, that is probably not the case. There are many such persons who could suit. Often, your choices are limited by the availability of mating partners within your geographic area and with whom you are compatible for other reasons (such as family background, past experiences, and education). From this same perspective, persons with unreasonable prejudices and biases may act in such a way as to conceal them simply because it is convenient not to let them show. A family of racial bigots may live in an integrated neighborhood because they can't afford to live elsewhere. A male chauvinist may espouse the principles of a liberated individual simply because to fail to do so would result in major inconvenience. The range of influences on overt behavior is very broad, which makes it extremely difficult to infer attitudes from behavior. According to one researcher (Wicker, 1969, p. 65) who undertook an in-depth study of the research that has dealt with the relationship between attitudes and behavior, attitudes are at best only slightly related to overt behaviors.

There is no real solution to the dilemma posed for attitude change researchers by this fact. However, a few important principles have been generated in response to the problem posed by research like LaPiere's and Wicker's. For one thing, it is now well recognized that no single act of overt behavior in an unstructured real-life situation is a reliable test of attitudes. It is insanity in general to infer attitudes from behavior; and it is doubly insane to infer attitudes from only *one* act of behavior. From your own experience you know this to be true. That is why you would object if your course grade were based on only one speech or one written test. "What!" you would say, "How can you gauge my overall ability on the basis of only one speech?" You know intuitively that a larger sample is required. The larger the sample, the more likely is the conclusion to be true. In light of this fact, the best test of a person's competence would occur over many repeated performances. Similarly, the best test of an attitude is to observe a person's behavior over a long period of time, in a variety of circumstances, and under many conditions. The difficulty that arises here, of course, is the problem of time and resources. Researchers rarely can afford the time or the money to conduct exhaustive longitudinal studies. Instead, they must rely on carefully controlled laboratory experimentation. But, as we saw with the LaPiere study, paper-and-pencil tests and laboratory conditions must approximate as closely as possible the actual conditions under which the behavior might occur. Further, the tests must be neither more nor less specific than the behavioral situation would demand. It is not enough to say that, in principle, a person is in favor of abortion. She must be tested in a more personal way—she must actually be put into a situation in which a decision to abort or not must be made. (Simulation games and role-playing exercises are often used for this purpose.) Then, perhaps, the results of the test would more closely approximate the actual behavior.

BELIEFS, ATTITUDES, INTENTIONS, AND BEHAVIOR

The astute reader has probably thought of another important flaw in La-Piere's questionnaire. What he was actually measuring was an intention; did the hotel and restaurant managers intend to serve Chinese guests? Furthermore, what exactly is the relationship between an intention and an attitude? between an attitude and a behavior? Is there a difference among them? What *is* an attitude? There is perhaps no more basic problem that plagues persuasion research than a lack of agreement on the meanings of key terms. According to Fishbein and Ajzen (1975, p. 2), who conducted a painstaking search of the literature on this very topic, there is little agreement on the meaning of the word attitude. Further, what agreement there is seems to conceal underlying disagreements. There are no fewer than five hundred different measuring instruments designed to assess attitudes, and since operational definitions are always tied to scores on these measures, it is not unreasonable to conclude that there may be as many as five hundred different definitions of the term. Of even more significance is the fact that different experimental results are frequently obtained, depending on which attitude test is used. Thus the same study done using different measures of attitudes would yield very different results. This dilemma suggests a great deal of conceptual ambiguity and wasted research effort.

Fishbein and Ajzen have been in the forefront of those concerned with clarifying key terms used in persuasion research. They have developed a conceptual scheme in which they distinguish among beliefs, intentions, attitudes, and behavior. You will see that by making these distinctions yourself, your thinking about the effects of persuasive messages will be clarified; further, your use of this scheme will permit more intelligent speech planning.

Traditionally, an attitude has been regarded as a learned predisposition to respond favorably or unfavorably with respect to a given object of judgment. If you have a positive attitude toward ice cream, for example, you are likely to eat it when you can, to associate pleasant feelings with it, and so on. A negative attitude would result in your avoiding ice cream and refusing to purchase it. While much is concealed in this seemingly simple definition (see Fishbein and Ajzen, 1975, pp. 6–11), a few points are obvious. For one thing, attitudes are learned; they are the result of past experience. The more ingrained the attitudes, the more one's past experiences have tended to reinforce them and the harder they are to change. Second, attitudes are predispositions—they make one inclined to respond to the given object of judgment in one manner or another. Fishbein and Ajzen go to great lengths, however, to show that attitudes are predispositions of the most general sort. They are not the same as intentions, which are far more specific and which possess an immediacy that is not characteristic of attitudes. An attitude exerts a latent, remote influence on behavior. It is extremely difficult to predict just how an attitude will affect a specific behavior in a particular context. For example, you may generally be favorably inclined toward a specific dating partner; however, whether or not you attend a dance with that person will depend on many factors. Have you arranged to go with someone else? Are you feeling up to attending a dance? Do study requirements make it impossible for you to attend? These are only three of the factors that may intervene between an attitude and a behavior.

A third characteristic of attitudes—the central one, according to Fishbein and Ajzen—is only implied by the definition given above. Attitudes are evaluative or affective in nature. They are not factual statements. They are not equivalent to one's knowledge, beliefs, opinions, or convictions. Instead, attitudes have to do with the attraction of a given object of judgment; they are concerned with your values and sentiments. For example, although you may believe that spinach is good for you, that does not mean you have a positive attitude toward spinach; you may still dislike it. Attitudes have to do with liking or disliking, feeling attracted to something or repulsed by it. Hence, they are measured by means of a test requiring that the person making the judgment evaluate a given object on a continuum with two opposite poles. On one side would be a term such as "like very much" and on the other, a term such as "dislike very much."

Fishbein and Ajzen argue that past measures of attitude have been inconsistent because they have failed to distinguish among beliefs, attitudes, and intentions. To eliminate this conceptual sloppiness, the two authors define beliefs as cognitions. They are not evaluative in nature. Rather, they are statements that link an object of judgment with some trait, quality, characteristic, property, or outcome. You may believe that a certain politician is dishonest, that a college education is a good investment, that people with artistic temperaments are undependable. Each of these statements represents a belief about these three objects of judgment. Although they may be associated with an attitude, none is equivalent to an attitude. Since you believe that the politician Erhardt is self-seeking, for example, you may have a negative attitude toward him. However, there is no necessary connection between your belief and your attitude. You might feel, for example, that while Erhardt is self-seeking, he possesses other traits so desirable as to make it possible for you to feel positive toward him. In the same way, you may believe that people with artistic temperaments are undependable. Despite that, however, you may feel they contribute so much to society that a little undependability can be put up with in the interests of esthetic pleasure.

Beliefs are measured by assessing the strength with which a person links the object of judgment to a specific quality or trait. In other words, how strongly do you believe that the object and the trait go together? With what degree of probability do you associate the two? The measurement of beliefs requires very personal decisions. You and I may agree in our belief that college teachers are forgetful, but we may differ in the strength of our belief. Put another way, we may link together the object (college teachers) and the trait (forgetful) with different degrees of probability. You may be more sure than I that the link-up exists.

Intentions are different from both attitudes and beliefs. Let's say you hear a speech about the difficulties associated with old age. One of the points the speaker makes is that loneliness is a major problem. After hearing the speech, you leave the auditorium firmly resolved to pay a visit to your widowed grandmother as soon as possible. This resolve represents an intention. It is quite specific, involving a particular person. Further, it links a behavior (visiting your widowed grandmother) with a measure of the likelihood that you will perform it (you are very firmly resolved to visit her). The surer you are that you will do what you have resolved, the stronger your intention. To measure an intention, the subject must gauge the probability that he or she will perform some action.

An important qualification exists. The longer the time lag between the point at which the intention is formulated and the point at which the actual behavior is performed, the less accurate is the intention as a predictor of the behavior. It is one thing to say that you're going to visit your grandmother next week; it is another actually to do it. Who knows what intervening factors may arise? Perhaps you will have a major assignment. Maybe some friends will invite you to a party on the very night you'd planned your visit. Fund-raisers have known about the time lag between intention and behavior for a long time; hence the most successful fund-raising efforts call for a minimum time lag between the appeal and the collection.

In light of the many problems associated with inferring attitudes from behavior, Fishbein and Ajzen emphasize that a person's behavior is not a measure of attitude. Thus, they recommend study of overt behavior in its own right. For example, a review of registration patterns at your school may indicate that a particular student tends to withdraw from a greater-than-average number of classes. The uncautious researcher might conclude that such behavior is indicative of inner ambivalence toward college studies. The more careful researcher would simply be interested in the behavior itself and would likely look more closely into the observable factors beneath it. For example, does the student work and are the class changes centered around the problem of scheduling? Perhaps the student tends to withdraw from courses in the physical sciences but not in the humanities. By seeking out observable trends or patterns, it might be possible to draw a number of likely conclusions regarding this student's behavior. To infer immediately that he or she possess ambivalent attitudes toward college studies would be rash and reckless.

The diagram in Figure 4.2 shows the relationships among beliefs, attitudes, intentions, and behavior.

According to Fishbein and Ajzen, beliefs are the building blocks of a person's cognitive structure. They constitute the "informational base that ultimately determines [a person's] attitudes, intentions, and behaviors." A person's attitudes are based on beliefs. The more firmly a person believes something to be true, the more influential is that belief in determining attitude. A person's evaluations of the attributes he or she associates with the object determine the direction of attitude. Similarly, the more a belief is uppermost in one's mind, the more influence it exerts. Thus, for instance, let's suppose you have always believed that a particular movie actress was a nice person. Based on a friend's testimony that she is generous with her time in helping needy children, plus what you have read and heard in the media, you believe quite strongly that the actress is a nice person. Let's suppose further that as part of your efforts as chairperson of a fund-raising campaign for starving children in Africa, you have written the actress to invite her to headline a fund-raising drive. Just a few hours ago, you received a letter from her, signed personally, in which she indicated that she is most interested, and requested further information so she can plan a trip to your campus. At this moment, the chances are very likely that you possess extremely positive attitudes toward the actress. First of all, you believed quite strongly from the outset that she is a nice person. Her personal response to your inquiry made this belief still stronger. On top of that, since you are deeply involved in the

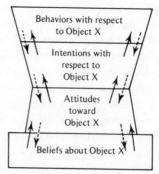

Figure 4.2. Relationships Between Beliefs, Attitudes, Intentions, and Behavior

funding campaign and since you received her letter only a few hours ago, your belief is salient, or uppermost in your mind. Both factors—the strength and the saliency of your belief—contribute to the extremely positive attitudes you hold.

Attitudes are related to intentions as beliefs are related to attitudes. That is, a person's intentions are determined by the totality of the attitudes held. While attitudes predispose you generally to act in one way or another, each intention is related to a corresponding behavior. An attitude is a general predisposition while an intention is more specific in that it predisposes a person to perform a particular behavior.

Note that the diagram in Figure 4.2 shows that the predominant influence (indicated by the arrows with solid lines) goes from bottom to top—that is, from beliefs through attitudes, through intentions, to behavior. But influence can work the other way as well, as indicated by the arrows with the broken lines. It is possible for an attitude to influence a belief; similarly, intentions may influence attitudes, and behavior can influence all three. (This represents a bit of a departure from Fishbein and Ajzen's conception of the relationships, since they say only that attitudes and behavior can affect beliefs.) Your own experience can serve as an illustration of the points being made here. Have you ever changed your beliefs about a person after you came to like her? Perhaps you believed initially that she was overly impressed with her own self-importance. But as you became closer to her, she revealed herself to be a down-to-earth person who had the same fears and hopes as you. If this has occurred, you know that changes in attitudes can bring about changes in beliefs. Similarly, a decision to learn how to dive can affect your attitudes toward diving; in this case, intentions affect attitudes. And certainly behavior can affect intentions (you may find yourself at a party without really having intended to go, but since your friends dragged you along, you decided to attend). Behavior can also affect attitudes (you may feel differently about the party once you are there); and behavior may affect your beliefs (you may come to believe that parties with this particular social group can be pleasant).

The chief point I wish to make about Fishbein and Ajzen's scheme is that, as a student of persuasive speaking, you should recognize the importance of clear concepts in planning for persuasive messages and in measuring their effects. To do so, it is important to know which of the four elements in Fishbein and Ajzen's scheme you are assessing. Then, it is critical to measure that component and not any other.

To plan a persuasive message, for instance, you might ask yourself what you are trying to change: the audience's beliefs? their intentions? their attitudes? Another question: What are the audience's beliefs? And how might these beliefs influence their attitudes? Or again, what attitudes would have to be changed in order to influence the audience's intentions? A host of other questions come to mind (see Student Activity Option 4.1). In planning your persuasive speeches, it is important to make an accurate assessment of your audience. This scheme can guide you in thinking through exactly what you are setting out to do. It can help you determine and clarify your purposes. It can guide your decisions about where to invest energy in research efforts and where to provide proofs in your speech. To give an illustration, consider the following case. A student gives a speech about the slaughter of the seals on the Canadian coast. Her message ends with an appeal to write your congressional representative and demand that something be done. How effective would such a speech be if it failed to address the audience's belief that such killing is a valuable conservation measure since it thins the herd and ensures its survival? Similarly, a speech advocating the use of marijuana, cocaine, or heroin would fail if it did not address the audience's belief that such drugs can be harmful to your health. As you can see, Fishbein and Ajzen's scheme can aid not only in clarifying and assessing the effects of persuasive messages, but in planning and implementing them as well.

Student Activity Option 4.1
Beliefs, Attitudes, Intentions, and Behavior

INSTRUCTIONS
For each of the following objects of judgment, list the beliefs your audience might hold. Make a chart such as the following. To the right of the column labeled Key Beliefs, write the implications of this conviction. How, for example, might that belief affect your audience's attitudes toward the object of judgment? How might their attitude affect their intentions?

Object of Judgment	Key Beliefs	Effect of this Belief on Audience Attitudes	Effect of this Attitude on Audience Intentions
Sex	1._____	1._____	1._____
	2._____	2._____	2._____
	3._____	3._____	3._____
Organized Religion	1._____	1._____	1._____
	2._____	2._____	2._____
	3._____	3._____	3._____
College Professors	1._____	1._____	1._____
	2._____	2._____	2._____
	3._____	3._____	3._____

Object of Judgment	Key Beliefs	Effect of this Belief on Audience Attitudes	Effect of this Attitude on Audience Intentions
Communism	1. _____	1. _____	1. _____
	_____		_____
	2. _____	2. _____	2. _____
	_____		_____
	3. _____	3. _____	3. _____
	_____		_____

On a chart such as the following, formulate a proposition about each object of judgment. In light of your previous analysis, discuss the strategy you would use in trying to change your audience's beliefs, attitudes, and intentions. What beliefs would you want to change? How would you go about it? What attitudes would you want to change? How? What intentions? How? Discuss your answers with your classmates.

Sex
Proposition: _____
Strategy: _____

Organized religion
Proposition: _____
Strategy: _____

College professors
Proposition: _____
Strategy: _____

Communism
Proposition: _____
Strategy: _____

SUGGESTED READINGS

The following books and articles are representative of many that address the problems in attitude change research. All of the books listed contain valuable and extensive bibliographies. With your instructor's consent, consider selectively reporting on one of the problems discussed in this chapter so far.

Cronkhite, Gary (1969) *Perusasion: Speech and Behavioral Change.* Indianapolis: Bobbs-Merrill. See especially Chapter One, A Definition of Persuasion, pp. 3–17.

Fishbein, Martin and Icek Ajzen (1975) *Belief, Attitude, Intention and Behavior: An Introduction to Theory and Research.* Reading, Massachusetts: Addison-Wesley Publishing Company. See especially Chapter One, Introduction, pp. 1–18 and Chapter Eight, Prediction of Behavior, pp. 335–384.

Lucas, Darrel B. and Steuart H. Britt (1968) "Measuring Advertising Effectiveness: Inquiries and Sales Measures," pp. 328–46 in Howard H. Martin and Kenneth E. Andersen, eds. *Speech Communication: Analysis and Readings.* Boston: Allyn and Bacon.

Martin, Howard H. (1968) "The Assessment of Communication Effects," pp. 278–96 in Howard H. Martin and Kenneth E. Andersen, eds. *Speech Communication: Analysis and Readings.* Boston: Allyn and Bacon.

Sherif, C. W., M. Sherif, and R. E. Nebergall (1965) *Attitude and Attitude Change: The Social Judgment-Involvement Approach*. Philadelphia: Saunders.

Webb, Eugene J. and Donald T. Campbell (1973) "Experiments on Communication Effects," pp. 938–52 in Ithiel de Sola Pool, Frederick W. Frey, Wilbur Schramm, Nathan Maccoby, and Edwin B. Parker, eds. *Handbook of Communication*. Chicago: Rand McNally College Publishing Company.

Wicker, A. W. (1969) "Attitude vs. Actions: the Relationship of Verbal and Overt Behavioral Responses to Attitude Objects." *Journal of Social Issues*, 25: 41–78.

Thus far we have looked at two problems that arise when a researcher considers the effects of a persuasive message. The first problem had to do with the relationship between attitudes and behavior. The second was concerned with the exact nature of attitudes, and their relationship to beliefs, intentions, and behavior. I now want to examine briefly two other major concerns shared by students of the persuasive process—reliability and validity. In an earlier discussion on the reliability of behavior as an indicator of attitudes, I said that a single-item test was not a reliable indicator of a person's attitudes. Many factors may intervene to shape the behavior so as to make it an unreliable indicator of attitudes. The same concern must be raised when a paper-and-pencil test of attitudes is used. The question of a test's reliability—the extent to which it gives consistent results—is a major one for students of persuasion. A second closely related question has to do with the validity of the test—that is, does it actually measure what it purports to measure? Does an attitude test actually measure attitudes, for example? On the pages to follow, I will distinguish between reliability and validity and present some of the tests of each.

RELIABILITY

How would you characterize a teacher who came to class only irregularly? Suppose you owned a car that started sometimes but failed to start at other times. In each of these cases, you are confronting a problem of unreliability. A person, a car, or a test is said to be unreliable when it fails to perform consistently. If you took an intelligence test last week and came up with an IQ rating of 124, then you took the same test this week under roughly the same conditions and came up with a rating of 157, something would be wrong. A few factors might explain the discrepancy. Either you became much more intelligent in a week's time, or the testing situations differed so much that neither provided a true measure of your intelligence, or perhaps the test itself was faulty. To answer the question of the reason for the discrepancy, a researcher might give the test a third time, under conditions nearly identical to one of the two prior sets of conditions. Suppose that in the third test you came up with a third score—say, a 69.

At this point, the researcher would almost certainly have to question the reliability of the measuring instrument, since under similar conditions you received such widely divergent scores.

Needless to say, an unreliable test of attitudes, beliefs, or intentions could pose major problems for persuasion researchers. How could they determine the effects of a persuasive message if they did not know whether different attitude scores were due to the message itself or to flaws in the test? To solve the potential problem, researchers make determined efforts to measure the reliability of the tests they use. Several methods are available to them (Guilford, 1954).

One way of determining the reliability of a measuring instrument is to use the *test-retest method.* In this method, the same test is given more than once. Often different forms of the same test are given in order to eliminate the effects of memory. Scores on one administration are compared with those on a subsequent administration, and a coefficient of reliability is arrived at. A reliability coefficient of .95 means that test results agreed with themselves 95 per cent of the time. This suggests a very high level of reliability. On the average, if the test were given 100 times, the same results would be gotten 95 times.

A second method of assessing the reliability of a measuring instrument is called the *split-halves method.* This involves comparing the results gotten on the first half of the test (say, the first 50 items on a 100-item multiple choice exam) with those gotten on the second half. Again, a reliability coefficient is arrived at, indicating the extent to which the scores on both halves of the test agree with one another.

A third technique is called the *odd-even method.* To use this technique, you would compare the results gotten on all odd-numbered questions with those gotten on all even-numbered questions. The extent to which the results agree is a measure of the test's inherent reliability.

You may be interested to know that, with the exception of projective tests (the Rorschach Ink Blot Test and the Thematic Apperception Test, for example, have been used unsuccessfully to measure attitudes), most attitude tests are highly reliable and give consistent results.

VALIDITY

The major problem that gave birth to Fishbein and Ajzen's scheme of beliefs, attitudes, intentions, and behavior was a problem in validity. Because of unclear conceptualizations, many so-called attitude scales did not measure attitudes at all. They measured beliefs (see, for example, Congruity Hypothesis in Chapter Five); they measured intentions (recall LaPiere's questionnaire to the hotel and restaurant managers); but they did not measure attitudes. A measuring instrument is said to be valid when it measures the variable it purports to measure. A valid test of attitudes, for example, actually measures attitudes; a valid test of intelligence actually measures intelligence.

Controversy over IQ tests centers on this very issue. Opponents of conventional intelligence tests contend that the tests do not measure intelligence at all—since interpreting the questions requires a knowledge of vocabulary and grammar, the tests actually measure verbal abilities.

Why do problems of validity arise? Sometimes test-makers become so enamored of their creations that they lose sight of what the test is designed to do. Or they place more weight on the results of the test than on a person's ability to perform the function the test is supposed to predict. David C. McClelland (1973; p. 10) tells the story of a black man who was denied admission to Harvard University's graduate school on the basis of his scores on the Miller's Analogies Test. (This test includes questions that ask for completion of verbal ratios: Albany is to New York as Hartford is to _____.) The test claims to predict writing ability, one criterion for admission to many graduate schools. Ironically, the black applicant had a substantial record of publications upon application to Harvard, but because his test scores indicated he could not write, his application was turned down. This case became a *cause célèbre,* and, fortunately, the decision of the admissions board was reversed. But their blunder indicates that even intelligent people can encounter problems of validity.

As in the case of reliability, there are a number of tests designed to assess the validity of a measuring instrument. One question that is asked in assessing validity is whether the test or operation possesses face validity. That is, on the face of things, does it seem as though this test measures what it is supposed to? For example, to test a mechanic's ability to fix a car, you might actually present him or her with an auto that does not run and see if the person can fix it. Similarly, a road test is a test of driving ability that has very high face validity. It is unlikely that an inexperienced or incompetent driver could handle a car well by luck.

Construct or convergent validity involves the comparison of results of two tests that claim to measure the same thing. To determine construct or convergent validity, you might give an audience two different tests. If the scores on these tests were in agreement, you could reasonably conclude at the very least that these two tests seemed to be measuring the same thing. There is no guarantee, of course, that attitudes are what actually was being measured. Both tests could err in the same direction—by, for example, measuring beliefs or by confusing beliefs and attitudes. However, crosschecking the results on two different tests gives you a counterbalancing measure that reduces the likelihood of error. (It is less likely that both tests are equally incorrect.)

A third test of validity is called discriminant validity. A comparison is made of two different tests that are supposed to measure two different things. Here, the researcher is looking not for agreement but for disagreement. The more dissimilar the two sets of scores, the less likely it is that the two tests measure the same thing. By inference, then, the more likely it is that each test is measuring what it claims to measure.

Having introduced a number of basic concepts that lie beneath all attitude-change research, we now can turn to the specific techniques used to assess the effects of persuasive messages. To do this properly, it is necessary first to discuss the ways in which those elements in a person's cognitive structure are measured. For persuasive effects are changes in those elements. And you cannot judge changes unless you have a point of reference, a "before" in the usual "before-and-after" scheme. Therefore, the question we will look at first is this: What techniques are used to measure a person's beliefs, attitudes, intentions, and behavior?

Traditionally, most emphasis has been placed on measuring attitudes. This emphasis has really been by default, however, since most tests of attitudes have failed to distinguish among attitudes, beliefs, and intentions. More refined measurement techniques, just now being created, more clearly distinguish among these three concepts.

Two other preliminary observations need to be made. First, with respect to beliefs, attitudes, and intentions, the researcher is confronted with a problem. How do you externalize something that's inside someone's head? No one has ever seen a belief, for example. (Technically, beliefs, attitudes, and intentions are called hypothetical constructs—concepts created by scientists to explain what they observe.) One of the tasks of measuring these cognitive elements, therefore, is to make external something that's inside a person's mind (Zimbardo, 197, p. 313). The solution is to construct some sort of measuring instrument that accurately reflects the internal state of the person. Put another way, the researcher must get the person to behave in such a way as to mirror the internal state.

To appreciate the second preliminary observation you need to recall the scientist's emphasis on quantitative data. The aim in nearly all techniques for attitude measurement is to represent an attitude quantitatively. Researchers have built their tests on the assumption that an attitude can be represented by some numerical value. This assumption can be disconcerting to students trained in the humanities and in other fields that do not place emphasis on quantification. Confronted by mathematical formulas and esoteric Greek symbols that conjure unpleasant memories of algebra and trignometry, you may be intimidated by descriptions of some of the attitude-measurement techniques. You need not be. The techniques require neither genius nor spectacular insight to be comprehended. As someone who used to be intimidated by these formulas and methods, let me assure you that the primary requirement in making sense of them is a generous endowment of common sense and some knowledge of basic mathematics. Further, in my explanations of each technique I have attempted to be as clear and complete as possible.

The table of techniques for measuring the effects of persuasion in Figure 4.3 is intended to serve as both a review and forecast. It is a review of the basic experimental paradigm discussed earlier in this chapter, together with a recapping of information on independent and dependent variables. It is a forecast and overview of measuring techniques to be discussed further. The column labeled "measurement techniques" contains a listing of the primary

Audience Premessage State	Intervention: Persuasive Message	Audience Postmessage State	Objects of Measurement	Representative Measurement Technique	Chief Weakness of This Technique
Measurable Dependent Variables[1] attitudes beliefs intentions behavior	Measurable Independent Variables (observable characteristics of persuasive message) Source variables (credibility, etc.) Message variables (organization, proofs, etc.)	Measurable Dependent Variables beliefs attitudes intentions behavior	*beliefs* content strength *intentions* content strength *attitudes*	 unipolar scale linking object of judgment with attribute subjective probability scale unipolar scale linking subject with behavior subjective probability scale *physiological measures* galvanic skin response *projective tests* Rorschach *nondisguised techniques* tests of recall and learning Guttman Thurstone Likert Osgood, et al. Fishbein *disguised techniques* Hammond Cook	 respondent's conception of object of judgment may differ from tester's probability may not remain constant respondent's conception of behavior may differ from tester's probability may not remain constant indicate degree of interest or arousal, but tell us nothing about direction of attitude not valid or reliable no correlation between amount of recall or learning and amount of attitude change • cumbersome • fails to distinguish clearly between beliefs, attitudes, intentions, and behavior • limited applications • respondent's meanings of key terms in belief and intention statements may differ from tester's • cumbersome • fails to distinguish clearly between beliefs, attitudes, intentions, and behavior • requires large pool of subjects • rests on assumption that subjects' own attitudes don't influence their categorization of statements • intervals may not be equal • fails to distinguish clearly between beliefs, attitudes, intentions, and behavior • rests on the assumption that an attitude is a linear function • misuse may result in failure to distinguish clearly between beliefs, attitudes, intentions, and behavior • seemingly evaluative scales may not actually be such under all conditions • may require cumbersome statistical procedures • different subjects' evaluations of attributes linked to objects may vary • respondents' meanings for key terms may differ from tester's • fails to distinguish clearly between beliefs, attitudes, intentions and behavior • fails to distinguish clearly between beliefs, attitudes, intentions, and behavior
			behavior	frequency counts	• no major flaws so long as no attempt is made to infer attitudes from behavior

Figure 4.3. *Techniques for Measuring the Effects of Persuasion.* Note that under certain conditions, audience variables can constitute independent variables.

techniques. Note that they are categorized; some are called nondisguised techniques, others projective techniques, and so on. These categories correspond to headings in this chapter. The last column, "principal problems," identifies the chief weakness of each measurement technique. In my discussion of each technique will be a brief evaluation, plus further details, and references you can turn to for additional information.

MEASURING BELIEFS

At the height of the Watergate scandal in the early 1970s, then-President Richard Nixon uttered his now-celebrated line, "I am not a crook!" At the time, there was serious disagreement among the American citizenry regarding the truth or falsity of the statement. If you had been charged with measuring a person's belief regarding Nixon, you might have concluded that it could easily have been assessed simply by asking the question, "Do you think President Nixon is a crook?" But more careful analysis would have indicated that there were two, not one, factors operating. First, did the person link the object (Nixon) to the attribute (a crook)? Second, in the person's mind, how likely was it that the two were linked? To answer the first question, you would have had to ask, "Do you believe President Nixon is a crook?" If he or she answered yes, you would also have needed to determine the strength of the person's conviction that the object and the attribute were linked. You might have asked, for example, "How strongly do you believe that President Nixon is a crook?" The answer you got would have told you the degree of conviction with which the object and the attribute were linked in the respondent's mind.

The first factor operating here is called *belief content;* the second, *belief strength*. If you analyze each belief you hold, you will find that it can be broken down into these two components. Content refers to what you believe; strength has to do with how firmly you believe it. Do you believe there is a God? With what degree of conviction? Do you believe your instructor cares about your progress in this course? How firmly do you believe it?

This distinction between content and strength is more than academic; it has real implications for the persuasive speaker. In analyzing your audience, you need to determine what they believe about the subject of your speech. And you need to determine how strongly they hold that belief. If your speech were in favor of abortion, for example, you would need to determine whether your audience believed the fetus is human from the moment of conception. If they did, you would be faced with a formidable obstacle. But your situation could be even more desperate: How firmly did they believe the fetus is human from conception? Were they 100 per cent convinced? Were they doubtful but inclined to think it is? Needless to say, the stronger the belief, the more resistant the auditor.

MEASURING INTENTIONS

Intentions are measured in the same way as beliefs. You must first assess the content of the intention. This means determining what it is that you (or your audience) intend to do. Secondly, you must measure the strength with which the intention is held. In other words, you must determine how firmly resolved you (or they) are to perform the action.

The technique for measuring beliefs can also be used to assess a person's intentions. But there are other methods as well. For example, a person can be given a statement of intention such as, "I will begin contributing to my tuition expenses." Asked to respond yes or no, the individual would provide information about the content of the intention. If the person said no, you could safely conclude that among the intentions, the determination to contribute to tuition expenses is not present. If the person were to answer yes, your next task would be to measure the strength of the resolve. You might do this by asking the individual to mark a point on a scale that runs from *probable* to *improbable* or from *likely* to *unlikely*. Where the mark is put would be a rough index of the strength of the resolve—the more probable the person thinks the action to be, the stronger the intention, and vice versa. Each scale unit could be assigned a numerical value—say, from 1 to 7. The value of 1 could be placed at the extreme end of the scale bounded by *highly improbable*. The number 7 could be placed at the opposite end of the scale, indicating that it is *highly probable* that the respondent will perform the behavior specified in the intention statement. By summing up the point values scored on each scale, you would arrive at a number indicative of the strength of the person's intention to perform the behavior in question.

This procedure is outlined in more depth and is applied in Student Activity Option 4.2.

Student Activity Option 4.2
Measuring Intentions: Study Habits

INSTRUCTIONS

Below is a set of statements of intention. Please answer *yes* or *no* to each statement. For each intention statement that you answer *yes*, please mark the scale adjacent to that response. Note that the scale runs from "highly improbable" to "highly probable." Numerical values appear beneath each line on the scale. After you have marked the scale for each of the four statements, transfer the numerical value beneath the lines you marked to the score line on the right of the scale. The sum of these scores is a rough measure of your intention to perform the behavior specified. You might want to compare your intention scores with those of some of your classmates.

Note: As a persuasive speaker, you can apply this same technique to get a reading of your audience's intentions regarding the subject of your speech. By crosschecking before-speech intentions and after-speech intentions, you can estimate the effects of your speech on your audience's intentions.

Statement

1. I will start doing my term papers by the sixth week of the semester.

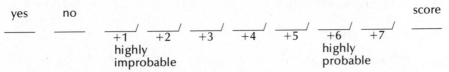

yes   no   score

_____   _____   +1   +2   +3   +4   +5   +6   +7   _____
                        highly   highly
                        improbable   probable

2. I intend to keep up with all course readings.

yes   no   score

_____   _____   +1   +2   +3   +4   +5   +6   +7   _____
                        highly   highly
                        improbable   probable

3. I will study for all tests.

yes   no   score

_____   _____   +1   +2   +3   +4   +5   +6   +7   _____
                        highly   highly
                        improbable   probable

4. I plan to meet with each instructor at least once this semester.

yes   no   score

_____   _____   +1   +2   +3   +4   +5   +6   +7   _____
                        highly   highly
                        improbable   probable

Total score:_____

It would be interesting to check at the end of the semester to see whether in fact you had performed the behaviors you intended to perform. If you failed to do so, you might try determining why. What factors affect your behaving as you intend to behave? This question is of interest not only in terms of your own self-understanding but also to you as a student of persuasive speaking. As a persuader, you need to be aware that while you may succeed in making your audience formulate an intention to do something, there is no guarantee that they will do it. Likely, the same sorts of things that interfered with your behaving as you intended to affect an audience and intervene between an audience's intentions and the performance of the behavior. An interesting research or term paper possibility is to try to systematize the sources and influence of forces that interfere with the performance of an intended behavior. Here are two readings on the subject that might be of interest:

Fishbein, Martin, and Icek Ajzen (1975) *Belief, Attitude, Intention and Behavior: An Introduction to Theory and Research.* Reading, Massachusetts: Addison-Wesley Publishing Company. See especially Chapter Eight, Prediction of Behavior.

Rose, Sheldon (1977) *Group Therapy: A Behavioral Approach.* Englewood Cliffs, New Jersey: Prentice Hall. See especially Chapters 3–6.

MEASURING ATTITUDES

Physiological measures

As indicated in Figure 4.3, several techniques are available for assessing attitudes, though not all are of equal quality. The first technique listed in the model consists of physiological measures. These include measures of the extent to which a person's pupils are dilated or contracted; and measures of the amount of sweat recorded on the palms of the hands. It stands to reason that a person excited by a persuasive message will respond physiologically. As the person becomes aroused, his or her pupils are likely to dilate. Heartbeat may speed up; the person's hands may start sweating. Researchers have attempted to use measures of these physiological reactions as indicators of an individual's attitudes. Unfortunately, their efforts have been unsuccessful because, while the responses indicate the degree of interest or arousal, they tell us nothing about the actual attitude. For example, increased heartbeat can mean a person is excitedly happy or excitedly angry. Dilation of the pupils can mean a person is intensely interested in and aroused by what he or she is seeing or hearing. But dilation in itself tells us nothing about the nature of that arousal. Is it due to positive feelings about the objects of perception? to negative feelings? No one can say. For this reason, physiological measures are not acceptable tests of attitudes.

Projective tests

The second technique is composed of projective tests. Did you ever study the shapes in a slowly moving mass of clouds and look for objects? Perhaps you saw a lion one minute, a teakettle the next. That pastime is a projective device. Projective tests consist of ambiguous stimuli like the clouds—inkblots, for example. The person taking the test is asked to look at the stimuli and to tell the experimenter what is represented. On the basis of the subject's interpretations of the stimuli, the experimenter arrives at an asessment of the subject's inner state.

These tests suffer from problems in both reliability and validity. Problems in reliability arise because the person who interprets the subject's responses may infer quite different things. Does the subject's seeing a shark in the inkblot mean that she possesses a great deal of aggression? Does it mean he is contemplating suicide by drowning? A person must have extensive training before being able to interpret projective tests intelligently. Still, there may be little agreement among experts as to the meanings of a subject's response on a particular test item. Furthermore, problems in validity arise because it is extremely difficult to determine whether these tests measure beliefs, attitudes, or intentions. Suppose a person takes the Thematic Aperception Test. The subject is shown a picture of an older woman and a younger man. The woman is frowning as she regards the man, who looks vaguely frightened. To explain the scene, the subject constructs a story that involves a stern mother who intimidates her compliant and easily frightened son. Does this interpretation mean that the subject believes his own mother to be stern? Does it mean he holds a negative attitude toward older women? toward mothers? toward all women? It is virtually impossible to assess exactly what is being measured by tests such as this. For that reason, projective tests are not used with any serious intent in attitude-change research.

Nondisguised techniques

Several nondisguised techniques make up the next category of measuring instruments listed in Figure 4.3. Nondisguised means that no attempt is made to hide from the respondent the fact that the attitudes on a particular subject are being assessed (sometimes, however, the subject is deceived into thinking that it's the attitudes toward A that are being measured whereas in fact the researcher is interested in the attitudes toward B).

The first of these techniques consists of tests of recall and learning. (Note that these can also be used to measure beliefs.) According to Howard H. Martin (1968, p. 191), until fairly recently advertisers made extensive use of tests of recall to assess the effects of their advertisements. It was assumed that a consumer's attitudes had been changed by an ad if he or she could recall the information it presented about the product. However, research has demonstrated that this assumption is invalid. You may see a cigarette commercial that tells you a great deal about the manufacture of a particular brand. You may learn, for example, that the tobacco blend created for use in this brand includes leaves grown in octagonal-shaped greenhouses on the highest peak of the Himalayan Mountains by bearded women wearing bikinis. However, does the fact that you recall this information indicate that your attitude toward this brand has changed? Are you more inclined or less inclined to buy this brand now? Research indicates that there is no necessary relationship between the amount of learning or recall that occurs as a result of an ad and the attitude changes induced (Hawkins, 1964). Hence, you may remember a particularly clever ad but still not be inclined to buy the product. You may even decide against the product, although you can appreciate the creativity that went into the commercial. In fact, one school of advertising thought argues that ads should not be too clever or cute; under such circumstances, consumers typically forget the product but remember the ad. Hence we may conclude that tests of recall and learning bear no necessary relationship to attitude or behavior change. (The clever reader, recalling the discussion of the relationship between attitudes and beliefs, may object to this principle. Since attitudes are a function of both the strength of one's beliefs about an object of judgment and also his or her evaluations of the attributes associated with that object, it is unlikely that changes in beliefs have no effect whatever. However, research indicates that no significant effect on attitudes is produced. One possible explanation is that the beliefs induced by a commercial are of so little weight that they do not have a noticeable impact on consumer attitudes.)

The next five nondisguised techniques for measuring attitudes are by far the most influential and frequently used. An appreciation of each method—its rationale, usefulness, and weaknesses—is important. If you are to make informed choices about techniques of persuasion, you need to be able to understand what the research shows and how the findings were arrive at.

GUTTMAN

Guttman's method of scaling was originally created to provide a method of organizing a wide range of qualitative data such as test scores. When applied to measuring attitudes, the Guttman method involves several steps. To get an idea of how the technique operates, imagine a mathematics test composed of ten questions of graduated difficulty. The first is the easiest, the tenth the hardest. One point is given for each correct answer, no points for each incorrect answer. Thus, a perfect score is ten while a zero means that no questions were answered correctly. Given these premises, you could accurately estimate a person's ability in mathematical computation. You would know that a person with a score of 5, for example, got the first five questions right but the last five wrong. A person with a score of 6 got one additional question right, and so on. Note that in this scheme it is assumed that no questions are gotten right simply by chance. Once you reach your level of ineptitude, you cannot exceed it by guessing. Thus, if I am a "level two" student and you are a "level eight" student, I will get two and only two questions right—that is the first two. You will get numbers one through eight correct. In this scheme, the probability is zero that a person will correctly answer a question beyond his or her ability level. Conversely, the probability that a person will correctly answer a question at or below performance level is one. To illustrate, if my ability a score is 3, then you know I got the first three questions right. Any question at a difficulty level equivalent to that in questions one, two, or three, I will get right. Any question beyond my ability level (equivalent in difficulty to questions four through ten), I will get wrong. This is like saying that a person in the third grade is able to do the work of a first or second grader but would not be expected to do the work of a fourth, fifth, or sixth grader.

A number of adjustments have to be made in applying this scaling technique to measuring attitudes, and the specifics of application become quite complex. However, I will show in essence how the application is made.* First, a number of statements are gathered that link together either an atti-

---

* If you are interested in a more technical treatment, see Guttman, 1944; Edwards, 1957; Green, 1954.

tude object and an attribute, or the subject and an intention to perform a specific behavior. For example, consider these statements:

1. Fig Newtons are sweet. (belief statement)
2. I plan to buy Fig Newtons. (intention statement)
3. Happy people eat Fig Newtons. (belief statement)
4. I would serve Fig Newtons to friends. (intention statement)
5. I could eat Fig Newtons every day. (intention statement)

Endorsements (in the form of agree-disagree statements) are gotten from the subjects. That is, subjects are asked to indicate which, if any, of the statements they endorse. Out of a pool of 50 subjects, let's suppose that 25 express agreement with statement number one (Fig Newtons are sweet), but only 3 endorse statement number five (I could eat Fig Newtons every day). Statements number two, three, and four each receive a specific number of endorsements as well. All the responses are collected, and the statements are placed in order. Each statement's ranking is determined by the frequency with which it was endorsed. That statement endorsed most frequently is placed first, the statement endorsed second most frequently is placed second, and so on, with the statement least frequently endorsed or not endorsed at all placed last. Then the responses of each subject are compared with those of the entire group of subjects. Let's say the pattern of frequency works out like this for the entire group:

Statement	Placement*
one	first
three	second
four	third
two	fourth
five	fifth

*by frequency of endorsement

This pattern represents an attitude typical of the sample group. If a subject's rankings deviate from the sample group's, that difference suggests that the subject holds an attitude different from the group's. The difference between the individual subject's scores and the ratings of the group as a whole are calculable mathematically. By computing that difference, it is possible to conclude that a particular subject's attitude is more strongly positive, less strongly positive, more strongly negative, and so on. Note here that as in ability testing, the theme in the Guttman scaling method is cumulative. The subject's ratings are summed, and that total represents the strength of his or her attitude. No deviation from the sample group's ratings results in a score of zero, which means the subject's attitude is typical of the group's.

Guttman's technique is not universally applicable. In some cases, it has been reported that data suggest subjects differed in the meanings they assigned to the various terms used in the belief or intention statements. Under these and other specific conditions, it is considered inadvisable to use the Guttman scale as a measure of attitudes. (Formulas have been developed to establish the circumstances under which it is inadvisable to use the scale.) Furthermore, the scaling technique is somewhat cumbersome, requiring a considerable amount of time to gather, order, and interpret data. Finally, the data this test provides are strictly cumulative. It provides rank orderings but no clear gradations of differences in degrees of liking between ratings. Nor does it provide an indication of the placement of attitude objects on a scale divided into equal segments or intervals. In order to achieve that goal, other tests of attitudes are used.

THURSTONE

Thurstone's method (1931) for measuring attitudes is the grand-daddy of more contemporary approaches. It differs from Guttman's in that it doesn't result in a purely cumulative set of items. Instead, the strength of a person's attitude falls somewhere on a scale of 11 equally spaced intervals. Thus, the strength of a person's attitude can be arrived at and can be compared with that of other individuals.

To measure an attitude using Thurstone's technique, first, a large group of statements about an attitude object is collected. (Later, this group of statements will be narrowed down to approximately twenty, each of which will specify a different quality attributable to the attitude object.) These statements are distributed to a group of subjects representative of the larger group whose attitudes are to be assessed. (The members of this first group are called judges.) So far, the technique is much like the method used in the Guttman scalogram method. Thurstone's instructions to this sample group of people (judges) differ from Guttman's, however. The judges in this instance aren't simply asked whether they agree or disagree with the statements. Instead, the judges are asked to rank each statement in terms of its degree of favorableness or unfavorableness toward the attitude object.

Judges are given 11 categories in which to place the statements. These categories range from most favorable, through neutral, to least favorable. If the statements are distributed on index cards, for example, subjects are told to place the cards into 11 piles. In the pile at one extreme end they are to place those statements reflecting a most favorable attitude toward the object of judgment. In the middle pile are statements reflecting an attitude that is neither favorable nor unfavorable, and so on.

Note two things here: First, the judge is not being asked to report his or her own attitudes, nor is the judge requested to rank the statements according to whether he or she agrees or disagrees with each statement. Instead, the judge is being asked to rank order the statements in terms of the extent to which he or she believes the statements to reflect degrees of favorableness or unfavorableness toward the attitude object. If you were a judge and you concluded that the statement "I could eat Fig Newtons every day" represented the most favorable sentiment toward Fig Newtons out of the group of 30 statements you had been given, you would place that statement in category one, indicating a "most favorable" rating. If you considered the statement "Fig Newtons can be hazardous to your health" to be the least favorable of the 30, you would place that statement in category eleven, indicating "least favorable."

Second, notice that in tabulating the results of the ordering, a researcher would eliminate statements that seemed to be ambiguous, confusing, or otherwise faulty. (For example, a statement such as, "Fig Newtons are generally available," which would be acceptable to two judges holding diametrically opposed attitudes, would be eliminated.) Usually, a Thurstone scale consists of approximately 20 statements about a specific attitude object.

Calculation and tabulation of these ratings involve determining the frequencies with which the various statements are placed in each of the 11 categories. For example, how often is a particular statement placed in the "most favorable" category? Thus a number of statements are identified as equally spaced along an imaginary continuum from "most favorable" to "most unfavorable." (The location of items and the equality of intervals are calculated mathematically, using simple formulas).

The person whose attitude the researcher wants to assess is then given the list of statements and asked to indicate whether he or she agrees with them. What this person doesn't know is that each statement has a numerical scale value that is determined by its placement on the continuum. (For example, a statement that falls into category one, "most favorable," is given a value of $+7.5$; a statement that falls into the next category is assigned a value of $+6.0$ and so on. A statement that falls into the category of "least favorable" is assigned a value of -1.5. By adding up the values of all the items the person agrees with and then dividing by the number of items responded to, the person's attitude score is arrived at. Again, this attitude is expressed numerically, with a plus sign indicating a positive attitude and a minus sign indicating a negative attitude. The larger the number, the more extreme the attitude. Thus, for example, a score of $+14$ would mean a most extreme positive attitude.

Like the Guttman scalogram, the Thurstone procedure is cumbersome and time consuming. It has also been criticized along several more important lines. First, it requires a rather large pool of potential subjects. From this pool must be drawn those who will serve as judges as well as those whose attitudes will be measured. Second, the entire procedure rests on the assumption that the judges' own attitudes do not influence their placing the various statements into each of the 11 categories. Fishbein and Ajzen report (1975, p. 71) that this seems a safe assumption under most circumstances. Nevertheless, the fact that judges' attitudes may affect the entire procedure is disconcerting, to say the least. Third, the key element in this procedure is that the intervals between the 11 categories are equal. (If they were not, precise mathematical values could not be assigned to each statement.) But there is doubt that the judges perceive the intervals as equal (Cronkhite, 1969, p. 117). Once again, the judges' own attitudes may distort their decisions as to where to place the statements. Finally, Cronkhite makes the point (1969, p. 118) that there is some doubt about the assumption that attitudes can accurately be represented as falling along a continuum. This criticism would affect not only the Thurstone procedure but also the Likert procedure.

LIKERT

One feature of the Thurstone method that bothered Likert (1932) was the dependence on judges in determining the scale ratings of the various statements with which the subjects would then agree or disagree. He devised a much simpler procedure that yielded a numerical value that reflected both the direction (positive or negative) and strength of an attitude. His method of summated ratings is a streamlined Thurstone procedure. It is one of the most frequently used techniques in contemporary attitude-change research. Like the Guttman and Thurstone procedures, Likert's procedure begins with a number of belief or intention statements about a particular object of judgment. Instead of having a group of judges determine whether each statement indicates a positive or negative attitude toward the object, this task is performed by the researcher. Items that are ambiguous, unclear, or otherwise flawed are eliminated. Note here that no discriminations are made regarding the degrees of favorableness or unfavorableness implied by the statements. The statements are merely grouped into categories of "favorable" and "unfavorable." Subjects are given a listing of statements and asked to indicate (usually by means of a multiple-choice format) whether they "agree strongly," "agree," "neither agree nor disagree," "disagree," or "disagree strongly." Each of these response categories is assigned a numerical value. For statements that fall into the "favorable" category, "agree strongly" is assigned a value of 5; "agree" is assigned a value of 4; "neither agree nor disagree" is assigned a value of 3; "disagree" is assigned a value of 2; and "disagree strongly" is assigned a value of 1. For statements that fall into the "unfavorable" category, "agree strongly" is assigned a value of 1, "agree" is assigned a value of 2; "neither agree nor disagree" is assigned a value of 3; "disagree" is assigned a value of 4; and "disagree strongly" is assigned a value of 5. This scale of ratings makes perfect sense, since a person with a positive attitude toward Fig Newtons is most likely to agree strongly with statements that reflect positive attitudes toward them and is most likely to disagree strongly with statements that reflect a negative attitude toward them. Conversely, if you really hate Fig Newtons, you are likely to agree strongly with statements that reflect a negative attitude toward Fig Newtons and to disagree strongly with statements that reflect a positive attitude toward them (see Figure 4.4). To arrive at a person's attitude score, his or her scores on individual items are summed. The result is a numerical value that is used to represent an attitude.

The Likert and Thurstone scales are different in a few ways, despite their

Attitude Object: Fig Newtons

Statement: I would serve Fig Newtons to friends.

Response Category	Value
a) agree strongly	5
b) agree	4
c) neither agree nor disagree	3
d) disagree	2
e) disagree strongly	1

Figure 4.4. Typical Likert Scale Item

similarities in method and in the assumption that attitudes are simple linear functions representable on a scale from 1 to n. First of all, recall that the intervals in the 11-point Thurstone scale are equal. No such contention is made in the Likert format. The psychological distance between the response of "disagree strongly" and the next one, "disagree," is not necessarily equivalent to the distance between "disagree" and "neither agree nor disagree." Secondly, recall that the items on a Thurstone scale must each reflect a different quality attributable to the attitude object. Each of the 20 or so items on the attitude test must be discrete. No such requirement operates in the Likert scale. In fact, according to Zibmardo et al. (1977, p. 216), "the items in a scale must be highly correlated with a common attribute and thus with each other."*

Despite these differences, research indicates that the Likert scale correlates highly with the Thurstone scale. A positive correlation of .72 and .92, as reported by Cronkhite (1969, p. 118), indicates much agreement between the results of the two attitude tests. Thus, the two can be used interchangeably; the Likert scale appears to be no less reliable than the Thurstone one. In light of these data, and because of the simplicity and streamlined nature of the Likert scale, it is far more widely used than Thurstone's procedure.

Despite its popularity and apparent utility, the Likert scale is open to a number of important criticisms. As has been implied, like so many other attitude scales, it fails to make a clear distinction among beliefs, attitudes, and intentions. Although Likert assumed that there is an equivalency between attitudes and beliefs and between attitudes and intentions, Fishbein has argued that this is an unwarranted assumption. In light of this argument, it can also be argued that the conceptualization beneath the Likert scale is faulty; hence, the scale itself seems less than perfect. Another problem with the Likert scale is that it rests on an additional questionable assumption—that an attitude is a linear function. Intellectually, it is simple and pleasing to view a person's attitudes as affective dimensions that can fall on a linear scale running from

---

* The particulars of the decisions regarding inclusion of the items were not covered in my discussion. If you are interested in the construction of the Likert scale, I recommend Likert, 1932, as well as Fishbein and Ajzen, 1975, which includes more details regarding procedures.

strongly negative to strongly positive. But do attitudes really lend themselves to such simplistic representations? In your own experience, aren't attitudes far more complex than that? You may love and hate the same person, for example. You may have ambivalent feelings about the same attitude object under different circumstances and conditions. Attitudes are not one-dimensional, as a linear scale implies, but multidimensional; they represent a point of convergence of many feelings, beliefs, wishes, intentions, and other cognitive elements. The Likert scale and all others reviewed thus far fail to reflect this multidimensionality feature. They are gross simplifications. Though they may be useful for purposes of measurement, you should not lose sight of the fact that these scales are meager representations of a very rich reality.

OSGOOD

The Osgood technique approximates the complexities of humankind's inner psychological space. Interestingly, it was constructed not by a student of attitude change but by a psychologist with an interest in meaning. In fact, the semantic differential scale was not even thought of as applicable to measuring attitudes until after the scale was developed. Geared to an entirely different purpose (the measurement of meaning), only after its construction did it become apparent that the scale represented a useful tool for the measurement of attitudes.

In an attempt to solve the riddle of meaning, Osgood and his associates hit upon an idea that hadn't previously been thought of. Recognizing that meanings are multidimensional, they postulated that there exists for each of us a semantic space. You can imagine this space as a cube of air bounded by imaginary lines. Within that space are many lines, each representing a particular dimension of meaning—for example, a "warm-cold" dimension or a "useless-useful" dimension. The meaning of a particular word or concept is that point in three-dimensional semantic space at which these various lines converge. Osgood reasoned that the meaning of a word could be determined by asking people to locate the concept on a number of scales, each traveling through semantic space. Thus, you might be asked to locate the concept "nuclear disarmament" on several scales, as depicted in Figure 4.5. Your instructions would be to mark the point on each scale that best represents the degree to which, in your judgment, the attitude object possesses or is related to the scale attribute. A mark at either end of the scale means "extremely." A mark in the middle line means "neutral," "undecided," or "does not pertain." Points in between mean "slightly" and "quite." Note that these scales are bipolar, which means that they are bounded by two different poles ("good" versus "bad," for example). This is in contrast to unipolar scales, which involve degrees of only one feeling or attitude (for example, they might measure only the extent to which a person feels less strongly or more strongly about an object of judgment). Unipolar scales are used in the Guttman scale.

By a statistical procedure known as factor analysis, Osgood has been able consistently to group responses on many scales into three recurring

Nuclear Disarmament

undecided
neutral
extremely / quite / slightly / does not pertain / slightly / quite / extremely

good	___	___	___	___	___	___	___	bad
active	___	___	___	___	___	___	___	passive
right	___	___	___	___	___	___	___	wrong
intelligent	___	___	___	___	___	___	___	stupid
attractive	___	___	___	___	___	___	___	unattractive
valuable	___	___	___	___	___	___	___	worthless
fast	___	___	___	___	___	___	___	slow
impractical	___	___	___	___	___	___	___	practical
beautiful	___	___	___	___	___	___	___	ugly

Figure 4.5. Semantic Differential Rating Scales

categories, each of which, he argues, represents a dimension of meaning. The three are (1) the activity dimension, which includes scales such as "active-passive" and "fast-slow"; (2) the potency dimension, including scales such as "strong-weak" and "hard-soft"; and (3) the evaluative dimension, made up of scales such as "good-bad" and "pleasant-unpleasant." It is this last dimension that has come to serve as a measure of attitudes toward the concept. Almost from the beginning of interest in attitude change, it has been recognized that attitudes involve evaluative responses such as feelings of attraction, repulsion, liking/disliking, and so on. It should come as no surprise therefore that Osgood's procedure could serve as a measure of attitudes. Intrigued by this possibility, Osgood and his associates compared the semantic differential technique with other attitude-measurement tools such as the Thurstone procedure. They found very high correlations between their attitude tests and others. They were able to provide statistical backing for the claim that their technique does indeed serve as a measure of attitudes. (The assumption here, as you have probably realized, is that the Thurstone method or any other method to which the semantic differential is compared really *does* measure attitudes and not something else. The least that can be said is that the semantic differential is no less valid a measure than is, for example, the Thurstone technique. If, as is generally assumed, the Thurstone method does measure attitudes, then so does the semantic differential. Thus, by the test of construct validity, the semantic differential technique seems to be a valid measuring instrument. Test-retest coefficients of reliability are also high, indicating that it is a reliable, or consistent, measurement method.)

Attitude scores in the semantic differential technique are arrived at by assigning values to each segment of the 7-point scale (from -3 for an extreme mark on the negative side of the scale to $+3$ for its opposite, with the mid-

	Nuclear Disarmament		scale points
good	X at +1	bad	+1
	+3 +2 +1 0 −1 −2 −3		
pleasurable	X at −2	painful	−2
	+3 +2 +1 0 −1 −2 −3		
dirty	X at +1	clean	+1
	−3 −2 −1 0 +1 +2 +3		
pleasant	X at −1	unpleasant	−1
	+3 +2 +1 0 −1 −2 −3		
worthless	X at +2	valuable	+2
	−3 −2 −1 0 +1 +2 +3		
fair	X at +2	unfair	+2
	+3 +2 +1 0 −1 −2 −3		

Attitude Score (sum of scale points): +3

Figure 4.6. An Attitude Score Using the Semantic Differential Technique

point assigned a value of zero), then summing a person's scores on each scale. Sometimes an average of these scores is used. Thus, for example, if you were to rate the concept of "nuclear disarmament" on six evaluative scales, you might come up with an attitude score of +3 (assuming a summative method), as depicted in Figure 4.6.

The procedure seems simple enough, but there are complicating factors in its use.* One interesting, potentially complicating fact is that not all bipolar scales that seem to measure evaluative responses do so under all conditions. Some pairs of words that seem to measure a subject's evaluation of a concept may not do so in all situations. For example, the concept "warm-cold" may be evaluative when applied to a person but factual when applied to another attitude object, such as fire. The same is true of adjective pairs such as "hard-soft," which may fall into the evaluative category when applied to a person but into the activity dimension when applied to a procedure, such as abortion. Similarly, "clean-dirty" may fall into the evaluative dimension when applied to a political party but into a different category when applied to another attitude object, such as abandoned house.

The fact that the semantic differential technique does not always measure evaluative responses makes its use complicated at times. It requires that the experimenter conduct a factor analysis of the subject's scores on each scale in order to see which scale scores seem to cluster together under the evaluative umbrella. In addition, the semantic differential technique falls victim to the basic flaw in all attitude tests discussed thus far—it fails to make a clear dis-

---

*If you are interested in details of scale use, see C. E. Osgood, C. J. Suci, and P. H. Tannenbaum, 1957; and C. E. Osgood and P. E. Tannenbaum, 1955; Fishbein and Ajzen, 1975, provide a reasonably complete discussion of the technique and its applications.

tinction among a subject's beliefs, attitudes, and intentions. These measures imply that a person's beliefs are related to his or her attitudes, which is true. They also imply that somehow or another a person's evaluations of the attributes associated with the object of judgment play a part in determining the attitude. However, as Fishbein and Ajzen rightly point out (1975, p. 86), these methods of attitude measurement do not take cognizance of the subject's own evaluation of the attribute associated with the object. Instead, it is recklessly assumed that the evaluation of the attribute is the same for all subjects; and the evaluation is nowhere specified by the researcher. To make this clearer, consider an example. Two people rate the attitude object gasoline as "extremely practical," a +3 rating on the semantic differential. This means that each person strongly associates the attitude object with the quality "practical." The question that arises, however, is whether each rater means the same thing when he or she marks the +3 space on the scale. Might they not have different evaluations of the attribute "practical"? Unless the researcher knows the value assigned to the attribute by the subject, it is impossible to arrive at a true estimate of that person's attitude toward the object; a +3 rating might mean different things to different people.

In light of these continuing problems, Fishbein developed a technique for measuring attitudes that clearly makes the conceptual distinctions among beliefs, attitude, and intentions.

FISHBEIN

According to Fishbein, a person's attitude toward an object is determined by his or her beliefs about that object. More precisely, two factors come into play in determining a person's attitudes. First are the person's beliefs about the object, including both the belief that the object in question (say, college athletics) is associated with a certain trait, quality, or outcome (for example, healthy); and the strength of the belief connecting the object with the trait. In other words, you and I may agree that college athletics are healthy. That is, our beliefs may have the same content. But we may disagree in the strength of our belief that the two are related. Our subjective probabilities may differ, to use Fishbein's jargon.

A second factor determining a person's attitude is the evaluation of the attributes he or she associates with the object. You and I may have different feelings about things that are healthy; we may evaluate that attribute differently.

Fishbein contends that it is possible to predict a person's attitudes toward a given object of judgment by multiplying the strength of the belief that an object and an attribute are linked times the person's evaluation of that attribute. Fishbein's formula appears in Figure 4.7. Note that in the formula, A_0 is the attitude toward some object, 0; b_i is the belief about the object (that is, the subjective probability that the object and the attribute are related); e_i is the evaluation of the attribute; n is the number of beliefs; and the symbol Σ

$$A_o = \sum_{i=1}^{n} b_i e_i$$

Figure 4.7. Fishbein's Attitude Formula

means "the sum of." By summing the products of b_i times e_i, you are multiplying the strength of a person's belief that an object and an attribute are linked by the person's evaluation of the attribute.

Let me return to the example of college athletics to illustrate. Let's suppose you were tested on the extent to which you believe that the object, college athletics, is associated with four attributes—healthy (attribute number one), competitive (attribute number two), fun (attribute number three), and school spirit (attribute number four). Let's suppose further that the strength of your belief that college athletics is associated with each attribute can be expressed numerically as follows: (1) strength of belief linking object (college athletics) with attribute one (healthy) equals .80; (2) strength of belief linking object with attribute two (competitive) equals .90; (3) strength of belief linking object with attribute number three (fun) equals .40; and (4) strength of belief linking object with attribute number four (school spirit) equals .70. Finally, let's postulate that when you were asked to evaluate each of the four attributes, you came up with these ratings: (1) healthy, +2; (2) competitive, −2; (3) fun, +3; and (4) school spirit, +1. By multiplying the strength of each of your beliefs by your evaluation of the attribute contained in the belief, you would come up with a product. By adding up all the products, you would come up with a sum of the products, in this case, 1.70 (see Figure 4.8). This sum represents your estimated attitude toward college athletics. In this case the attitude is positive overall, despite the fact that one negative value appears in the equation. On the basis of this calculation, someone might conclude that you have a mildly positive attitude toward college athletics. (Note that the highest possible score on this equation is +12; the lowest possible score is −12.)

Object of Judgment: College Athletics

Belief	b (strength of belief linking college athletics with this attribute)	e (your evaluation of the attribute)	be (the product of b times e)
healthy	.80	+2	1.60
competitive	.90	−2	−1.80
fun	.40	+3	1.20
school spirit	.70	+1	.70
	Estimated Attitude: Σ *(the sum of) be*		1.70

Figure 4.8. Fishbein's Attitude Formula Applied to Your Attitude Toward College Athletics

Student Activity Option 4.3
Fishbein's Summative Theory

INSTRUCTIONS

Below are a number of values representing a person's beliefs about three objects of judgment. Note that the values refer both to the strength of the beliefs and to the person's evaluation of the attributes associated with the objects in each belief statement. Apply Fishbein's formula and arrive at an estimate of this person's attitude about each object of judgment.

1. Object of Judgment: sexually aggressive males

Attributes associated with that object	Strength of belief linking the object and the attribute (b)	Evaluation of the attribute (e)	Product of b times e (be)
frightening	.80	−3	_____
exciting	.60	+2	_____
warm	.70	+1	_____
immature	.90	−2	_____

Estimated attitude: Σ (the sum of) be _____

2. Object of Judgment: cole slaw

Attributes associated with that object	Strength of belief linking the object and the attribute (b)	Evaluation of the attribute (e)	Product of b times e (be)
nutritious	.90	+2	_____
fattening	.80	−1	_____
delicious	.40	+3	_____
sloppy	.50	−2	_____

Estimated attitude: Σ (the sum of) be _____

3. Object of Judgment: textbook authors

Attributes associated with that object	Strength of belief linking the object and the attribute (b)	Evaluation of the attribute (e)	Product of b times e (be)
eggheaded	.80	−2	_____
capable	.90	+1	_____
intelligent	.90	+3	_____
creative	.40	+1	_____

Estimated attitude: Σ (the sum of) be _____

Disguised techniques

As indicated earlier, a problem can arise when subjects are aware of the fact that their attitudes are being measured. Particularly in pre- and post-measurement situations, individuals may deliberately and well-meaningly distort the results of an attitude test. For this and other reasons, disguised tests of attitudes are sometimes used, as shown in Figure 4.3 as the fourth major category of attitude tests. I will discuss here two of the more popular influential disguised tests of attitudes: the Hammond method (called the "error choice technique") and that of Cook (called the "plausibility technique").

Hammond. The subterfuge employed in a Hammond technique is to give subjects the impression they are responding to test items that have right and wrong answers. It appears as though their knowledge of factual material is being tested, whereas in fact the test yields a measure of the subjects' attitudes. A typical Hammond test item might look like this:

1. Capital punishment
   a. acts as a deterrent to crime
   b. does not act as a deterrent to crime

In this case, it is not factual matter about capital punishment that is being tested, but the subject's attitudes about capital punishment. (Note that more precisely, it is the subject's *belief* that is being assessed. As with other attitude tests, the Hammond technique blurs the distinction between beliefs and attitudes.) In cases such as this example, it has been shown that a subject's answer to the question is determined by his or her attitude toward capital punishment. If the subject supports capital punishment he or she believes that it acts as a deterrent. If the subject opposes it, he or she does not think it acts as a deterrent. Thus, the Hammond technique can serve as a measure of attitudes.*

Cook. Consider the following statement: "Because prayer in the public schools implies official governmental acceptance of a religious ideology, the practice is in violation of the Bill of Rights." Do you think that is a plausible argument? Read this one: "By failing to provide children with an opportunity to pray in the public schools, we undermine their moral and religious values." Suppose you had to judge the plausibility or effectiveness of the argument contained in the second passage. Would you judge it plausible? effective?

Judgments about these statements seem to deal with plausibility or effectiveness; in fact, they constitute a way of measuring attitudes. Research by Cook and his associates demonstrates that a person's judgments of the plausibility or effectiveness of a statement or argument is profoundly affected by his or her attitudes toward the subject matter. If you are in favor of prayer in the

---

*If you are interested in more particulars on the use of this attitude measure, see K. R. Hammond (1948) "Measuring Attitudes by Error-Choice: An Indirect Method," *Journal of Abnormal and Social Psychology,* 43: 38–48.

public schools, it is likely that you disagreed with the first statement above and that you agreed with the second.

In other words, the Cook technique is a disguised method of attitude assessment. The ploy is to delude subjects into thinking they are being asked to estimate the plausibility or effectiveness of an argument, seemingly an objective judgment. In fact, however, their responses are indicative of the attitudes they hold. Like all other attitude measures discussed here, the Cook technique results in a numerical value.*

Several other techniques are used to measure attitudes and new methods are being developed daily. The following Student Activity Option provides a number of readings and classroom activities that can result in your updating the material on attitude measurement. If you have an interest in psychological tests and measurements, I think you will find these activities interesting.

Student Activity Option 4.4
Attitude Tests and Measurements

INSTRUCTIONS
The following activities represent important learning tools in acquiring a knowledge of testing procedures. If classroom time permits, consider completing one or more of the options that follow.

1. Arrange to test your classmates' beliefs, attitudes, or intentions on a given topic. You may wish to use one or more of the testing procedures discussed in this chapter. With the consent of the instructors involved, you might even test the views of more than one class. Perhaps arrange for you and your classmates to be guest speakers in a number of classes on a variety of topics. It might be possible to conduct a few simple experiments in which the premessage states of various listeners are compared with their postmessage states.

2. Ask your instructor whether he or she has conducted any descriptive or experimental research on attitude change. If so, ask the instructor to discuss measurement techniques, as well as such related topics as experimental design and hypothesis. Or you might invite to your class a member of the department of speech-communication or psychology who has done such research. Read your guest's published research (or unpublished research, if you can get hold of it) prior to the class visit. Prepare a number of questions regarding measurement techniques, experimental procedure, and the like. Set as your goal to learn all you can about the scientific approach to the study of persuasion.

3. Read and report on one of or more of the following books and articles. Seek out more details on the testing methods briefly discussed in this chapter. Look

---

* Specifics on the scoring technique and other facts about this method of attitude assessment can be gotten from the following primary sources: (1) J. C. Brigham and S. W. Cook (1970) "The Influence of Attitude and Judgments of Plausibility: A Replication and Extension," *Educational and Psychological Measurement*, 30: 283–92; (2) P. Waly and S. W. Cook (1965) "Effect of Attitude on Judgements of Plausibility," *Journal of Personality and Social Psychology*, 2: 745–49.

for tests that have been developed more recently. Try to determine the improvements characteristic of testing procedures. Working alone or in a small group, demonstrate how a particular testing instrument is used.

SUGGESTED READINGS

Brigham, J. C. and S. W. Cook (1970) "The Influence of Attitude and Judgements of Plausibility: A Replication and Extension," *Educational and Psychological Measurement,* 30: 283–92.

Cronkhite, Gary (1969) *Persuasion: Speech and Behavior Change.* Indianapolis; Bobbs-Merril. See especially Chapter Six, "Measuring Persuasive Effects."

Edwards, A. L. (1957) *Techniques of Attitude Scale Construction.* New York: Appleton-Century-Crofts.

Fishbein, Martin, ed. (1967) *Readings in Attitude Theory and Measurement.* New York: John Wiley.

Fishbein, Martin and Icek Ajzen (1975) *Belief, Attitude, Intention and Behavior: An Introduction to Theory and Research* Reading, Massachusetts: Addison-Wesley.

Green, B. F. (1954) "Attitude Measurement," Vol. 1, pp. 335–69 in Gardner, Lindzey, ed *Handbook of Social Psychology.* Two vols. Reading, Massachusetts: Addison-Wesley.

Guttman, L. A. (1944) "A Basis for Scaling Quantitative Data," *American Sociological Review,* 9: 139–150.

Likert, R. (1932) "A Technique for the Measurement of Attitudes," *Archives of Psychology,* no. 140.

Linn, Lawrence S. (1965) "Verbal Attitudes and Overt Behavior: A Study of Racial Discrimination," *Social Forces* Vol. 43: 353–64. Reprinted on pp. 495–506 in Ralph L. Rosnow and Edward J. Robinson, eds. (1967) *Experiments in Persuasion.* New York: Academic Press.

Lucas, Darrel B. and Steuart H. Britt (1968) "Measuring Advertising Effectiveness: Inquiries and Sales Measures," pp. 328–46 in Howard H. Martin and Kenneth E. Andersen, eds. *Speech Communication: Analysis and Readings.* Boston: Allyn and Bacon.

Martin, Howard H. (1968) "The Assessment of Communication Effects," pp. 278–96 in Howard H. Martin and Kenneth E. Andersen, eds. *Speech Communication: Analysis and Readings.* Boston: Allyn and Bacon.

McClelland, David C. (1973) "Testing for Competence Rather than 'Intelligence,' " *American Psychologist* (January), 1–14. An excellent, down-to-earth discussion of validity problems in intelligence testing.

Osgood, Charles E; G. J. Suci; and Percy H. Tannenbaum (1957) *The Measurement of Meaning.* Urbana, Illinois: University of Illinois Press.

Osgood, Charles E. and Percy H. Tannenbaum (1955) "The Principle of Congruity in the Prediction of Attitude Change," *Psychological Review,* 62: 42–55.

Pollio, Howard R. (1974) *The Psychology of Symbolic Activity.* Reading, Massachusetts: Addison-Wesley.

Sechrest, L. "Testing, Measuring, and Assessing People," pp. 529–625 in E. F. Borgatta and W. W. Lambert, eds. *Handbook of Personality Theory and Research.* Chicago: Rand McNally.

Sherif, M. and C. W. Sherif (1967) "The Own-categories Procedure in Attitude Research," pp. 190–98 in Martin Fishbein, ed. *Readings in Attitude Theory and Measurement.* New York: John Wiley.

Thurstone, L. L. (1931) "The Measurement of Attitudes," *Journal of Abnormal and Social Psychology.* 26: 249–69.

Thurstone, L. L. and E. J. Chave (1929) *The Measurement of Attitude.* Chicago: University of Chicago Press.

Waly, P. and S. W. Cook (1965) "Effect of Attitude on Judgements of Plausibility," *Journal of Personality and Social Psychology,* 2: 745–49.

Webb, E. J., D. T. Campbell, R. D. Schwartz, and L. Sechrest (1966) *Unobtrusive Measures: Nonreactive Research in the Social Sciences.* Chicago: Rand McNally.

Zimbardo, Philip G., Ebbe B. Ebbeson, and Christina Maslach (1977), *Influencing Attitudes and Changing Behavior,* 2nd ed. Reading, Massachusetts: Addison-Wesley. See especially Postscript B: Techniques of Attitude Measurement, pp. 213–221.

MEASURING BEHAVIOR

It is also important to refer to some of the techniques used to measure behavior. Note that I am not talking about using behavior as an index of attitudes but about examining behavior in its own right. Given this limitation, you might ask why anyone would want to study behavior. The reason is that the study of behavior is often a starting point in scientific investigation. The scientist has a commitment to analyzing that which can be seen, observed, and counted. There is no better target for such analysis than overt behavior. Frequency counts are the most popular tools by which overt behavior is systematically observed. If, for example, you wanted to gain a sense of how a particular individual spends her day, you might follow her around during a particular period with a pad and pencil and simply note (1) what she does, (2) for how long, (3) and how often. This sort of behavioral inventory can give you a picture of how this individual structures her day.

Often, such a technique is used by persons who study time management. If you were concerned about making better use of your time, for example, you would first want a profile of how you use your time now. This profile could be gotten from such a behavioral inventory procedure. According to one therapist who specializes in time management, most people who undertake such a survey are astonished at how much time they fritter away on trivial and inconsequential activities. She reports that in several cases, individuals who undertook such self-behavior analyses found that by consolidating tasks and coordinating activities systematically, they were able to "discover" time that had eluded them before. They were actually able to accomplish more in a given day, simply because they became aware of how they were spending their moments.

In the following Student Activity Option, you are given the opportunity to take an inventory of your own time-management habits. The results may indicate that to function more efficiently as a student, some changes in your time-management habits may be required.

Student Activity Option 4.5
Behavior: Frequency Counts

INSTRUCTIONS:
Select a three-hour period of your waking day and divide those three hours up into twelve segments of fifteen minutes each. On the left-hand side of a sheet of paper, write down each time frame, following the example shown below. (Leave several lines between each notation, so that you have space to write.) To the right of the time frame, make five columns as follows: (1) behavior, (2) frequency (number of times performed during the particular time frame), (3) duration of behavior, (4) antecedent conditions (those conditions or circumstances that preceded the performance of the behavior), (5) consequences (of the be-

havior). When you are done with your self-inventory form, it should look like this:

Behavior Frequency Self-Inventory Form

Time Frame	Behavior	Frequency	Duration of Behavior	Antecedent Conditions	Consequences
3:00–3:15					

On a given day, use this form to take an inventory of all the behaviors you perform within each time frame during the three-hour period. You might want to ask a friend or classmate to do the survey for you by actually following you around. This technique will result in a more accurate count. In turn, you can perform the service for him or her.

When you have completed the form, examine it carefully and try to evaluate the manner in which the time was spent. Did you make the most use of your time? Total the "wasted" minutes you spent. How many were there? (You may be startled at the result!) On what activity did you spend most time? the least? What does the way you budget your time tell you about your value system? Try analyzing the behaviors you consider undesirable (for example, smoking or snacking). What were the conditions that preceded them? Are you more likely to grab a cookie when you're hanging around the kitchen? What were the consequences? Did you feel angry with yourself? regretful? How about behaviors you want to perform (for example, studying or exercising)? What antecedent conditions preceded them? What were their consequences?

Behavior modification experts know that one of the best ways to discourage unwanted behaviors and to encourage desired ones is to change the conditions that precede them. For example, you might eliminate the habit of munching on junk food simply by spending less time in the kitchen. You might make a pact with yourself that each time you find yourself in the kitchen thinking about what to eat, you will substitute a desired behavior—perhaps go into another room and touch your toes ten times or review an assignment.

A carefully constructed behavior modification program is much more complex than this. For instance, it also includes reinforcement schedules whereby each time you perform a desired behavior, you are allowed to reward yourself by doing something you enjoy. Nevertheless, this brief discussion provides an accurate perspective on the essence of behavior modification. The following readings will provide you with more information on behavior frequency counts and behavior modification.

SUGGESTED READINGS

Bandura, A. (1969)) *Principles of Behavior Modification.* New York: Holt, Rinehart, and Winston.

Fensterheim, Herbert and Jean Baer (1975) *Don't Say Yes When You Want to Say No.* New York: Dell. Although this book focuses on assertive training exclusively, the principles of behavior assessment and change are applicable to other situations.

Rathus, S. A. and J. S. Nevid (1977) *Behavior Therapy: Strategies for Solving Problems in Living.* New York: Doubleday.

Rose, Sheldon (1977) *Group Therapy: A Behavioral Approach.* Englewood Cliffs, New Jersey: Prentice-Hall.

Wolpe, J. (1973) *The Practice of Behavior Therapy.* New York: Pergamon Press.

This activity brings to a close our discussion of the wide variety of different techniques used to measure beliefs, attitudes, intentions, and behavior. Note that thinking scientifically about persuasion requires at least a basic familiarity with the tools used in persuasion research. In addition, awareness of these methods can lead to more effective persuasion practice, because it permits more careful and accurate audience assessment, strategic planning, and evaluation of effects.

SUMMARY

This chapter was devoted to the tools used to evaluate outcomes of persuasive messages. A persuasive message is technically called an intervention, because it intervenes between the premessage state of an audience and its postmessage state. As a result of careful observation and the exercise of controls on extraneous influences to which an audience is subject, it is possible to determine the effect of a speech on an audience by measuring the differences between the premessage and postmessage states. I reviewed a few of the general concerns in measuring persuasive effects—for example, who is affected by a persuasive message? How many are affected? How much change is brought about? How formidable are the obstacles faced by a persuader? What kind of changes are brought about?

You were also introduced to the more specific concerns of persuasion theorists, chief among them the question of validity. The complex relationship between attitudes and behavior, coupled with vague conceptualizations (for example, there are over 500 definitions of the word *attitude*), have made much research in persuasion inconclusive. Following Fishbein and Ajzen, I distinguished among four concepts—beliefs, attitudes, intentions, and behavior—that are often confused in persuasion research. A belief is a statement that links together an object and an attribute. It is measured by assessing the strength with which the two are linked in an individual's mind. An attitude is an evaluation of some object of judgment. It is measured by locating the judge on a bipolar affective or evaluative dimension in regard to the object of judgment. An intention links an individual with a behavior he or she is likely to perform. Intentions are quite specific, unlike attitudes, which constitute more general predispositions. Intentions are measured by assessing the strength with which an individual links himself or herself with the behavior in question. Overt behavior, while not a reliable test of attitudes, grows out of the complex set of ties between and among beliefs, attitudes, and intentions. You saw that beliefs are the building blocks of a person's cognitive set. They affect attitudes, which in turn affect intentions. While influence goes both ways—an intention can affect an attitude and an attitude can influence a belief—the predominant influence goes from beliefs, through attitudes and intentions, to behavior. You saw the ways your planning for persuasion can be improved by keeping this scheme in mind; by intervening at any point in a person's cognitive set, it is possible to affect changes in other parts or to affect the person's overt behavior.

I introduced the concepts of reliability (the extent to which a measuring instrument gives consistent results) and validity (the extent to which a measuring instrument measures what it was designed to measure). I discussed the tests for reliability: the test-retest method, the split-halves method, and the odd-even method. The differences among face validity, construct or convergent validity, and discriminant validity were spelled out.

Next, you learned about the characteristics, strengths, and weaknesses of several types of tests used to measure attitudes, including physiological measures, projective tests, nondisguided techniques (the Guttman, Thurstone, and Likert scales, Osgood's semantic differential, and Fishbein's summative method), and disguised techniques (the methods of Hammond and Cook). You saw that it is possible to adapt these tools to help you gain a clearer understanding of your audience's premessage state and to plan your persuasive strategy. Finally, I presented a brief discussion of techniques used to measure behavior, chiefly the behavioral inventory.

Chapter 5

Representative Approaches to the Study of Attitude Change

In Chapter 4 you learned what a theory was. You saw, too, that a scientific approach to persuasion requires some understanding of why persuasive effects occur. On the pages to follow, I will survey a representative sample of attitude-change theories in order to familiarize you with several of the more important theories that serve to explain persuasive effects. You will see that it is possible to analyze systematically the complex events that characterize the transmission and reception of a persuasive message. Sense can be made of what may appear to be a phenomenon that defies analysis. Further, I hope that as a result of this survey, you will form the habit of approaching your persuasive tasks systematically by making use of those principles that have been validated by research. Approaching persuasive tasks systematically also means becoming aware of the assumptions upon which you operate as a persuasive speaker—and, when necessary, revising or abandoning them.

Two preliminary observations are in order here. First, recall that there is a distinction between theories of assessment and theories of intervention. The vast majority of attitude-change theories are theories of assessment, geared primarily to understand why, how, and under what circumstances attitudes are changed. They are intended to deepen our understanding of how people work. In the words of Karlins and Abelson (1970, p. 139), most research in the persuasion area is conducted "to test theory to help build theory . . . . Thus, the primary interest of [researchers is] not to manipulate behavior, but to extend our knowledge of how people learn and how our personalities function." Theories and research, therefore, are not geared to telling you *how* to persuade. They sometimes lead to interventive principles but, in general, theory in this area is insufficiently developed to generate any meaningful or integrated system of practice principles. Instead, particular studies point the

149

way to individual principles, but these principles have not yet been integrated into a comprehensive theory of intervention.

Second, there are many ways of categorizing theories of attitude change. Traditionally, theories have been classified as either learning theories or consistency theories (see, for example, Simons, 1976). Learning theories refer to those theories that have their roots in the stimulus-response approach of behavior or learning theory. Consistency theories refer to that group of theories that originates in field theory, popularly referred to as the group dynamics orientation. Consistency theories emphasize the importance of cognitive balance in the functioning of the individual. This system of classification blurs some important distinctions (Fishbein and Ajzen, 1975). For example, congruity principle is usually classified as a consistency theory. But it is in fact the brain child of psychologists whose origins were clearly in the learning theory tradition. In light of this problem in categorizing theories, I will make no attempt to classify them as falling inexorably into one class or another. Instead, I will use an "issues in persuasion" organizational format, attempting to show the evolution of theory as a response to issues raised by research.

REINFORCEMENT THEORY

The first systematic, long-term attempt to understand the dynamics of persuasion was undertaken by Carl Hovland and his associates at Yale University. This program of research, begun in the 1940s, is the precursor of all serious contemporary research into persuasion and persuasive effects. On its own, the Yale program spawned several influential books and hundreds of journal articles. The researchers enjoyed the exhilaration of sailing in virtually unchartered waters; they followed the currents to wherever logic and their own interests suggested. Consequently, the Yale approach is noteworthy for its wide-ranging pursuit of the many variables that operate in the persuasive process. Hovland and his associates are rightly credited with having undertaken the first systematic study of the operation of key variables in the persuasive process.

As its name implies, reinforcement theory has its origins in behavior or learning theory. It is a theory of assessment, primarily concerned with the circumstances under which attitudes are changed rather than with generating prescriptions for persuasion. Several features distinguish reinforcement theory from other theories of attitude change. Each is examined briefly in the following pages.

Lasswell's model

Lasswell's model is characterized by the question, *Who said what to whom with what effect?* This simple model of communication, formulated in 1948, summarizes the major thrusts of the Yale approach. The researchers were interested in *who* acts as a persuader, including his or her credibility and expertness. Students of Aristotle's *Rhetoric* know that the ancient Greek was among the first to recognize the influence exerted on the audience by the orator. However, since Aristotle lacked the tools for careful study of the effects of this variable, it was left to Hovland and his colleagues to investigate systematically the impact of *ethos*. Research continues in this area now, and many people are at work trying to specify the nature of the influence exerted by the source of a message, and to describe the circumstances under which that influence occurs.

The *what* in Lasswell's model refers to the message being sent. The Yale group sought to determine the effects of certain message variables on the outcome of a persuasive effort. They studied the effects of such message variables as organization, the order of proofs (what different effects can be observed when the strongest arguments come first or last), and the appeals used (for example, fear appeals).

The study of audience characteristics is suggested by the *whom* in Lasswell's model. Reinforcement theorists were interested in determining the effects of different audience variables, including personality, intelligence, self-esteem, and sex. Their attempts to study the effects of these variables were often simplistic; there is no one-to-one relationship between sex and persuasibility, for instance, nor is there even any one factor of "persuasibility." Nevertheless, the theorists pointed the way to subsequent more refined research efforts that have yielded fruit.

The *effect* mentioned in Lasswell's model concerns the outcome of a persuasive message. The focus of the Yale group's research efforts was attitudes and attitude change. Their attempts to specify persuasive effects were hampered by inadequate conceptualizations. For instance, as noted in Chapter Three, the distinctions among beliefs, attitudes, and intentions went largely unmade for many decades. The Hovland group assumed that it was possible to infer attitudes from verbalized statements of opinion. However, no systematic study was made of the exact relationship between attitudes and opinions, nor was their assumption about inferred attitudes ever tested or validated. This is not to say the Yale research group failed to contribute to persuasion theory. In many respects, theirs was an outstanding contribution. But it is important to recognize that their work hardly represents a final product.

The persuasive message

The subject of attitude change can be studied from many angles. One feature that sets research programs apart from each other is the instrument of attitude change. It is possible, for example, to study attitude change induced by a person's participation in an event or a simulation. In this case, the instrument is not a persuasive message but the event itself. (The group dynamics approach to the study of persuasion has studied systematically the effect of participation in a group activity.) The Yale group focused on the persuasive message, usually written, as the key instrument of attitude change. Hence the popularity of their research with teachers and students of speech communication whose primary interest is in learning how to construct the most effective persuasive messages possible.

Determinants of effectiveness

In their attempt to impose order on the persuasive process, the Yale researchers identified four factors—attention, comprehension, acceptance, and retention*—as playing a major role in influencing effectiveness. Their conceptualization has spawned countless research articles dealing with one or more aspects of these four factors. One cluster of research studies examines the subject of attention. What determines whether an audience attends? When is attention withdrawn? What is the effect of lack of attention? of differing degrees of attention?

Comprehension was seen by Hovland and his associates as a prerequisite to persuasion: A person cannot be persuaded by what he or she does not understand. Although the Yale group failed to resolve adequately the question of the relationship between comprehension and acceptance (or between attention and comprehension, for that matter), their identification of this key component in the persuasion process did open the way for careful research in this area. (See Chapter Three on the relationship between recall and attitude change.)

Acceptance was seen as the third determinant of effectiveness. Much of the research conducted by Hovland and his fellows centered on this topic. They attempted to answer such questions as these: What incentives does a persuader use to induce acceptance of the message? How can principles of reinforcement be shown to operate in a persuasive communication situation?

As Insko (1967, p. 13) has observed, from the vantage point of the Yale group, a persuasive message is a stimulus that raises questions and provides answers. Since a persuader must necessarily cause auditors to think about a subject that was not on their minds, he or she runs the risk of having them revert to their formerly held conclusions and viewpoints. The way to avoid that eventuality is to provide them with incentives to answer the questions differently from the way they answered them before. These incentives take the form of reasons and evidence (proof) for the position advocated. Note that reinforcement theory emphasizes the rational, information-processing side of human beings. It is assumed that given adequate reasons and logical proofs, a reasonable person will change opinions because he or she is logically satisfied of the rightness of the position advocated.

A second strategy is available to the speaker in order to ensure that the au-

---

* I have elected, with Zimbardo et al. (1977, p. 57), to include retention. Insko (1967) as well as Fishbein and Ajzen (1975) do not consider retention as one of the determinants of effectiveness but as simply another subject investigated by the Yale group.

dience will answer in the desired manner the questions raised. According to this theory, the speaker can point out rewards or reinforcements that will follow from the adoption of new opinions, and punishments that will follow from the failure to adopt them. For example, the conceptualization behind research on fear appeals was as follows: It was argued that escape from or avoidance of fear is reinforcing. Hence a fear appeal ("Your teeth will fall out if you don't brush them regularly") contains both built-in punishments for nonacceptance and rewards for acceptance of the message. By doing what the advocate suggests—brushing regularly—the auditor knows that he or she can avoid the fear associated with losing one's teeth.

Retention, the fourth determinant of effectiveness, was considered important in those cases where auditors are asked to think or behave in the manner suggested by the speaker at some future time. This clearly is a sizable number of instances. Anything the persuader does to help his or her auditors remember the persuasive appeal at the crucial time (including striking illustrations, slogans, and vivid imagery) aids retention.

The following Student Activity Option allows you to test out these notions: (1) behavior that is rewarded tends to occur with greater frequency than behavior that is not rewarded, and (2) reinforcement influences opinions.

Student Activity Option 5.1
Keep Talking

INSTRUCTIONS

Is it true that reinforcement increases the likelihood of a given response? Can reinforcement affect stated opinions? The following activity may answer these questions. It requires only a telephone, a lined pad, and a pen or pencil.

Begin by selecting a current, controversial subject. It can be a campus issue or a local, national, or international one. Phrase the issue in such a way as to invite both pro and con statements. For example, if you select a local or national election, phrase the question so the persons you contact will be able to indicate pros and cons about a particular candidate. If you select the abortion issue, present it in such a way as to invite comments in favor of or opposed to abortion.

On the pad, write the name of the person you are contacting as well as the date and time you spoke with the person. On a separate sheet for each respondent, make two columns that go halfway down the page. Label one column *pro* and the other *con*. Mark with an asterisk which of the two kinds of comments you will reinforce during the phone conversation. (You will need to decide in advance whether to reinforce pro or con statements).

Telephone three or four people, identify the controversial subject, and ask them to list the pros and cons on the subject. With your pencil or pen, place a check in the appropriate column each time a pro or con statement is uttered. Each time your respondent utters a comment that falls into the category you've decided to reinforce, answer with a positive-sounding remark: "That's good," "Yes," "Right!" "Very interesting," "Very good," and so on.

Continue tallying the number of comments the person offers on both sides of the issue. When the conversation nears an end, ask the person to tell you his or her overall position on the subject. Be certain to thank your respondent.

If it is true that reinforcement increases the likelihood of behavior as well as of stated opinions, you should find the following to be true: (1) the respondent made more comments on the side of the issue you reinforced, and (2) the overall position verbalized was in agreement with that side of the issue you were reinforcing.

Discuss your data with those of a few classmates. Did you find the same things? Was the principle validated that reinforced behavior occurs more frequently? Did respondents tend to verbalize opinions that were in agreement with the side of the issue your classmates reinforced? If not, why do you suppose the discrepancy occurred? Were you faithful about reinforcing responses only on one side of the issue? Might other factors have confounded the results of the exercise (for example, the respondent's involvement with this issue)?

If you are interested in doing some reading in this area, see one or more of the following:

SUGGESTED READINGS

Hildum, D. and Brown, R. (1956) "Verbal Reinforcement and Interview Bias," *Journal of Abnormal and Social Psychology*, 53: 108–111.

Insko, C. (1965) "Verbal Reinforcement of Attitude," *Journal of Personality and Social Psychology*, 2: 621–23.

Krasner, L.; J. Knowles, and L. Ullmann (1965) "Effects of Verbal Conditioning of Attitudes on Subsequent Motor Performance," *Journal of Personality and Social Psychology*, 1: 407–12.

Acceptance is also rendered more likely by a set of expectations that most audiences hold. The effective persuader induces acceptance by playing upon these three expectations. The first is the expectation of being right or of not being wrong. Isn't it true that you feel good when you're about to make a right decision? Don't you feel inclined to accept a person's advice when you have confidence in his or her judgment? According to this theory, audiences tend to accept a message if they expect that they will be right. This expectation is influenced in large measure by their evaluation of the expertness of the speaker. Audiences tend to believe that experts are right, hence, by accepting what experts have to say, audience members anticipate that they, too, will be right. Thus, they anticipate all the rewards and past reinforcements associated with being right. Conversely, they tend not to accept a message if they lack confidence in the expertness of the source; then they associate acceptance of the message with the punishments and past experiences associated with being wrong.

A second set of expectations concerns trustworthiness versus manipulative intent. Audience members will accept a message if they expect that a speaker has their best interests at heart. But if they expect that the speaker is being manipulative or exploitive, they will associate the message with past occurrences of nonreinforcing exploitations. Hence, they will not accept the message. Note that this expectation, like the preceding one, is tied to the audience's perceptions of the speaker. The more expert and trustworthy he or she appears to be, the more likely are the audience members to anticipate positive reinforcements if they accept the message; hence, the more likely they are to accept it. The less the speaker appears expert or trustworthy, the less likely they are to accept the message.

The third expectation involves social approval or disapproval. If audience members expect to win social approval by acceding to the demands of a speaker, they are likely to accept what he or she has to say. If they fear social disapproval, they are very unlikely to accept the message. The expectation of social approval is usually created in two ways. First, the speech may contain explicit or implicit statements linking the desired audience response to social approval. Hence the hackneyed appeal of the advertiser—"Be the first on your block to own this fine product!" or "Impress your friends!" or "Show your good taste!" Second, the communicator may be presented as a prestigious source, likely to have anticipated popular opinion. Hence, by doing what he or she recommends, the audience members can expect to be ahead of their time: They may anticipate social approval by following the recommendations of a trend setter. This is part of the rationale behind testimonials used in advertisements. "Can you go wrong," asks the advertiser, "by following the beauty advice of this glamorous, successful movie star?" Or "Wouldn't you sad sacks do better if you cared for your hair and body the way rugged, well-known football players do?"

According to this theory an audience's reaction to your messages will be profoundly affected by the members' judgments of your expertise, trustworthiness, and prestige. You would do well to make every effort to create the proper expectations in your audience's mind by presenting yourself in such a way as to inspire confidence.

This brief sketch of reinforcement theory was not intended to be exhaustive but merely to suggest the scope of the scientific inquiry undertaken by the Yale group and their disciples. The Yale group is noted for its impressive contribution to the study of persuasion and attitude change, yet criticisms are valid and must be levied. Theirs was a preliminary effort, seriously hampered by flawed conceptualizations and unclear relationships (for example, among the determinants of effectiveness). Reinforcement theory is hardly a theory in the strict sense of the word, it is a rather loosely organized set of research undertakings, tied together by common threads of interest and effort. Hovland and his associates never intended to do more than to break ground, to offer a preliminary analysis. In their own words, the theory was designed as "an initial framework for subsequent 'theory building' "—and nothing more (Hovland, Janis, and Kelley, 1953, p. 17). In that it succeeded admirably.

Student Activity Option 5.2 ———————————————
Reinforcement Theory

INSTRUCTIONS

Read one or more of the following books and articles. Consult your instructor on the possibility of your reporting to your classmates the results of your work. The Insko book is especially valuable for a perceptive summary and evaluation of this and other theories of persuasion.

SUGGESTED READINGS

Hovland, C. I., I. L. Janis, and H. H. Kelley (1953) *Communication and Persuasion.* New Haven: Yale University Press.

Hovland, C. I. and I. L. Janis, eds. (1959) *Personality and Persuasibility.* New Haven: Yale University Press.

Insko, C. A. *Theories of Attitude Change.* New York: Appleton-Century-Crofts. See especially pp. 12–63.

———————————————————————————————————

SOCIAL JUDGMENT THEORY*

This theory has its roots in the Yale research program and was the outgrowth of questions raised by Hovland and his associates. Specifically, those questions had to do with the internal processes that operate in an auditor's decision to accept or reject a persuasive appeal. It is simple enough to see and to measure attributes of a message and the perceived attributes of a source. But the internal processes that operate inside the mind of a receiver of a persuasive message are obscured from view, nor are they measurable in any scientific sense. The problem that arises, therefore, is this: Exactly what goes on inside a receiver between the time he or she attends a message, comprehends its meaning, and decides to accept it or not? These internal processes fascinated Hovland and others, and a few preliminary studies were undertaken with the goal of identifying and clarifying the nature of these internal processes.

McGuire (1959) began the process of clarification by making finer distinctions between concepts that had previously been considered unitary. He noted that the original conceptualization offered by Hovland and the Yale group failed to explain why a message might be attended to and comprehended, yet not accepted. To explain the phenomenon, McGuire proposed the introduction of an additional mediating process that he called yielding. He said that there are in reality only two processes at work when a person hears a persuasive message—*reception,* which consists of attention and comprehension, and *yielding.* The yielding factor may vary from high to low; moreover, it bears no necessary relationship to the processes of attention and compre-

———————

*This theory is also known as assimilation-contrast theory. A close relation is adaptation-level theory. (See Insko, 1967, p. 64.)

hension. Later (1968, 1969) McGuire added still more mediating steps and came up with a four-step persuasive process, consisting of reception (that is, attention and comprehension), yielding, retention, and action.

Still, the McGuire scheme failed to explain just why one degree of yielding or another might occur at any given time. In response to this need, the theory of persuasion known as the social judgment theory was developed.

Research by Hovland and Sherif (1961), and Nebergall (1965) provides a framework for explaining the differing degrees of yielding. The researchers explained the phenomenon by suggesting the presence of latitudes of acceptance, rejection, and noncommitment. The latitude of acceptance consists of the range of Thurstone-type scale statements acceptable to a receiver. It includes the auditor's own position and all other acceptable positions. The latitude of rejection consists of all statements likely to be rejected by the recipient. The latitude of noncommitment or neutrality consists of that gray area where latitudes of acceptance and rejection meet. These latitudes may be pictured as falling along a continuum (see Figure 5.1). In the center of the continuum is the recipient's own position; extending for a short distance to either side is the latitude of acceptance. Farther out on the continuum is the latitude of rejection. The latitude of noncommitment lies where the other latitudes meet—that is, it represents points at which the auditor is undecided, or noncommitted. Note that the size of the latitudes of acceptance and rejection do not remain constant for every person on every issue but vary with the extent of the person's ego involvement. The more ego-involved the person, the smaller the latitude of acceptance and the larger the latitude of rejection. This makes perfect sense. Those persons most fanatically attached to a given point of view are most likely to reject an opposing viewpoint because they have a lot at stake in their beliefs. On the other hand, those with only a casual interest in a subject area (i.e., those with a low level of ego-involvement) are probably most willing to listen to just about any point of view.

From the vantage point of this theory, the extent to which a person can be expected to yield to a persuasive message is determined by the degree to which he or she perceives that message as falling within the latitude of accep-

Figure 5.1. Latitudes of Acceptance, Rejection, and Noncommitment (Social Judgment Theory)

tance. The closer the advocated position to his or her own, the more likely the person is to accept it—in the language of this theory, to assimilate the point of view advocated. The more the person perceives the message as falling outside the latitude of acceptance, the more likely he or she is to reject it. In Insko's words (1967, p. 67), "if the communication advocates a position that is not too discrepant from that held by the communication recipient, assimilation will result—i.e., the individual will perceive the communication as advocating a less extreme position, will favorably evaluate the communication, and will be strongly influenced." If the communication does the opposite, the recipient will contrast it with his or her own position; in the end, the recipient will either be influenced very, very slightly, or a boomerang effect will occur—that is, the recipient will become more firmly convinced of his or her own position (Cohen, 1962).

According to this theory, a person's own position serves as an internal anchor or a point of reference in light of which he or she evaluates and responds to communications dealing with this subject matter. A persuasive message is an external anchor. It represents another point of reference, one which the auditor is invited to adopt. Thus the process of persuasion can be seen as a tug of war between these anchors or points of reference. The farther the auditor's position from the one advocated, the more pronounced the tug of war. When the advocated position is close to the one the auditor holds, little real struggle occurs; the two sides join hands in a sense and become one as a result of assimilation.

Student Activity Option 5.3
Latitudes of Acceptance, Rejection, and Noncommitment

INSTRUCTIONS
In this exercise I have described three audiences that are about to hear speeches on designated topics. You are to guage the level of each audience's ego involvement in the subject. In addition, you are to sketch a continuum on which you estimate the size of this audience's latitudes of acceptance, rejection, and noncommitment. Finally, you are to write down at least three strategies you might use in order to increase the size of the audience's latitude of acceptance. In other words, how would you minimize the discrepancy between the position you are advocating and the one held by the audience? How would you increase the likelihood that the audience would assimilate the position you are advocating rather than contrast it with their own?

1. A speech in favor of the resumption of atmospheric nuclear testing
Audience: A gathering of environmental conservationists. The persons in your audience have been members of this and similar groups—such as the Sierra Club—for several years. Considering themselves protectors of the environment, they organize and participate in antinuclear demonstrations several times a year.

Estimated degree of audience ego involvement
  a. Very high
  b. High
  c. Average
  d. Low
  e. Very low

Latitudes of acceptance, rejection, and noncommitment

Strategies: _____
_____
_____

2. A speech in favor of price and wage controls
Audience: A national convention of labor leaders. Representatives of 20 major unions are present. With high inflation and increasing unemployment, these union officials are angry at the treatment they feel their rank and file are getting at the hands of big business. They have their eyes on huge salary increases as one way of recouping their losses. Incidentally, their future as union leaders depends on how effectively they protect the interests of the people they represent.

Estimated degree of audience ego involvement
  a. Very high
  b. High
  c. Average
  d. Low
  e. Very low

Latitudes of acceptance, rejection, and noncommitment

Strategies: _____
_____
_____

3. A speech against returning lands to American Indian tribes
Audience: A group of college students. The major fields of persons in the group are mixed, but a majority are students of political science and law.

Estimated degree of audience ego involvement
  a. Very high
  b. High
  c. Average
  d. Low
  e. Very low

Latitudes of acceptance, rejection, and noncommitment

Strategies: _____

_____

_____

SUGGESTED READINGS

Sherif, M. and Hovland, C. (1961) *Social Judgement*. New Haven: Yale University Press.
Sherif, C. Sherif, M. and Nebergall, R. (1965) *Attitude and Attitude Change*. Philadelphia: W. B. Saunders.
Cohen, A. A. (1962) "A Dissonance Analysis of the Boomerang Effect," *Journal of Personality*. 30: 75–88.

Social judgment theory was an important first step in investigating the effects of discrepancies between the position advocated by a communicator and the initial position of a receiver. Sherif, Hovland, and a large number of researchers have done a service in generating the theory. It is of particular interest because it lends itself to rather specific testing. For example, if it is true that there is a direct relationship between a person's ego involvement and the smallness of the latitude of acceptance, it follows that less attitude change should occur when the same speech is presented to audiences varying only in the extent of their ego involvement. This predictive capacity is a strong point of the theory. Unfortunately, its predictions have not been validated consistently. Insko (1967, pp. 69–90), reporting on many research studies, concludes that the results are inconsistent and that social judgment theory, at least at present, is not a serious contender as an adequate theory of attitude change. Nevertheless, its creators can be credited with having initiated efforts to study systematically the effects of differing degrees of discrepancy between a position advocated by a persuasive message and the one held by a recipient.

Because of the unsatisfactory results of research on this theory, other theories have been developed; they are aimed at accounting for audiences' reactions to messages that present viewpoints differing from their own. Among the more popular are dissonance theory, balance theory, and congruity principle.

BALANCE THEORY

Have you ever had an experience like the following? Next semester you are planning to take a certain philosophy course of which many sections are offered. You are uncertain which instructor is best, so you ask your good friend Cynthia, who has had the course, which instructor she would recommend. You respect this woman's judgment and make it a point to register for the specified section taught by Professor Darwimple, despite a large number of inconveniences. But when at last you enter Professor Darwimple's course, you and he are at loggerheads almost from the first moment. He seems a stuffy, self-righteous bore who delights in insulting students and showing off his erudition.

This is the sort of situation with which balance theory deals. Originally formulated by Fritz Heider, this theory has many variations. It is the grand-daddy of a host of theories whose key element is the importance of balance, congruity, congruence, and consonance or consistency in the psychological life of the individual. Heider's original formulation, flawed and simplistic as it is, opens the way to an understanding of more sophisticated formulations. Once you understand Heider's scheme, you will possess the fundamentals upon which to build an understanding of later variations on his theme.

Before presenting the assumptions upon which balance theory rests, it should be noted that the concept of balance is not a new one, nor did it even have its origins in psychology. Biologists, for example, have long discussed the concept of homeostasis, having to do with the processes whereby body balances are maintained. But it was Heider and his associates who initially took the concept and applied it to the subjects of attitude and attitude change. And it is only since his theory was constructed that systematic steps have been taken to explore in depth the behavioral and attitudinal consequences of psychological imbalance.* Balance theory rests on the two following assumptions.

Assumption one: Human beings seek to maintain balance and to reduce imbalance. A state of psychological balance is experienced as pleasant. You and I like to feel that things make sense, that our cognitive set holds together. We feel good when our friends share our opinions, we like to feel that choices we make would be validated by our associates if we asked their opinion. The opposite of balance is experienced as unpleasant. It is difficult to be aware of holding two inconsistent beliefs simultaneously. Discrepant attitudes among close friends is a source of some tension and dismay. For example, if your friend Cynthia had disliked Professor Darwimple as much as you did, there would be no discomfort. But because she loved him and you hated him, tension is created.

Heider postulated that imbalance is much like any drive state: It generates tension. This is a basic principle in psychology. If you are hungry, you will experience tension until that hunger is satisfied. Sexual tension seeks reduction as do thirst and other basic drives. In the same way, people seek a psychologically balanced or consistent view of the world.

The assumption that psychological balance is experienced as pleasant has been validated experimentally. Jordan (1953), for example, presented a number of subjects with 64 hypothetical situations not unlike the one with

---

* Used in this context, the words *balance* and *psychological imbalance* have nothing to do with sanity and insanity. The terms refer to the harmony that characterizes a person's beliefs, attitudes, and other elements of the cognitive structure, a fitting together of the components of the person's belief set, attitude set, and so on.

Cynthia and Professor Darwimple. His respondents were asked how pleasant or unpleasant each situation would be to them. The results indicated that the balanced situations were experienced as more pleasant than the unbalanced ones.

Assumption two: Once a state of imbalance is experienced, a limited number of options by which to restore balance are open to the individual. By internal processes as yet poorly understood, a person will choose one or more of the options in order to achieve consonance.

In the situation involving Professor Darwimple, one alternative you might use to restore balance is to think less of the friend who had recommended the instructor. "Maybe," you might say to yourself, "my friend Cynthia is not so swell a gal after all!" Or you might make a fine discrimination between your friend's judgment of instructors and her more desirable qualities in another area. "Cynthia's a good friend and she sure knows a lot about dancing and football. But she's no expert on the quality of teachers!" A third option would be to begin looking for desirable qualities in Professor Darwimple. "Maybe he is pompous and dull," you might say. "But he sure knows his stuff!" Or you might talk to Cynthia to try to convince her of how awful Professor Darwimple is. "If I can change her mind so the two of us can see eye to eye, then we'll be in agreement again."

This assumption about the state of imbalance provides a frame of reference for considering the effects of a persuasive speech. A persuasive message has as its objectives (1) to create imbalance and (2) to have your listeners reestablish balance by changing their attitudes in the direction you wish. (This is exactly what you seek to do if you try to change Cynthia's evaluation of Professor Darwimple.) One option open to persons who experience imbalance as a result of a persuasive message is to change their attitudes in the direction advocated by the communicator. With adequate proof and other appeals, it might be possible to bring about a new balanced state incorporating the ideas you want your listener to adopt.

Heider provides a simple and interesting way of conceiving of the balanced or unbalanced relationships between two persons and an object of judgment. Called the Heider triangle, this model presents all the possible relationships. Heider assumes the existence of two persons, called person one (P1) and person two (P2), and one object of judgment (O). He says that person one has attitudes (or sentiment relations) toward person two and toward the object of judgment. Person two is also assumed to have attitudes toward the object of judgment. Finally, Heider says that person one is aware of person two's attitudes toward the object. Positive attitudes are depicted by means of a plus sign; negative ones by a minus sign. Thus, the situation with Cynthia could be depicted in the following manner: You (person one) have positive attitudes toward Cynthia (person two). But you have negative attitudes toward Professor Darwimple (object of judgment). The Heider triangle in Figure 5.2 captures these relationships. Note that this is an unbalanced situation, and the prediction is that person one will do something to restore balance.

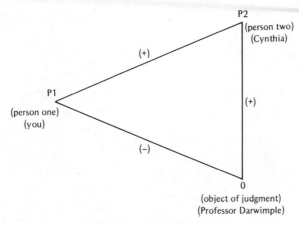

Figure 5.2. Heider Triangle

How do you determine whether a Heider triangle reflecting a real-world situation is balanced or unbalanced? Most simply, you can do this by multiplying the signs according to the laws of algebra—two like signs yield a positive result, two unlike signs yield a negative product. Thus, $(+) \cdot (+) = (+)$; $(-) \cdot (-) = (+)$; $(+) \cdot (-) = (-)$; and $(-) \cdot (+) = (-)$. In our example, person one's attitude toward person two is positive $(+)$. Person two's attitude toward the object of judgment is also positive $(+)$. Thus, step one yields a positive product: $(+) \cdot (+) = (+)$. If you were to multiply this product by the product linking person one and the object of judgment (a negative one, because you dislike Professor Darwimple), you would get a negative product: $(+) \cdot (-) = (-)$. When the final result of these procedures is a negative sign, as it is in this case, the situation is said to be unbalanced. When the final product is positive, the situation is said to be balanced.

Another way of determining whether a Heider triangle is balanced or unbalanced is simply to ask yourself how many plus and minus signs there are. If there are three plus signs, the situation is balanced. If there are two minus signs and one plus sign, the situation is also said to be balanced. But if there are two plus signs and one minus sign, the situation is unbalanced. And if three minus signs are present, it also is unbalanced. Figure 5.3 shows all the possible combinations.

Student Activity Option 5.4
Heider Triangles

INSTRUCTIONS
Depict the following situations by means of a Heider triangle. To convert a situation into Heider's terminology, follow these steps: First, label the three ele-

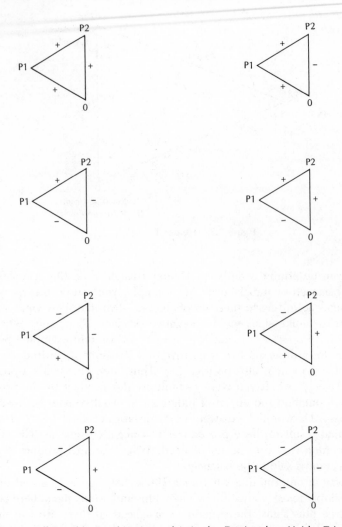

Figure 5.3. All Possible Combinations of Attitudes Depicted on Heider Triangles

ments P1 (person one), P2 (person two), and O (object of judgment). Note that an individual can be an object of judgment, as was Professor Darwimple in our example. Second, convert such terms as *love, like, favor, support,* or *endorse* into plus signs. Convert such terms as *dislike, hate,* or *loathe* into minus signs. Third, sketch a triangle, label each corner, and fill in the plus or minus signs along each leg of the triangle. To determine whether a triangle is balanced, multiply the signs algebraically. Remember to multiply the product of the first multiplication by the remaining sign on the triangle. You may also use the "sum of the signs" method described in the preceding section to determine whether the situation is balanced.

1. *Situation One*
George likes Martha.
George likes grade B movies.
Martha likes grade B movies.

Name of person one (P1) _____
Name of person two (P2) _____
Name of object of judgment _____

Sketch a triangle. Label each corner. Fill in the signs.

Is this situation balanced or unbalanced?

2. *Situation Two*
Brian likes Kathleen.
Kathleen hates Fig Newtons.
Brian likes Fig Newtons.

Name of person one (P1) _____
Name of person two (P2) _____
Name of object of judgment _____

Sketch a triangle. Label each corner. Fill in the signs.
Is this situation balanced or unbalanced?

3. *Situation Three*

Carlos dislikes Anthony.
Carlos doesn't enjoy tennis.
Anthony doesn't enjoy tennis.

Name of person one (P1) _____
Name of person two (P2) _____
Name of object of judgment _____

Sketch a triangle. Label each corner. Fill in the signs.

Is this situation balanced or unbalanced?

4. *Situation Four*

Professor Darwimple likes garlic.
Cynthia likes Professor Darwimple.
Cynthia hates garlic.

Name of person one (P1) _____
Name of person two (P2) _____
Name of object of judgment _____

Sketch a triangle. Label each corner. Fill in the signs.

Is this situation balanced or unbalanced?

5. *Situation Five*
Margo loves Hector.
Hector endorses Cheerios.
Margo likes Cheerios.

Name of person one (P1) _____
Name of person two (P2) _____
Name of object of judgment _____

Sketch a triangle. Label each corner. Fill in the signs.

Is this situation balanced or unbalanced?

SUGGESTED READINGS

Heider, F. (1946) "Attitudes and Cognitive Organization," *Journal of Psychology*, 21: 107–112.
Heider, F. (1958) *The Psychology of Interpersonal Relations*. New York: John Wiley.
Insko, C. (1967) *Theories of Attitude Change*. New York: Appleton-Century-Crofts, pp. 161–76.
Jordan, N. (1953) "Behavioral Forces that are a Function of Attitudes and of Cognitive Organization," *Human Relations*, 6: 273–87.

A number of flaws in Heider's scheme might have become apparent to you as you worked out the simple problems in Student Activity Option 5.4. One flaw is that the model does not take into account degrees of liking or disliking. Heider's scheme is limited by its use of plus or minus signs as the only indicators of attitudes. This is a basic flaw, since the extent to which one person cares for another or for an object of judgment can make a tremendous difference. A situation that in Heider's scheme would be considered balanced might in fact be an occasion for attitude change. For example, suppose you are an avid fan of a famous football player. In addition, you possess mildly positive attitudes toward a popular brand of toothpaste. One day you see a commercial in which the football player endorses that particular brand of paste. What do you suppose would happen? According to Heider, this situation is balanced; the attitudes all around are positive. Yet a degree of tension might well be created because of the degree of liking you feel for the football player and for the brand of toothpaste. The fact that you admire him so much might cause a degree of imbalance, prompting you either to like him less or to like the toothpaste more. For another example, suppose you like Paul much better than you like Timmy. When you find that Paul cares for Timmy very much, some change in your opinions or attitudes toward either one or both is likely to occur. When situations like this arise, tensions or imbalances are created.

Implied in this discussion has been another flaw in Heider's scheme. I've suggested that a number of options are open to the person who feels the tensions created by imbalance. In the example just given, for instance, I indicated that in light of the imbalance created by the differing degrees of liking felt toward Paul and Timmy, some change in your attitudes toward either one or both is likely to occur. But toward which person would your attitudes change? Why would you come to like Paul less as opposed to coming to like Timmy more? To use another example, why would you hold your friend Cynthia in lower esteem as opposed to thinking more of Professor Darwimple? The balance model does not offer any insight into the reasons why one method of restoring balance is chosen over another.

Nor does the balance theory admit the possibility that some change in a person's attitudes toward both attitude objects might occur, resulting in the establishment of a suitable midpoint at which balance is restored. Instead, in Heider's scheme, one set of attitudes, toward either person two or toward the object of judgment, changes radically—from positive to negative or vice versa. Thus, it is an all-or-nothing situation. This failing to include degrees of attitude change is tied to the theory's failure to take into consideration degrees of initial liking or disliking.

An additional weakness is that the principles of balance theory may not be universally applicable. To raise a variation of a question once asked by Leon Festinger (the formulator of cognitive dissonance theory), would it follow that because you love your cat and your cat loves to eat raw fish heads, you, too, love to eat raw fish heads? Or that you would start disliking your cat? There seem to be some situations in which balance model does not apply.

Another basic flaw is that this theory doesn't take into account situations involving more than two people and one object of judgment. It is thus severely limited in its applicability.

Nevertheless, balance theory remains an important and seminal contribution with far-reaching applications. While Heider's initial formulation was extremely simplistic, it held within itself the seeds of far more sophisticated and comprehensive theories of attitude change. Insko (1967, p. 174) believes that in the decades ahead, balance theory and its offshoots will spawn much valuable research. It promises to maintain its place as a cornerstone of what one day may be an adequate theory of persuasion.

In response to the rather apparent weaknesses of balance theory, congruity hypothesis developed. It overcomes many of the weakness of Heider's conceptualization, though at the cost of considerably more complexity.

CONGRUITY PRINCIPLE*

If it is true that science strives to comprehend the world accurately, then the best scientific explanations are those that accurately capture many of the nuances that characterize reality. Simplistic formulations such as Heider's, like the early drawings of a child, are rather gross representations of reality; they overlook a great many observable factors and simplify reality excessively. Yet they often capture an essential truth. Progress, in science as in the maturation of the child, involves capturing ever more accurately the richness and complexity of reality.

This progress can be seen in congruity principle. While it is far from being a final statement of the truth about attitude change, it is a vast improvement over earlier and simpler schemes like Heider's.† A comparison with balance theory reveals several important differences. For one thing, congruity principle predicts both direction and degree of attitude change, while balance theory predicted direction of change only. Second, it allows for degrees of liking or disliking on the part of the person whose attitudes are being measured. Whereas balance theory spoke only of positive or negative attitudes, congruity principle can take into account degrees of positiveness or negativeness (and also neutrality) in the person's attitudes. Third, whereas Heider's formulation predicted that balance would be restored by means of a total shift in attitudes toward either the second person or the object of judgment, congruity hypothesis allows for some additional change in degree toward both attitude objects.

In congruity principle, attitudes are measured on a seven-point bipolar evaluative scale. The values on the scale range from +3 to −3. The poles are represented by the terms *good* and *bad*. Thus, a typical attitude scale looks like that pictured in Figure 5.4. The person whose attitudes are being measured is asked to mark the scale at the point which best represents the evaluation of the individual or concept being rated. (These rated objects—persons, concepts, or things—are alternately called attitude objects or objects of judgment. The latter is the preferred terminology when discussing congruity principle. Simply put, an object of judgment is something toward which a person's attitudes are being measured.)

If the respondent marks the +3 space, he or she is said to have an extremely positive attitude toward the object of judgment being rated. If the respondent marks the opposite end, the −3 space, he or she is said to possess

---

*Congruity principle is also referred to by various authors as congruity hypothesis, congruity theory, and congruity model. It is hardly a theory in the strict sense of the term, nor is it just a model, although part of its statement does include a model. While it can be considered simply an hypothesis, I have chosen to use the term *congruity principle*, because it most closely approximates the essential nature of this formulation: It is an hypothesis-generating principle relating to attitude change.

†To avoid confusion, I want to make clear that the formulators of this principle were not motivated only by a desire to improve on Heider's scheme. They were also interested in prestige suggestion generally and in attribution theory as well.

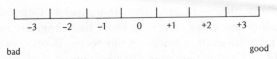

Figure 5.4. Attitude Scale

an extremely negative attitude. Any marks between these two poles represent less extreme evaluations. A mark at the midpoint of the scale can mean a number of things, including mixed feelings, neutrality, indecision, or a firm, middle-of-the road evaluation. (The ambiguity associated with a mark on the middle point of the scale is a major weakness of congruity principle. Since such a mark can mean different things, the measuring instrument is less than perfect. Technically, this is a problem in validity.)

Like balance theory, congruity principle assumes the existence of two persons and some concept or object. The rater (the person whose attitudes are being measured) is assumed to have attitudes toward both the second person (technically referred to as object of judgment one) and the concept or object (called object of judgment two). Further, this formulation assumes that the rater becomes aware of some message that links the second person and the concept. It is not an entire speech, complete with persuasive appeals. (This, too, is a weakness of congruity principle.)

To illustrate, let's say that you are the rater, the person whose attitudes are being measured. The second person (object of judgment one) is the late *John Wayne*. The concept of object (object of judgment two) is *harsh discipline*. In Figure 5.5, I have provided two attitude scales and an assertion linking both objects of judgment. Mark the scales at that point which best represents your

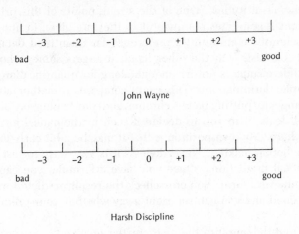

Linking assertion: *John Wayne* supports *harsh discipline.*

Figure 5.5. Two Attitude Scales and a Linking Assertion

feelings toward the objects of judgment being rated. Depending on where you marked each of the scales, it is very likely that congruity principle would predict that some change in attitudes would occur. If you rated *John Wayne* +2, for example, indicating that your attitudes toward the late star were quite positive, and you rated *harsh discipline* −3, congruity hypothesis predicts that some shift in attitudes would occur. Note that the assertion that links the objects of judgment can be either positive or negative. In Figure 5.5, the linking assertion is positive. This kind of assertion is called an associative bond.

Here are more examples of associative bonds:

1. Farah Fawcett Majors uses Maybelline eye makeup.
2. Joggers make better lovers.
3. Cigarette smoking is harmful to your health.

Dissociative bonds are negative linkages: They dissociate one object of judgment from another. Instead of stating that a positive relationship exists between the two objects of judgment, they state that a negative relationship exists, or that no relationship exists between them. (This ambiguity is another weakness of congruity principle.) Here are some examples of dissociative bonds:

1. Former dictator Idi Amin was not kind to some people.
2. Jimmy Carter fired one-time HEW secretary Joseph Califano.
3. Oil companies fight price controls.

Whether a bond is associative or dissociative, congruity principle predicts with precision (although not always accurately, unfortunately) what will happen to a person's attitudes. (One of the strong points of this principle is that the predictions it generates are quantified; they are given in numerical terms. Given the scientific community's preference for quantified data, this pleases many social scientists. On the other hand, it angers some, who say that the field of attitude change is not far enough along for quantification; we ought to stick to simpler formulations. This camp compares a mathematical model in attitude change to putting fancy chrome and pinstriping on a battered old jalopy. I will leave it to you to decide if such mathematical formulations are out of place here. My own position is that it may be a bit early to begin mathematical prediction-making. Nevertheless, it is very easy to test the accuracy of mathematical predictions. Once you have a formula, you can arrive at an answer in numerical form. You crosscheck the result predicted with the result actually obtained and you can see right away whether your prediction was accurate.)

Even without delving into the mathematics involved, you can see that congruity principle makes sense. Let's suppose that someone toward whom you hold positive attitudes is linked by an associative bond to something toward which you have negative attitudes. One of three things will happen: (1) your positive attitudes toward the person will become less positive, (2) your negative attitudes toward the second object of judgment will become less negative, or (3) both will occur.* Regardless of what the options are, one principle is clear: Changes in attitude are always in the direction of increased congruity. Put another way, you and I seek congruence or balance among the attitudes we hold. When a situation arises that is out of kilter we seek to reestablish balance or congruence. Insko (1967, p. 113) sees this effort to regain congruence as part of the tendency of attitudes to move toward maximum simplicity. It is more tiring and unsettling to hold inconsistent attitudes than it is to bring them into harmony. We seek to simplify our attitudinal sets by just such a process. Regardless of how the process is explained, there is little doubt that under such circumstances, congruence is sought—the attitudes toward both attitude objects tend to be brought into harmony.

Common sense can tell us something else that would be likely to occur under the circumstances described. The amount of change in attitudes toward a particular object of judgment would likely depend on the initial attitude rating given that object. The more extreme the attitude, or the more polarized it is, the more it resists change. The less extreme, the less it resists change. Thus, extreme attitudes at either end of the scale tend to change less than those that fall at less extreme positions of the scale. Conversely, the less extreme the attitude, the greater its tendency to change. Thus, if you held extremely positive attitudes toward *John Wayne* and only mildly positive negative attitudes toward *harsh discipline*, we might predict that your positive attitudes toward *Wayne* would change less than your less polarized attitudes toward *harsh discipline*.

All this may sound vaguely familiar to you. You may recall earlier discussions about latitudes of acceptance, rejection, and noncommitment. I noted then that messages that fall within a person's latitude of noncommitment are more likely to have an affect than those that fall at the outer reaches of the latitude of rejection. The same thing is being said here, but from a different vantage point. Here I am saying that resistance to attitude change increases as does the polarity of attitudes. Essentially the same truth is presented in both these formulations.

You might also be asking yourself what would happen in the case of a dissociative bond—that is, a negative linkage. Suppose, for example, someone toward whom you hold positive attitudes is linked by a dissociative bond to something toward which you have negative attitudes. Such a situation would exist if you ranked *John Wayne* +2 and *harsh discipline* −1 and the linking assertion was "*John Wayne* abhors *harsh discipline*." Common sense tells us that your positive feeling toward *John Wayne* might well become even more positive, since you and he both feel negatively about harsh discipline. Another possibility is that your negative attitude toward harsh discipline might

---

* Recall that this third option was not possible in balance theory, although it is very likely to occur in reality.

well become more negative, since someone whom you admire is linked to it negatively—that is, he went on record as opposed to it. Still another possibility, of course, is that both would occur—your positive feelings toward *John Wayne* might become even more positive, while your negative attitudes toward *harsh discipline* might become more negative. Furthermore, in light of our preceding discussion, we might predict that the less polarized attitude (−1 for *harsh discipline*) might be expected to change more than the more extreme attitude. In other words, it's likely that your negative attitudes toward *harsh discipline* might become negative to a greater degree than your positive attitudes toward *John Wayne* might become more positive.

All this is common sense. It has, however, taken us nearly two pages to wade through these observations. Osgood and Tannenbaum compressed these thoughts into a simple algebraic formula. That is the beauty, and simplicity, of mathematical formulations. The two variations of the formula, one for object of judgment one and another for object of judgment two, are the same except for simple substitutions.

Variation One
    Attitude Change
    for Object of
    Judgement One

$$Ac_{oj1} = \frac{|d_{oj2}|}{|d_{oj1}| + |d_{oj2}|} \times P_{oj1}$$

Variation Two
    Attitude Change
    for Object of
    Judgement Two

$$Ac_{oj2} = \frac{|d_{oj1}|}{|d_{oj1}| + |d_{oj2}|} \times P_{oj2}$$

As forbidding as these formulas may look, I want to reassure you that they are simple to work out. You will also have the chance to try your skill in Student Activity Options 5.5, 5.6, and 5.7.

Let's begin with the bracketed figures in the fraction. The numerator of the fraction contains one bracketed figure; in Variation One, this figure is $|d_{oj2}|$. This is the initial evaluative scale position of object of judgment two. The brackets mean that you are to disregard the plus sign or minus sign on the scale and only fill in the absolute value. For example, let's suppose you had ranked *John Wayne* (object of judgment one) +2 and *harsh discipline* (object of judgment two) −1. Your two attitude scales would look like those in Figure 5.6. The initial evaluative scale position for *John Wayne* is +2. Stripped of its sign, it is simply 2. The initial evaluative scale position for *harsh discipline* is −1. Stripped of its sign, it is simply 1. Thus, in Variation One, the formula for attitude change for *John Wayne*, the numerator of the fraction is $|d_{oj2}|$ (the initial scale position of object of judgment two, stripped of its sign), which equals 1.

The denominator of the fraction contains two items, which are to be added together. In both variations, the denominator is represented as follows:

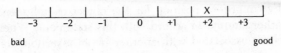

bad   good

John Wayne

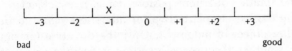

bad   good

Harsh Discipline

Linking assertion: *John Wayne* supports *harsh discipline.*

Figure 5.6. Marked Attitude Scales and Linking Assertion

$|d_{oj1}| + |d_{oj2}|$. These figures are arrived at in the same way as was the numerator: $|d_{oj1}|$ means the initial attitude scale position of object of judgment one, stripped of its sign; $|d_{oj2}|$ means the initial evaluative scale position of object of judgment two, stripped of its sign. Thus, in Variation One, the fraction is filled in as shown in Figure 5.7.

$$AC_{oj1} = \frac{|d_{oj2}|}{|d_{oj1}| + |d_{oj2}|} \times P_{oj1} = \frac{1}{2+1} = \frac{1}{3} \times P_{oj1}$$

Figure 5.7. Completed Fraction in Variation One (formula for Attitude Change for Object of Judgment One)

Exactly the same steps are followed in completing the fraction in Variation Two of the formula to give you attitude change for *harsh discipline*. Note that the numerator in Variation Two is different; here, the numerator is the initial evaluative scale position of object of judgment one, stripped of its sign. Thus, the fraction in Variation Two is completed as shown in Figure 5.8.

The next element in the formula is *P*, which stands for pressure toward congruity. P_{oj1} means pressure toward congruity for object of judgment one; P_{oj2} means pressure toward congruity for object of judgment two. Note that it is this figure that provides a plus or minus sign in the answer to the problem, since the fractional value arrived at with absolute numbers is itself an absolute number—it has no sign.

P is calculated by means of a three-step process. The first step is to deter-

$$AC_{oj2} = \frac{|d_{oj1}|}{|d_{oj1}| + |d_{oj2}|} \times P_{oj2} = \frac{2}{1+2} = \frac{2}{3} \times P_{oj2}$$

Figure 5.8. Completed Fraction in Variation Two (Formula for Attitude Change for Object of Judgment Two)

mine the totally congruent position for the object of judgment in question. This is done rather simply, in accord with this statement: Whenever one object of judgment is associated with another by an assertion, its [totally] congruent position along the evaluative dimension is always equal in degree of polarization (d) to the other object of judgment in either the same direction (positive assertion) or opposite (negative assertion) evaluative direction.

This elaborate statement sounds complicated, but it's really quite simple. It means that the totally congruent position for a given object of judgment is always equal in degree of polarization (or numerical value) to the scale position of the other object of judgment. Only the direction (or sign) may vary, depending on whether the linking assertion is positive or negative. For example, note that in our previous example the initial scale rating for *John Wayne* is +2 and the initial scale rating for *harsh discipline* is −1. Degree of polarization refers to the number. Thus, an attitude rating of 1 (regardless of sign) is less polarized than an attitude rating of 2. The higher the number, the higher the degree of polarization, regardless of the sign. The lower the number, the lower the degree of polarization. In addition, note that the direction is determined by the sign. A plus sign means a positive direction (that is, a positive attitude). A minus sign means a negative direction (a negative attitude).

This principle tells us that the totally congruent position for *John Wayne* is 1—that is, it is equal in degree of polarization to the initial scale rating for *harsh discipline*. The totally congruent position for *harsh discipline* is 2, equal in degree of polarization to the initial scale rating for *John Wayne*.

The only element that can change is the sign in front of the number. When the linking assertion is positive, as it is in our example, then the direction (represented by the plus sign or the minus sign) of the totally congruent position is the same as the direction for the object of judgment that also determines the degree of polarization. Thus, the totally congruent position for *John Wayne* is −1. It is a 1 because the position is equal in degree of polarization to the initial scale position for *harsh discipline*. It is in the same evaluative direction because the linking assertion is positive. The sign, in other words, corresponds to the sign of the other object of judgment. If the linking assertion were negative ("*John Wayne* abhors *harsh discipline*"), then the degree of polarity would remain equal to that of *harsh discipline* (a 1), but the sign would be exactly opposite—that is, the totally congruent position for *John Wayne* would be +1.* And, assuming a negative linking assertion (or a dissociative bond), the totally congruent position for *harsh discipline* would be equal in

---

* You may have noticed that this prediction is not in accord with what we speculated common sense would tell us. We speculated that under these circumstances, a person's attitudes toward *John Wayne* might become more positive rather than less positive. This kind of discrepancy points to a weakness in congruity principle (unless common sense is wrong) and suggests the need for refinements in the principle. Research, by the way, suggests that common sense is correct in this case.

degree of polarization to the initial scale position of *John Wayne* (i.e., a 2), but the sign would be opposite. From a plus sign (the direction of the initial attitude toward *John Wayne*), the sign would shift to a minus sign.

Let's try a few examples to make sure this is clear.

Student Activity Option 5.5:
Finding Totally Congruent Positions

INSTRUCTIONS
For each object of judgment in the problems below, find the totally congruent position. Be sure to include both degree of polarization (numerical value) and direction (sign).

Problem One

```
/ X / / / / / / /
-3 -2 -1  0 +1 +2 +3
bad                  good
        Professor
        Darwimple
```

Linking assertion:
Professor Darwimple drinks *Hawaiian Punch.*
Is the linking assertion positive or negative?

```
/ / / / / X / / /
-3 -2 -1  0 +1 +2 +3
bad                  good
      Hawaiian
       Punch
```

Totally congruent position for *Professor Darwimple:* _____
                                                        (sign)   (value)

Totally congruent position for *Hawaiian Punch:* _____
                                                  (sign)   (value)

Problem Two

```
/ / / / / X / / /
-3 -2 -1  0 +1 +2 +3
bad                  good
      Paul Newman
```

Linking assertion:
Paul Newman likes *Robert Redford.*
Is the linking assertion positive or negative?

```
/ / / / / / X / /
-3 -2 -1  0 +1 +2 +3
bad                  good
    Robert Redford
```

Totally congruent position for *Paul Newman:* _____
                                               (sign)   (value)

Totally congruent position for *Robert Redford:* _____
                                                  (sign)   (value)

Problem Three

```
 /   /   /   /   /   / X /   /
-3  -2  -1   0  +1  +2  +3
bad                      good
         Senator
     William Proxmire
```

Linking assertion:
Senator William Proxmire opposes *aid to cities.*
Is the linking assertion positive or negative?

```
/ X /   /   /   /   /   /   /
-3  -2  -1   0  +1  +2  +3
bad                      good
       aid to cities
```

Totally congruent position for *Senator William Proxmire:* _____
                                                              (sign)   (value)

Totally congruent position for *aid to cities:* _____
                                              (sign)   (value)

Problem Four

```
 /   /   /   / X /   /   /
-3  -2  -1   0  +1  +2  +3
bad                      good
       Woody Allen
```

Linking assertion:
Woody Allen scorns *Oscar awards.*
Is the linking assertion positive or negative?

```
/ X /   /   /   /   /   /   /
-3  -2  -1   0  +1  +2  +3
bad                      good
       Oscar awards
```

Totally congruent position for *Woody Allen:* _____
                                             (sign)   (value)

Totally congruent position for *Oscar awards:* _____
                                              (sign)   (value)

Once you have found the totally congruent position for a particular object of judgment, only two other steps are required to find pressure toward congruity for that object. First, simply count the attitude scale units between the object's initial scale position and the point on the scale at which that object would be in its totally congruent position. Next, give that number a sign. If, in your counting (starting at the initial position and working toward the totally congruent position), you move from left to right, give the number a plus sign; if you move from right to left, give the number a minus sign. To illustrate, consider the example in Figure 5.6. *John Wayne*, with an initial scale position of +2, is linked to *harsh discipline*, with an initial scale position of −1, by an associative bond (or a positive linking statement). We have determined that the totally congruent position for *John Wayne* is −1 (the same degree of

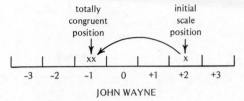

JOHN WAYNE

Initial scale position: +2
Totally congruent position (positive linkage): −1
Difference in attitude scale units: 3
Direction: right to left
Sign: minus

Pressure toward congruity for John Wayne: −3

Figure 5.9.

polarization as the initial scale position of *harsh discipline,* and the same sign because the linking assertion is positive). We have also determined that the totally congruent position for *harsh discipline* is +2.

To find pressure toward congruity for John Wayne, first count the difference in scale units between his initial position and his totally congruent position. This is illustrated in Figure 5.9. Note that the difference in scale units is 3. Note, too, that the direction is from right to left, hence, a minus sign is attached to the 3. Thus, the pressure toward congruity for *John Wayne* is −3.

The same method can be applied in finding pressure toward congruity for *harsh discipline.* The initital scale position for this object of judgment was −1. Its totally congruent position was +2. The difference in attitude scale units is 3. The direction is from left to right; hence, the sign is positive. Thus, pressure toward congruity for *harsh discipline* is +3 (see Figure 5.10).

If the linkage is negative, the same procedure is used. If the bond were

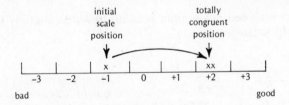

Harsh Discipline

Initial scale position: −1
Totally congruent position (positive linkage): +2
Difference in attitude scale units: 3
Direction: left to right
Sign: plus

Pressure toward congruity for harsh discipline: (positive linkage): +3

Figure 5.10. Finding Pressure Toward Congruity for Harsh Discipline, Assuming a Positive Linkage

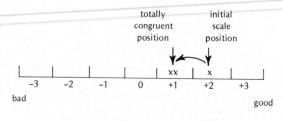

John Wayne

Initial scale position: +2
Totally congruent position (negative linkage): +1
Difference in attitude scale units: 1
Direction: right to left
Sign: minus
Pressure toward congruity for John Wayne (negative linkage): −1

Figure 5.11. Finding Pressure Toward Congruity for John Wayne, Assuming a Negative Linkage

"John Wayne abhors *harsh discipline,"* then the pressure toward congruity for *John Wayne* would be −1. This is arrived at as follows: The initial scale position for this object of judgment was +2. Its totally congruent position was +1. The difference in attitude scale units is 1. The direction is from right to left; hence, the sign is negative (see Figure 5.11).

To test your ability to find pressure toward congruity, work out the problems in Student Activity Option 5.6.

Student Activity Option 5.6
Finding Pressure Toward Congruity

INSTRUCTIONS
Using the data provided below, find pressure toward congruity for the designated objects of judgment.

Problem One

−3 −2 −1 0 +1 +2 +3
bad   good
Rosalynn Carter

Linking assertion:
Rosalynn Carter supports the
Equal Rights Amendment.
Is the linking assertion positive
or negative?

−3 −2 −1 0 +1 +2 +3
bad   good
*Equal Rights
Amendment*

A. Find pressure toward congruity for *Rosalynn Carter.*
  1. Initial scale position: _____
  2. Totally congruent position: _____

3. Difference in attitude scale units: _____
4. Direction: _____
5. Sign: _____
6. Pressure toward congruity for *Rosalynn Carter:* _____

B. Find pressure toward congruity for *Equal Rights Amendment.*
1. Initial scale position: _____
2. Totally congruent position: _____
3. Difference in attitude scale units: _____
4. Direction: _____
5. Sign: _____
6. Pressure toward congruity for *Equal Rights Amendment:* _____

Problem Two

```
/__/__/__/_x_/__/__/__/
 -3 -2 -1  0 +1 +2 +3
bad                good
      Ralph Nader
```

```
/__/__/__/__/__/__/_x_/
 -3 -2 -1  0 +1 +2 +3
bad                good
        consumer
        protection
```

Linking Assertion:
Ralph Nader supports *consumer protection*
Is the linking assertion positive or negative?

A. Find pressure toward congruity for *Ralph Nader.*
1. Initial scale position: _____
2. Totally congruent position: _____
3. Difference in attitude scale units: _____
4. Direction: _____
5. Sign: _____
6. Pressure toward congruity for *Ralph Nader:* _____

B. Find pressure toward congruity for *consumer protection.*
1. Initial scale position: _____
2. Totally congruent position: _____
3. Difference in attitude scale units: _____
4. Direction: _____
5. Sign: _____
6. Pressure toward congruity for *consumer protection:* _____

Problem Three

```
/_x_/__/__/__/__/__/__/
 -3 -2 -1  0 +1 +2 +3
bad                good
       Richard Nixon
```

```
/__/__/__/__/__/_x_/__/
 -3 -2 -1  0 +1 +2 +3
bad                good
         free press
```

Linking assertion:
Richard Nixon came out against a *free press.*
Is the linking assertion positive or negative?

A. Find pressure toward congruity for *Richard Nixon.*
1. Initial scale position: _____
2. Totally congruent position: _____
3. Difference in attitude scale units: _____
4. Direction: _____
5. Sign: _____
6. Pressure toward congruity for *Richard Nixon:* _____

B. Find pressure toward congruity for *free press.*
1. Initial scale position: _____
2. Totally congruent position: _____
3. Difference in attitude scale units: _____
4. Direction: _____
5. Sign: _____
6. Pressure toward congruity for *free press:* _____

Once you have found pressure toward congruity for the object of judgment in question, that value is plugged into the formula for attitude change and simple mathematics does the rest. Assuming both initial scale ratings we've been working with (+2 for *John Wayne,* −1 for *harsh discipline*), attitude change for *John Wayne* would be calculated as shown in Figure 5.12.

$$AC_{oj1} = \frac{|d_{oj2}|}{|d_{oj1}| + |d_{oj2}|} \times P_{oj1}$$

$$= \frac{1}{2+1} \times -3$$

$$= \frac{1}{3} \times -3$$

$$= -1$$

Figure 5.12.

The figure −1 means that congruity principle predicts that in light of the associative bond linking *John Wayne* and *harsh discipline,* a shift in attitudes would occur in the person whose attitudes are being measured such that the evaluation of *John Wayne* would become slightly less favorable: It would move 1 attitude scale unit to the left. This is in accord with our earlier common-sense predictions.

Under the same circumstances, attitude change for *harsh discipline* would be calculated as shown in Figure 5.13. The figure +2 means that congruity predicts that the evaluative scale rating of the person whose attitudes are being measured would move 2 scale units to the right, from an initial position of −1 to a position of +1. This, too, is in accord with our common-sense predictions.

$$AC_{oj2} = \frac{|d_{oj1}|}{|d_{oj1}| + |d_{oj2}|} \times P_{oj2}$$

$$= \frac{2}{2+1} \times +3$$

$$= \frac{2}{3} \times +3$$

$$= +2$$

Figure 5.13. Attitude Change for Harsh Discipline, Assuming a Positive Linkage

Now let's assume a negative linkage ("*John Wayne* abhors *harsh discipline*"). We'll assume the same initial scale positions with which we've been working. In this case, attitude change for *John Wayne* would equal $-\frac{1}{3}$ (see Figure 5.14). Congruity principle predicts that a shift in attitudes would occur on the part of the person whose attitudes are being measured such that the evaluative scale rating of *John Wayne* would move $\frac{1}{3}$ of a scale unit to the left. While this is a very slight shift, it is not in agreement with our common-sense predictions. This disagreement represents a flaw in the principle. It is a case of the tail wagging the dog, because users of the formula are forced into a position of arguing for a point that lacks face validity—that is, it simply seems not to jibe with reason. Osgood and Tannenbaum correct for this error by tacking onto the formula an "Assertion Constant" that has a value of $\pm.17$. A value of $+.17$ is used in the case of an associative bond; $-.17$ is used in the case of a dissociative bond.

Such tacked-on corrections suggest the presence of essential weaknesses in congruity principle. There is one other, called the Correction for Incredulity, used to take into account the fact that an individual is likely to disbelieve an assertion that links two objects of judgment in a way that runs counter to reasonable expectations—for example, "Jimmy Carter advocates the overthrow of the government." If you are interested in learning more about these corrections, I suggest you look at any of the readings listed in Student Activity Option 5.7. In this exercise, you will also find a number of simple problems that tie together the skills you have recently acquired.

$$AC_{oj1} = \frac{|d_{oj2}|}{|d_{oj1}| + |d_{oj2}|} \times P_{oj1}$$

$$= \frac{1}{2+1} \times -1$$

$$= \frac{1}{3} \times -1$$

$$= -\frac{1}{3}$$

Figure 5.14. Attitude Change for John Wayne, Assuming a Negative Linkage

Student Activity Option 5.7
Finding Attitude Change

INSTRUCTIONS

Use the appropriate formula to find attitude change for the designated objects of judgment.

Problem One

```
L__/__/__/__/__/_x_/__/
 -3 -2 -1  0  +1 +2 +3
bad                good
        Amy Carter
```

```
/x_/__/__/__/__/__/__/
 -3 -2 -1  0  +1 +2 +3
bad                good
     The Flintstones
```

Linking assertion:
Amy Carter laughs at
The Flintstones.
Is the linking assertion positive
or negative?

A. Find attitude change for *Amy Carter:*
B. Find attitude change for *The Flintstones:*

Problem Two

```
L__/__/_x_/__/__/__/__/
 -3 -2 -1  0  +1 +2 +3
bad                good
       Chrissy Evert
```

```
/x_/__/__/__/__/__/__/
 -3 -2 -1  0  +1 +2 +3
bad                good
     Jimmy Connors
```

Linking assertion:
Chrissy Evert no longer cares for
Jimmy Connors.
Is the linking assertion positive
or negative?

A. Find attitude change for *Chrissy Evert:*
B. Find attitude change for *Jimmy Connors:*

Problem Three

```
L__/__/__/__/__/__/_x_/
 -3 -2 -1  0  +1 +2 +3
bad                good
   Federal Department
       of Energy
```

```
/x_/__/__/__/__/__/__/
 -3 -2 -1  0  +1 +2 +3
bad                good
     Nuclear power
```

Linking assertion:
The *Federal Department of
Energy* advocates the
use of *nuclear power.*
Is the linking assertion positive
or negative?

A. Find attitude change for *Federal Department of Energy:*
B. Find attitude change for *nuclear power:*

Problem Four

```
 /   /   /   /   / x /   /   /
-3  -2  -1   0  +1  +2  +3
```
bad   good

    inner-city banks

```
 / x /   /   /   /   /   /   /
-3  -2  -1   0  +1  +2  +3
```
bad   good

    red-lining

Linking assertion:
Inner-city banks practice
red-lining.
Is the linking assertion positive
or negative?

A. Find attitude change for *inner-city banks:*
B. Find attitude change for *red-lining:*

SUGGESTED READINGS

Insko, C. (1967) *Theories of Attitude Change.* New York: Appleton-Century-Crofts. See pp. 112–140.
Kerrick, J. (1958) "The Effect of Relevant and Nonrelevant Sources on Attitude Change," *Journal of Social Psychology,* 47: 15–20.
Osgood, C. and P. Tannenbaum (1955) "The Principle of Congruity in the Prediction of Attitude Change," *Psychological Review,* 62: 42–55.
Stachowiak, J. and C. Moss (1965) "Hypnotic Alterations of Social Attitudes," *Journal of Personality and Social Psychology,* 2:77–83.

For all its flaws, congruity principle represents a step forward in the scientific/analytical approach to the study of persuasion. It accounts for reality more adequately than did Heider's balance theory. In addition, quantification of data makes possible accurate assessment of the prediction's worth. Research has indicated that congruity principle accurately predicts the direction of change likely to occur when two objects of judgment are linked by an associative or a dissociative bond, but it has failed to validate its predictions regarding the degree of change. Still, the fact that research can clearly confirm or negate the predictions of congruity principle (due to its capacity to quantify data) is a strong point.

Congruity principle may also be evaluated positively along other dimensions. For one thing, the formulation is relatively clear, straightforward, and simple. (Recall that one test of an hypothesis or theory is that it explain reality in as simple a manner as possible.) Cronkhite (1967, p. 56) has also observed that congruity principle has generated much productive research. He notes, too, that the principle has many interesting implications, among these one called mediated generalization. This formulation captures the tendency for audience attitudes to generalize from one concept to another when the same source presents them, despite the fact that the two concepts are unrelated to one another. In other words, a highly prestigious source may be evaluated so highly for accomplishments or expertise in one area that an audience will evaluate positively any object of judgment positively associated with the source, regardless of its tie to the person's area of specialization. Hence, prestige suggestion, also known as the "halo effect," can be validated scientifically.

Bettinghaus (1973, p. 55) maintains that congruity principle has important practical implications for the persuader as well. For one thing, it can be predicted that only rarely will a single speech produce a major change in an audience's attitudes. Most especially is this true when the audience's attitudes are highly polarized—when feelings run high and audience members have a large emotional investment in their convictions. In light of this implication, two options are open to the persuader. One, a persuasive campaign, like an advertising campaign, is extended over time; it consists of many messages, perhaps sent over many media and channels, all geared at producing the desired audience result. A second strategy is what I call the incremental approach to attitude change. This involves seeking many small changes over a period of time the cumulative effect of which is to bring about a large change. But if the large change were blatantly argued for at the outset, the response would be one of resistance and hostility.

Many observers report that social progress comes about by means of such incremental changes. Consider the following examples, each of which, added to the others, has resulted in our country's becoming a welfare state, to a greater degree than ever before; (1) income tax, an amazingly successful form of income redistribution; (2) the New Deal, a response to the Depression of the 1930s that established the place of the federal government in managing economic and unemployment problems; (3) Social Security, protection for the aged and infirm, which, through the auspices of a large central government, guarantees each citizen adequate income and care under conditions of illness or old age; (4) unemployment compensation, protection for those who have lost the capacity to earn an income; and (5) aid to dependent children, social welfare legislation that places more of the burden of child care on the state in order not to victimize children by economic and family circumstances beyond their control. Such changes, gradual as they are, will ultimately add up to a major change in the way this nation is run. Had all these revisions been advocated at once, however, they most certainly would have been rejected. (In fact, socialist Presidential candidates like Norman Thomas did incorporate all these proposals, and more, into their national platforms. Not surprisingly, the candidates were roundly defeated, though they are rightly credited with having been ahead of their time.) Because these changes have been introduced gradually, they have won support—sometimes reluctant, but adequate to ensure passage of the required legislation. Incremental advocacy means asking in stages for minor changes, which collectively add up to a major change.*

According to Bettinghaus, a second practical implication of congruity hypothesis is that as a speaker you can expect audiences' attitudes toward you to be affected by the popularity of the cause you advocate. The less popular the

---

* See Abne M. Eisenberg and Joseph A. Ilardo: *Argument: A Guide to Formal and Informal Debate,* 2nd ed. Englewood Cliffs, New Jersey: Prentice-Hall, 1980, pp. 154–158.

cause in their eyes, the more likely they are to downgrade their evaluations of you. The opposite is also true. Since some positive feelings toward a persuader are important, you can anticipate that your ability to persuade at all will be adversely affected if your audience associates you only with unpopular causes.

The situation of former President Richard Nixon is a case in point. Because of his close association with the Watergate conspiracy, he lost whatever credibility he had had as an individual. During the final days of his disgraced administration, even the office of the Presidency, to which he had referred so often, failed to provide a modicum of credibility. Nor did it earn him respect.

A third implication is that a speaker may impede his or her chances of exerting influence if associated too steadily with only one cause. The speaker becomes type-cast, and the ability to be considered credible when speaking about other subjects may be adversely affected. This is what happens to performers, for example, when they become associated with only one kind of music.

Congruity hypothesis has significant advantages over earlier formations, and it even has a few practical implications for persuaders. But I have noted throughout this discussion that congruity principle is far from perfect. What are some of its specific flaws?

When discussing the meaning of a mark on the zero point of the attitude scale, I reported that such a notation might mean many things. It could mean true neutrality or noncommitment, as Osgood and Tannenbaum suggest. In such a case, the rater might easily be influenced, since he or she is neither strongly in favor of the concept being rated nor strongly opposed to it. However, a mark at or near the midpoint of the scale can also mean that the rater possesses firm and definite attitudes that just happen to fall midway between extremely negative and extremely positive feelings. Take the example of student ratings of faculty. After a semester's experience with a particular instructor, you are asked to indicate your attitudes toward him or her. You weigh the matter carefully and mark the midpoint in the scale. In all likelihood this does not mean that you are undecided about the instructor; after 16 weeks of exposure, I suspect you have pretty firmly held attitudes. Thus, a mark at the midpoint of the scale suggests that you possess mixed feelings that are neither extremely positive nor extremely negative.

This discussion of the meaning of a mark midpoint on the scale suggests that a basic tenet of congruity principle might be open to question. Formulators of the principle based their work on the assumption that less polarized attitudes are more inclined to change than are more polarized ones. This, it appears, may well not be the case. What matters is not the degree of polarization; this is only one dimension of attitudes. In addition to degree of polarity, it is important to consider the conviction with which the attitudes are held, regardless of where on the seven-point scale they happen to fall. Cronkhite (1969, p. 54) dubs this second dimension *tenacity*, a well-chosen word, suggesting that the firmness with which an attitude is held can affect the ease with which the attitude can be changed. Recent research has confirmed this suspicion, and a few changes in congruity principle have been required. They more faithfully reflect the reality of the two dimensions of attitudes—tenacity and polarity.

A second major weakness of congruity principles is that in its original form, it failed to consider the fact that many messages that link two objects of judgment consist of more than a simple linking assertion. Far more often they are extended over time, as are speeches, essays, motion pictures, or ad campaigns. Yet congruity principle did not take into consideration the effects of appeals, proofs, and other features characteristic of such extended linking assertions. Common sense suggests that a single, stark assertion is qualitatively as well as quantitatively different from a speech or essay. The more reasonable the arguments that are part of an associative bond, the greater the likelihood of change. If you are well regarded by your audience and you talk about a subject to which they are opposed—say, unilateral disarmement—congruity hypothesis predicts that the audience will lower its ratings of you and increase its rating of unilateral disarmament. But must the price of reduced personal popularity always be paid? I suspect not, for if you were to offer many convincing and uncontestable proofs in support of the unpopular cause, it is likely that attitudes toward it would change for the better, while your own popularity would not suffer at all. In fact, you might become still more highly esteemed. The weight of evidence might just tip the scales both in favor of unilateral disarmament and in your own personal favor.

A related weakness consists of the conceptual content of messages that link two objects of judgment. The superficial observer might say that a speaker is discussing gay rights when talking about the right of gays to work at whatever jobs they choose and when arguing in favor of gays gaining custody of children from their former marriages. Beneath this broad label of gay rights, the two subjects discussed might be tied together. However, more careful scrutiny reveals that two very different concepts are likely involved. The right of gays to work where they wish is one thing; their right to raise children is likely regarded as quite another by most people. Thus, a message that contains more than one concept, or perhaps many of them, cannot fairly be considered as having dealt with only one concept. Artificial laboratory conditions make possible the linking of two objects of judgment by a single, simple assertion. In the real world, however, associative and dissociative bonds are far more complex than that. An adequate theoretical formulation takes into account the complexities of the real world. A principle that fails to do so can only be considered inadequate.

A third weakness of congruity principle is that it offers only three ways of restoring congruity—by changing attitudes toward the first object of judgment, by changing attitudes toward the second object of judgment, and by changing one's attitudes toward both. In reality, there are many more strategies available to the person who is experiencing incongruity. The person can, for example, disbelieve the linking assertion. The correction for incredulity reveals an awareness of this congruence-restoring strategy, yet it is tacked onto the congruity principle in a manner wholly unsatisfactory (Insko: 1967, p. 139).

Two other major failings of congruity principle warrant brief discussion. The first is that it fails to consider the strength of the associative or dissociative bond. Consider the following statements:

> Pamela likes Roy.
> Pamela loves Roy.
> Pamela adores Roy.

or again,

> Pamela dislikes Roy.
> Pamela hates Roy.
> Pamela loathes Roy.

The first three statements would all be considered associative bonds by congruity principle. Yet the strength of the linking assertion differs in each case. Similarly, the assertions in the second set would all be considered dissociative bonds. But each of the distinctions is different from the others. The failure to take these distinctions into account constitutes an important weakness of congruity principle.

The last major weakness is that congruity principle fails to consider the relevance of the linkage assertions to the person whose attitudes are being measured. If you don't care about Anita Bryant or orange juice, then a linking assertion to the effect that Anita Bryant drinks orange juice would likely be of little relevance to you. It seems that the less relevant the concepts in a linking assertion, the less involved the respondent and the less attitude change is likely to occur. A certain degree of personal involvement or concern is necessary to bring about the engagement that precedes attitude change. However, it should also be noted that beyond a moderate level, involvement works against any attempts at changing attitudes. Only in the middle range, where involvement is neither too low nor too high, can a persuader expect optimum conditions to exist. The situation is depicted in Figure 5.15. Note that the phenomenon depicted here is a little like the latitudes of acceptance, noncommitment, and rejection referred to earlier. There are ranges within which attitudes are open to change. But as soon as a message falls beyond normal parameters, the likelihood of change is sharply reduced. Involvement, along with many other factors (such as emotional investment, past experience, and familiarity with the subject matter of a message), plays a major role in determining whether any attitude change, regardless of direction, is likely to occur at all.

It is possible to ennumerate still other weaknesses of congruity principle. Scholars have objected to the lack of a clear definition of associative and dis-

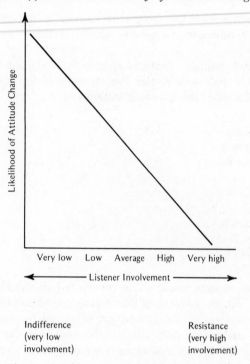

Figure 5.15. Listener Involvement and the Likelihood of Attitude Change

sociative bonds. Others have found fault with the ambiguity associated with the concepts that appear in linking assertions. If you are interested in reading more about the flaws in congruity principle, I suggest you see any of the sources referred to in the Student Activity Options as well as Roger Brown, *Social Psychology*. New York: Free Press (1962). See especially Chapter 11, which includes an excellent critique of congruity principle as well as other theories of attitude change.

COGNITIVE DISSONANCE THEORY

Earlier in the chapter, when discussing assimilation-contrast theory, I noted that attitude-change theorists have been particularly interested in accounting for audience reactions to messages that present viewpoints differing from those of auditors. I observed that cognitive dissonance theory was one formulation designed to account for reactions to this kind of discrepancy. This theory had dual parentage; it sprang both from the reinforcement and assimilation-contrast theory tradition on the one hand, and from the consistency theory tradition on the other.

Zimbardo and his coauthors (1977, p. 56) have observed that dissonance theory stands apart from most other attitude-change formulations because it is formally stated as a theory. Unlike congruity principle or balance theory, which are extremely sketchy formulations, dissonance theory is fully developed. It should be noted, too, that dissonance theory is more than a theory of attitude change; it is a theory of behavior in the broad sense. Its applications to the field of attitude change are many, and its implications reach into other areas as well.

Another feature that distinguishes dissonance theory from other formulations is that it details an impressively large range of options open to the person who has been exposed to a set of dissonance-producing circumstances. Balance theory oversimplifies reality tremendously by suggesting that in the face of conflict-production information, a person would radically shift evaluations of an attitude object from pro to con. Congruity principle offers a slightly more accurate account of what might occur; Osgood and Tannenbaum's formulation predicts possible changes in attitudes toward both objects of judgment. Cognitive dissonance theory goes still further, suggesting that more options are open to the person who experiences dissonance. Thus, it more accurately reflects reality.

Unlike congruity principle, which is stated in quantitative terms, dissonance theory is essentially a verbally stated formulation. It is possible to convert Festinger's statements into quantitative terms (see, Fishbein and Ajzen, 1977, p. 40); nevertheless, the original statement of the theory was verbal. This may be considered a weakness or a strength of the theory, depending on one's point of view. It is a weakness in that the theory is less precise. Indeed, verbal ambiguity is one of the major flaws of dissonance theory; everyday language is invariably less precise than mathematical symbolism. On the other hand, dissonance theory is a formulation easily understood and capable of explanation without reference to algebraic formulas and mathematical jargon. Thus, what dissonance theory lacks in precision, it makes up for in its straightforwardness and ease of intelligibility.

What, then, is dissonance theory? To answer, it is necessary first to define cognitions or cognitive elements and then to specify the relationships that can exist among them. A cognition or a cognitive element is a belief or a bit of knowledge; it is anything people know about themselves, their behavior, or their surroundings (Festinger, 1957, p. 9). Here are some examples of cognitive elements: (1) I am reading a book; (2) I attend college; (3) Bolivia exports tin.

Since the beliefs you hold and the pieces of knowledge you possess are part of a single cognitive set (your interlocking network of beliefs, attitudes, and intentions), it follows that they exist in some sort of relationship to one another. There are three such relationships among beliefs and knowledge. The first is an irrelevant one: Two beliefs that have no bearing on one another are said to be irrelevant to each other. For example, the belief that "apples are sweet" and the belief that "Oklahoma is west of the Mississippi" are irrelevant to one another. Only under the most exceptional circumstances might they be tied together in such a way that a relationship other than irrelevancy might arise.

Two beliefs are said to be consonant when one tends to follow from the other. They are in harmony or agreement, and no tension is felt when the two cognitive elements are juxtaposed. For example, your awareness that you are reading a book is consonant with your awareness that you are a college student. These awarenesses tend to go together or to follow from one another: College students tend to read books, at least some of the time! Other examples of cognitive elements that are in consonant relationship to one another are these: (1) "Smoking causes cancer" and "I do not smoke"; (2) "I have a test tomorrow" and "I am studying for the test"; and (3) "I do not want to get pregnant" and "I am taking precautions to ensure that I do not get pregnant."

In Festinger's own words, two cognitive elements are in dissonant relationship to one another when "the obverse of one element would follow from the other." To state it more formally, x and y are dissonant if *not-x* follows from y (Festinger, 1957, p. 13). In other words, dissonance arises when two inconsistent cognitive elements are juxtaposed and the opposite of one element would follow from the other. Here are some examples: (1) "Smoking causes cancer" and "I smoke"; (2) "I have a test tomorrow" and "I am not studying for the test"; (3) "I do not want to get pregnant" and "I am taking no precautions to ensure that I do not get pregnant." Note that in all three cases, the person is aware of inconsistencies between one belief and another or between belief and behavior. Consider this additional example. You might have been taught that members of a particular minority group possess certain undesirable traits. Let's suppose that you have met Tom, a member of such a group, and you find that he displays none of the traits he is supposed to possess. Instead, he seems to be just the opposite; his group is reputed to be cheap, loud, and vulgar, but he is generous, refined, and intelligent. In such a case, dissonance arises, not between your beliefs and your behavior, but between the beliefs you were taught and the beliefs that have resulted from your own perceptions.

Festinger's concept of dissonance is very much like Osgood and Tannenbaum's concept of pressure toward congruity. Dissonance is said to be psychologically uncomfortable; hence the person experiences a pressure to reduce dissonance. This pressure is directly proportional to the magnitude of the dissonance. In Festinger's own words,

> The existence of dissonance, being psychologically uncomfortable, will motivate the person to try to reduce the dissonance and achieve consonance. . . . The strength of the pressure to reduce the dissonance is a function of the magnitude of the dissonance (Festinger, 1957, p. 18, italics omitted).

As Zimbardo et al. (1977, pp. 67–68) have pointed out, the magnitude of dissonance depends on four things. The first is the importance of the cognitive elements involved. You would obviously feel little dissonance if it was pointed out to you that two trivial cognitive elements were in dissonant relationship to one another. Perhaps you believe that fluoride helps prevent tooth decay, and that one brand of toothpaste contains flouride while another does not; yet you use the brand that doesn't contain fluoride. Under these circumstances, you would likely feel but little dissonance. Far more dissonance would be felt if the cognitive elements were really important, for example, if you believed your survival depended on daily injections of insulin, yet you were not taking the necessary steps to ensure an adequate supply.

A second determinant of the magnitude of dissonance is the ratio of consonant to dissonant relationships. The more consonant elements in your cognitive set, the more at peace you feel; the fewer consonant ties and the more inconsistent ones, the more dissonance you experience. You can conceive of this ratio as a simple seesaw: The more consonance-producing cognitive elements on one side of the seesaw, the less dissonance you feel, and vice versa. For example, suppose you believe that sugar is harmful to your health; nevertheless, you eat it. Taken alone, these two elements could produce considerable dissonance. However, dissonance could be reduced by adding to your cognitive set such elements as these: (1) I have cut down on my sugar intake; (2) a little sugar is less harmful than smoking and drinking, neither of which I do; (3) in other respects my nutritional habits are good. What occurs in a case like this is a weighing process: The more beliefs that fit together and reinforce your behavior, the less dissonance you experience. Thus, you would not be very strongly motivated to change your behavior. Needless to say, the opposite ratio would be experienced as most uncomfortable; under the circumstances, a psychologically healthy person would be motivated to change behavior. For example, if you believed that passing a certain course depended on your completing a term paper, yet you could not bring yourself to do it, an objective observer might legitimately conclude that you are exhibiting self-defeating behavior.

The magnitude of dissonance is also a function of the extent to which a person is freely committed to a given conviction or course of behavior. This notion, which was added to cognitive dissonance theory by two of Festinger's followers (Brehm and Cohen, 1962), has a great deal of importance. The more deeply committed you are to a point of view, the more dissonance you will feel if it is contradicted. Similarly, the more people perceive themselves as having chosen freely to behave in a specific way, the more dissonance they are likely to feel if their behavior is in conflict with their basic beliefs. Conversely, the more coerced their choice, the less dissonance they are likely to feel. If you are threatened with death unless you denounce a close friend, you will likely do it with some regret, but with little dissonance. But if you are urged to denounce your friend and offered only a small reward, your willingness to denounce him or her might well create considerably more dissonance. "Was my action worth the reward?" you might ask yourself. "What have I gained? What have I lost?"

According to this line of thought, coercion reduces one's freedom of choice; hence, under extreme coercion, people might feel that their choice is not really theirs. Because they would assume less responsibility for their choice, less dissonance would arise.

Interestingly, Erich Fromm has argued eloquently that freedom of choice can be narrowed. The more a person chooses to do good deeds, the easier they become, until a point is reached at which the choice to do evil is actually next to impossible. Conversely, with each successive choice to do evil, a person's range of options is narrowed and the choice to do good becomes ever more remote. Thus, behaving well or behaving badly is a function of one's past choices and behavior (Fromm, 1964). You may think that your decision to behave in a specific way is a function of the immediate circumstances surrounding your decision. In reality, your choice may well be dictated by all the decisions and alternatives you have chosen up to this particular point. It should be noted that the ethical concerns raised by Erich Fromm are really aside from dissonance theory. Festinger and his colleagues have not been concerned with the ethics of behavior, only with its determinants. I have introduced this ethical dimension because it grows so naturally from the emphasis on freedom and commitment in dissonance theory.*

The fourth determinant of the magnitude of dissonance is the degree of cognitive overlap between the cognitive elements. The concept of cognitive overlap refers primarily to the similarlity between cognitive elements. Zimbardo and his coauthors (1977, p. 68) refer to it as "the functional equivalence of the objects or activities represented by each cognition." The more similar the cognitions or the objects they represent, the less dissonance is felt. Thus, a choice between buying one brand of automobile or another would produce less dissonance than the choice between buying a new automobile or taking a trip to Europe. If you want a new car and you also want to go to Europe, but you have only four thousand dollars to spend, you have to make a hard choice. No matter how you look at it, a new car and a European vacation are not functionally equivalent. Hence, the choice of one over the other would produce considerably more dissonance than the choice of one type of new car over another. Cronkhite (1969, p. 57) talks about the presence or absence of opportunities to compromise when he discusses cognitive overlap. He observes that the more opportunities to compromise (choosing a fuel-efficient auto over a good-looking one, for example), the greater the cognitive overlap and the less dissonance is felt. The opposite is also true. Regardless of how cognitive overlap is conceptualized, the important point is to note that the more mutually exclusive the choices, the more dissonance is felt. The less exclusive the choices are, the less dissonance is felt.

---

*See my book, *Taking Chances* (1981) Cornerstone/Simon and Schuster, for more on the matters of freedom, choice, and responsibility.

DISSONANCE-PRODUCING SITUATIONS

We will now look at each of the four prime situations in which dissonance can arise—choice, discrepant information, encountering someone who disagrees with you, and forced compliance. You will see throughout that my discussion has important implications for you as a persuasive speaker.

1. *Choice*

A situation in which you make a choice is typically one that produces dissonance. Festinger states that the situation just prior to making a choice is a conflicted one. You feel torn in one direction or the other, depending on the extent to which the two alternatives are equally attractive. Little conflict is felt when the two options are vastly different in attractiveness—the choice between a broken-down motorcycle that doesn't run and a shiny new one, for example. Once the choice is made, however, you are open to experiencing dissonance. Suppose you look carefully into the strong points of two stereo systems that are roughly equally attractive; they both sound good, use good components, and are equivalent in other ways. A few features on one are absent on the other, and vice versa. You decide ultimately to buy system A. According to dissonance theory, afterward you would be susceptible to dissonance. Any information you might get indicating that system B, the unchosen alternative, was better would likely create psychological discomfort. You might reject such information, or you might match each bit of information with a corresponding advantage of the system you purchased. "True, system B had a larger wattage capacity," you might say, "but the speakers in system A are superior." By such tactics, you would seek to reduce dissonance and to restore or maintain consonance.

Once again, the freer the choice, the greater the dissonance you are likely to feel. If an old friend, an expert in stereo components, laced into you for choosing your system, you might experience much dissonance. "What did you buy that one for?!" your friend might bellow. "What a mistake! System B stands head and shoulders above the cheapy you bought. Incidentally, the one you got ought to sell for about half the price of B. What did you pay for it? Oh, no, you're kidding me!" Here, responsibility is being placed squarely on your shoulders for having made the choice. If you had received the system as gift, however, you might wiggle out of the uncomfortable situation by disclaiming responsibility: "Oh, yeah, I know what you mean," you might say. "But my parents got it for my birthday, and what do they know about stereo systems!"

To review the other general principles, the magnitude of dissonance in a free-choice situation depends on (1) the importance of the choice (the more trivial the choice—say, between two brands of shampoo—the less dissonance you feel) (2) the cognitive similarity between the alternatives, (3) the ratio of consonant to dissonant relationships, and (4) the freedom with which the choice was made. Of these, the first two are of special interest here. In the case of the stereo system, you might content yourself with the thought that regardless of the quality of the two systems, the one you bought *will* allow you to play your stereo records, to listen to your favorite FM-stereo radio station, and to record directly from the radio onto your 8-tracks. Thus, the two systems would be seen as functionally equivalent, and dissonance would be reduced.

Implied in this discussion are some of the ways to cope with dissonance. You could seek to reduce dissonance by (1) seeking out areas of cognitive similarity, (2) revoking your decision (bringing back system A and exchanging it for the other), (3) seeking out data that support the choice you made (you might reread articles and advertisements that sing the praises of the system you purchased, talk again to friends who recommended the purchase, and so on), (4) downplaying or avoiding data that indicate you made the wrong choice (only a masochist would seek out people who would underline the foolish choice).

This last alternative of avoiding or downgrading negative data has pertinence for the persuasive speaker. If your audience would feel dissonance by accepting you and your message, you can be reasonably confident that most of the members will denigrate your qualifications, disbelieve your proofs, and use other strategies to avoid experiencing psychological discomfort. They might even avoid coming to hear you speak at all. Indeed, this is a major problem in persuasive communications. Often, the very persons whom you most want to reach are the very ones who avoid hearing your talk. How likely is it, for example, that a racial bigot would come to hear a speech on the accomplishments of blacks or Hispanics? Would a loyal Democrat come to hear a campaign speech of a leading Republican, except to gather materials for refutation?

Consider your own behavior when confronted by someone who challenges a basic belief you hold. Aren't you likely to ridicule the person, to downplay his or her qualifications, to point to the preponderance of people who agree with you and disagree with the speaker. Such responses are perfectly human, and perfectly in accord with the predictions of cognitive dissonance theory.

2. Discrepant information

When you are involuntarily exposed to discrepant information that contradicts your beliefs or runs counter to your ways of behaving, you experience dissonance to one degree or another. It has been observed (Boulding, 1956) that we live in the midst of a stream of through-put: We are constantly exposed to new thoughts and new information. The mass media have so greatly extended the range of input available to us that we can hardly escape to a safe haven where all our convictions go unchallenged. Instead, we are bombarded every day by messages that contain data that can be irrelevant, consonant, or dissonant in relation to elements in our cognitive sets.

The amount of dissonance you feel is directly proportional to the importance of the cognitive element challenged by the discrepant information. A second factor determining the magnitude of the dissonance is the extent to which the information directly contradicts your belief. If the information only obliquely contradicts your belief, you can comfortably put it aside and so restore consonance relatively easily. If the data directly contradict your belief, your task is more difficult. A third determinant of the amount of dissonance is the degree to which the information you receive is incontestable. The more irrefutable the data, the more difficult a time you have to restore consonance.

Consider the case of a woman whose boyfriend is unfaithful to her. Her belief in her boyfriend's faithfulness is an important cognitive element in her psychological set. Exposed to information that he is being unfaithful, she would likely experience considerable dissonance. If the information were only in the form of rumors, she might counter it quite easily by denying the allegations on the basis of the fact that no hard evidence is available. Even if the rumors were supplemented by circumstantial evidence—say, a strange perfume in her boyfriend's car or growing coldness on his part toward her—she might stll deny the contention that he is being unfaithful. When the information becomes uncontestable, and when it directly contradicts her belief in his faithfulness, she might have no alternative but to accept it, confront the awful hurt, and accept reality. The incontestable evidence might consist of her seeing him on a date with someone else. At such a point, rumors no longer can be discounted, nor can circumstantial evidence be argued away. The cognition directly contradicts her belief, and some sort of accommodation must be made. She might accomplish this by denying that she ever really cared for him and so reduce dissonance.

Thus, the major strategies used to restore consonance (or to reduce dissonance) when a person happens to come into contact with unwanted information are (1) downplaying the importance of the cognitive element that is being contradicted, (2) contesting the information by denying it, misperceiving it, or otherwise using a strategy that Insko appropriately calls "defensive misperception" (1967, p. 203), and (3) changing the belief or the cognitive element. A fourth strategy was only implied in the example of the unfaithful boyfriend. This strategy consists of seeking out cognitive overlap—some point of compromise, some way of justifying or explaining the apparent inconsistency and so bringing the two discrepant cognitions into harmony. This might occur if the woman were to accept her boyfriend's unfaithfulness, yet continue to see him, contending that a certain set of circumstances that is not likely to be repeated led to his aberration.

Here I wish to make explicit what may have gone unnoticed up to this point—namely, that dissonance theory sets forth many, many strategies by which consonance can be restored. In my eyes, it gives due credit to the ingenuity of the human mind, which seems infinitely capable of coming up with ways to preserve the internal order upon which cognitive balance depends. Balance theory, as I hope you can now see, is an enormous oversimplification of the way we cope with reality. Congruity principle, while more complex than balance theory, is an embarrassment because of its tunnel vision and simplicity. Dissonance theory is the first formulation we have discussed that accurately reflects the extraordinary resourcefulness of human beings.

As an exercise, you may wish to list the ways in which Festinger says dissonance can be restored. Don't, however, simply copy down the strategies as I have presented them but put them in your own words and feel free to add other strategies that have not been discussed. Remember that these strategies are the very ones audience members are likely to use if you present them with information that creates cognitive dissonance.

3. Encountering someone who disagrees with you

There are two interrelated functions that operate in the typical persuasive situation in which one person encounters another who is arguing for some proposition that runs counter to the listener's point of view. The first function involves the listener's reactions to the message and its source. The second involves the presence or absence of social supports for the listener and the listener's beliefs.

In the case of this typical persuasive encounter, several variables affect the magnitude of the dissonance experienced. The most important variable is the listener's perception and evaluation of the speaker: The more well-liked, well-respected, and credible the speaker, the greater will be the magnitude of the listener's dissonance. It is far easier to disregard the opinions and admonitions of someone for whom you have little liking or respect. The case of Cynthia and Professor Darwimple is a typical one. Because you admire Cynthia, and because the two of you agree on many things, your disagreement over the quality of Professor Darwimple's teaching is a source of considerable dissonance. If the two of you were strangers, it is unlikely that any significant degree of dissonance would develop.

There is an important exception to this incidence of dissonance: In some circumstances, dissonance theory predicts that a disliked source will actually produce more attitude change than a well-liked one. This nonobvious prediction, which has been validated by research, is an important testing point for dissonance theory. That it can generate such a nonobvious prediction, and that the prediction can be validated, is indeed a crucial bit of verification for Festinger's formulation. Fundamentally, the prediction stems from the two following starting points: first, the less overt justification for a change in outward behavior, the more change in attitudes occurs. When overt justification is minimal, only by bringing inward convictions into line with outward behavior can a person restore consonance. In the example concerning the size of the reward given for denouncing a friend, the threat of death would bring about the denunciation with only minimal dissonance. But denouncing a friend for a paltry reward would likely create much dissonance. Once the dissonance had developed, you would be faced with the problem of bringing into harmony your outward comment about your friend and your inner beliefs. To restore consonance, you might well change your inner conviction about the friend. You might come to believe that the unkind things you said about your friend are true. Under these circumstances, changing your inner beliefs is far less complicated than undoing what you have done by issuing a retraction, apologizing, or by other means. In a case like this, minimal reward brings about maximum attitude change. In the case of denunciation under penalty of death, outward change in behavior might occur, but no real attitude change would follow. To paraphrase Zimbardo and his coauthors (1977, p. 72), might brings about compliance—outward behavior in accord with expectations—but not attitude change.

The second starting point from which originates the nonobvious prediction that a disliked communicator can bring about more attitude change than a well-liked one is that a well-liked communicator represents adequate justification for behavior change, while a disliked speaker represents inadequate justification. From this vantage point, a well-liked communicator is akin to the threat of death: He or she constitutes ample reason to behave in the desired way. The force of the communicator alone is sufficient to bring about the outward change in behavior. The disliked communicator is like the smaller reward offered for denunciation: He or she does not constitute justification for the act. Thus, if a person can be pressured to behave in the desired way, two things will occur. First, dissonance will develop as tension is felt between inner convictions and outward behavior. Second, the person will seek ways to restore consonance by changing inner beliefs to bring them into line with outward behavior. The pressure to change inner beliefs is directly proportional to the degree to which the communicator is disliked. The more the person dislikes the communicator, the greater will be the pressure to bring about the inner change, and vice versa.

Zimbardo et al. (1977, pp. 105–109) summarize a study designed to test the validity of this line of thought. A carefully structured situation was devised in which army reservists were induced to eat fried grasshoppers. Independent variables consisted of the source of persuasive appeals to do so. On the one hand, a "positive communicator," a well-liked and well-respected officer, urged that they eat the food. On the other hand, the urging was done by a "negative communicator," the experimenter, who acted in a cool, unfriendly, and somewhat authoritarian manner. (In the "positive communicator" condition, the experimenter acted warmly, in a relaxed and friendly manner, prior to the talk by the well-respected officer.) Dependent variables consisted of the reservists' attitudes toward eating fried grasshoppers. These attitudes were measured before and after the talks were given and the grasshoppers were eaten. The results of the study showed that those reservists subjected to the negative communicator condition changed their attitudes more than those reservists who had been subjected to the positive communicator. It was as though each member of the negative communicator group were saying, "I dislike you. The fact that I ate the grasshoppers had nothing to do with your capacity to influence me! I simply don't mind eating them." A typical member of the positive communicator group, on the other hand, was saying in effect, "I ate them because I like and respect you, but I still feel a bit squeamish about eating grasshoppers."

No simple relationship exists between the extent of liking and the magnitude of dissonance. Other factors are also involved in determining the magnitude of dissonance that arises when a person encounters someone who argues for a point of view with which the listener disagrees. A second factor is the importance and extent of the disagreement. If you and a close friend were to disagree about something trivial—which brand of ice cream tastes better, for example—in all likelihood little dissonance would develop. But if a husband and wife were to disagree about family finances, child rearing, or the obligations of spouses, then a more serious and extensive range of disagreements would exist. Much dissonance would probably be felt, and considerable effort would likely be exerted to reduce it.

A third determinant of the magnitude of dissonance is the degree to which the point of clash can be resolved by observation and testing. The more the disagreement centers on a matter of opinion, the more dissonance is likely to be felt. When the clash can easily be resolved by reference to external, observable facts, relatively little dissonance is experienced. Thus, if you were driving with your parents and your father insisted that on the next street corner you would pass a pizzaria but you said that a movie theater was on the next corner, it would be a relatively simple matter to wait a moment and simply see who was right. But when the disagreement is over something less tangible—say, the values by which one should live—then the clash is less easily resolved and more dissonance producing.

The magnitude of dissonance in interpersonal conflict or in a persuasive situation is also affected by the weight of facts and opinion on both sides of an issue. Indeed, evidence—hard data, informed opinion—in a speech enables your listener to recognize that in accepting the viewpoint you are advocating, he or she will not be alone. It can be postulated that the scantier the evidence and the less compelling the supporting materials, the more comfortable your audience will be in holding firmly to prior beliefs and convictions. Only by presenting an impressive array of facts and testimony can you create the dissonance that is a prerequisite to persuasion.

This fourth point leads us to the concept of social support. Generally speaking, the more social support you feel, the less dissonance you experience. Conversely, the less support you feel, the more dissonance you are likely to experience. Thus, one way to reduce dissonance, whatever its origin, is to seek out others who agree with your viewpoint. That is why members of various political parties tend to read newspapers reflecting that party line. It is why clerics tend to read religious publications and why academics attend academic conventions. It is why teenagers steep themselves in adolescent culture and why parents commiserate with other parents. It is the rare person who deliberately fails to seek out such social supports; without them, he or she is prone to self-doubt and the fears that are associated with being a minority of one.

Once exposure to a person who disagrees with you has resulted in dissonance, what steps can be taken to reduce the dissonance and to restore consonance? One method, obviously, is seeking out social supports. Another is to downplay the areas of disagreement. You might seek to minimize the fact that Cynthia regards Professor Darwimple highly while you think little of him. Another method of restoring consonance is to try to convert your adversary. Festinger has done an interesting study of a religious cult whose members believed that the world would end on a certain day. When it did not, the members of the cult reacted in a way that may seem surprising—they set out to win more converts. This reaction, however, was in accord with Festinger's prediction. On the one hand, seeking new believers would have the effect of reconfirming the members' beliefs in their doctrines, which had been severely shaken by the failure of the prophecy. By winning converts, the cult members were acting to reduce dissonance by attempting to convert nonbelievers. The act of proselytizing itself can serve to reduce dissonance.

A fourth dissonance-reducing technique is to change your attitude toward the source of the communication. If a well-liked person advocates something with which you disagree, you may come to like this person less. By reducing your liking for the source, you reduce the discrepancy between your evaluation of the speaker and your evaluation of the proposition he or she is advocating.

Conversely, you can come to like more a source whom you previously disliked. If you found yourself in agreement with a person of whom you formerly thought little, you would feel a degree of dissonance. To reduce it, you might well upgrade your evaluation of this person.

A final alternative to reduce dissonance is to change your attitudes. If someone advocates a position with which you disagree, and does so with incontestable evidence and a great deal of sincerity, you may reduce the dissonance thus created by changing your opinion. This is rarely an easy thing to do. The greater the turnabout you must make, the more dissonance you are likely to feel. Astute practitioners of the art of persuasion have long recognized the importance of giving people in such a situation an "out"—an excuse for making the change and for saving face as they do so. Mahatma Gandhi, for example, was well aware of the Indian concept of Satyagraha, the requirement that both sides in a confrontation coerce and injure one another as little as possible. To give the other person the courage to change, it is important not to place him or her in a position in which the person must react defensively.

4. Forced Compliance

I have suggested that externally induced behavior that runs counter to one's internal beliefs is a source of cognitive dissonance. Extensive research has been done on the effects of forced compliance. Investigators have been especially interested in examining the effects of inducing changes in behavior by offering rewards or by threatening punishments. Some rather interesting findings have been uncovered.

In general, dissonance is unavoidable under conditions of forced compliance; hence, some attitude change in one direction or another is almost bound to occur. But the direction of the attitude change and the interrelationships of the variables involved warrant close scrutiny. In many cases, the interconnections are surprising and the effects of changes in variables are not what would be expected.

The starting points in forced compliance research are these: First, assume an individual who will be offered rewards or threatened with punishments for acting (or failing to act) in designated ways. Consider the case of your being asked to denounce a friend. You could be offered rewards, large or small, for making the denunciation. Further, you could be threatened with punishments, mild or severe, for failing to do so. Second, assume that the freedom of this individual is not entirely curtailed; the person retains the option of behaving as he or she chooses, though the range of freedom is limited. Third, assume that the individual's beliefs and attitudes, which can be measured prior to and after the forced compliance situation, run counter to the behavior to be engaged in.

Review in your mind the discussion of dependent and independent variables that appeared in Chapter 3. Analysis reveals that while there is only one set of dependent variables (the attitudes of the person involved), there are many independent variables, all of which can have an impact on the person's attitudes. Here is a listing of the independent variables in the forced compliance situation:

1. the importance of the pertinent beliefs in the cognitive set of the individual (if you were asked to denounce a friend, the extent to which you thought well of the friend and valued the friendship would be roughly equivalent to the importance of the beliefs in question);
2. the extent to which the specified behavior directly contradicts the beliefs in question;
3. the size of the promised rewards, which can vary from large to paltry;
4. the severity of the threatened punishments, which can vary from severe to mild;
5. performance or nonperformance of the behavior in question.

This last variable is critically important, because the amount of dissonance felt is tied irrevocably to whether the behavior is performed or not. Let's suppose you are offered a reward for denouncing a friend. Let's suppose further that you go ahead and do so. Under these circumstances, the magnitude of dissonance would be determined by all the factors just listed. The more you value the friendship, for example, the more dissonance you are likely to feel.

But there is a qualification: The larger the size of the reward, the less dissonance you'll feel. (Recall my earlier comments on justifying the change: The less outward justification—a small reward—the more dissonance is felt, since a person can't justify behavior by thinking of the huge reward to come.) Conversely, the smaller the reward, the more dissonance will be felt, and hence the more attitude change.

Now let's suppose you were threatened with punishment and therefore performed the desired behavior. Once again, the more you valued the friendship, the more dissonance you would feel. But a similar qualification exists: The amount of dissonance is inversely proportionate to the severity of the threatened punishment. That is, the less severe the punishment, the more dissonance you would feel, and hence the more attitude change would occur. Conversely, the more severe the punishment, the less dissonance you would feel, and the less attitude change would occur. (Might can bring about compliance, remember, but not necessarily changes in attitude.)

Let's take the situation in which you refuse to perform the desired behavior. Offered a large reward for denouncing your friend, you would experience considerable dissonance for refusing to perform the behavior. Two factors influence the magnitude of the dissonance you'd feel under these circumstances. On the one hand, your noncompliance with a behavior that runs counter to an important belief would tend to reduce the amount of dissonance. On the other hand, however, refusing the large reward would tend to generate considerable dissonance. If you were offered only a small reward, your refusal to comply would generate little dissonance.

How about punishment? Your refusal to denounce your friend would be the occasion of considerable dissonance if you were threatened with severe punishment. Once again, two factors would cross paths. On the one hand, your refusal would cause considerable dissonance, since you would face severe punishment for refusal. On the other, however, your refusal to betray someone whose friendship you value would have the effect of reducing the amount of dissonance you felt. And, if the threatened punishment were trivial, your noncompliance would occasion very little dissonance. (If you are interested in more particulars of the precise interrelationships that operate in all of these circumstances, I suggest you consult the sources listed in Student Activity Option 5.8.)

To summarize the strategies used by the person who experiences dissonance under circumstances of forced compliance: The number of options open is relatively small. (1) If the person complies and performs the behavior, he or she can reduce dissonance by minimizing the importance of the belief in question. In other words, if you were to denounce your friend, you might downplay the extent to which you think well of your friend and value the friendship. In this manner, you would seek to reduce the magnitude of dissonance. (2) Another option is to inflate the size of the reward you have received, thereby increasing the justification of your betrayal and reducing dissonance. (3) Finally, you might actually change your beliefs about and attitudes toward your friend. This would have the effect of bringing your outward behavior into line with your inner cognitive set. (4) If you did not comply, you might reduce dissonance by minimizing the size of the reward offered for compliance. (5) If threatened with punishment for noncompliance, you might downplay the severity of the anticipated punishment. (6) And if the belief were important to you, you might remind yourself that you held steadfastly to a critical principle. "I have not betrayed my friend," you might say, "though I could have secured a sizable reward for doing so. I held true to my convictions." Or if punishment were involved, "I will face this punishment with peace of mind, knowing that at least I have not betrayed someone whom I hold in high regard."

Dissonance theory has many implications for persuasive strategy. First of all, it suggests a specific way of conceptualizing audience resistance to persuasive appeals. As a speaker, you need to know that because of the tendency to avoid dissonance, your audience will automatically resist any message that contradicts basic beliefs; the more basic the beliefs, the greater the resistance. Second, the audience evaluation of you will rise or fall to the extent that you advocate ideas that agree with or contradict convictions and attitudes. Of even more interest to me is the fact that persuasive appeals calling for active participation on the audience's part are almost invariably far more effective than those in which the audience serves as a passive recipient of a message.

In a classic study designed to test the influence of group participation on attitude and behavior change, Kurt Lewin (1952; pp. 459–73) set out to change one of the most resistant forms of human behavior, eating habits.* A hospital set the goal of inducing new mothers to feed their children cod-liver oil and orange juice immediately upon discharge from the hospital. Mothers were assigned to one of two groups, or experimental conditions. For roughly 25 minutes, Group One listened to a persuasive talk by a member of the hospital staff that stressed the benefits of feeding cod-liver oil and orange juice to neonates. The members of Group Two heard no such talk. Instead, mothers in groups of six talked with one another and with a hospital staff member about the same topic. These group discussions, which also lasted about 25 minutes, were informal, with plenty of opportunities for questions and for self-persuasion.

Two weeks, and again four weeks later, the mothers were surveyed: How many members in each of the two experimental conditions were feeding their children cod-liver oil and orange juice? with what frequency? The results clearly indicated that many more mothers who had participated in the informal group discussions were doing the feeding, and with much more frequency. After four weeks, for example, 90 per cent of the group discussants

---

* Lewin's study was not designed to test the validity of dissonance theory; nevertheless, it lends support to the contention that active audience involvement enhances attitude change. Technically, Lewin's study falls under the heading of "group dynamics," another branch of persuasion theory.

were continuing the feedings; only 50 per cent of the mothers who had heard the speech were doing so.

Other studies, some of which are tied directly to dissonance theory, have been designed to measure the effect on attitude change of behavior that runs counter to a person's private beliefs. In Chapter One, I mentioned the controversy over debating both sides of an issue. Some people have contended that while such training is excellent preparation for argument, it tends to lower ethical sensibilities and to glorify mental gymnastics at the expense of sincerity and good will. There is still another aspect to the matter of debating both sides: By arguing a point of view with which one does not agree, a person's attitudes can be changed and the convictions eroded.

A good many studies have been conducted on the effects of public statements that run counter to one's own beliefs. One such study predates dissonance theory but nevertheless can be construed as supporting it; the study is of special interest because it involves a class very much like this one. In 1954, Janis and King sought to measure the effects of what they called "counterattitudinal advocacy"—that is, arguing publicly in a way that runs counter to one's attitudes. A group of students in a speech communication class was selected from a pool of students who had answered an attitude questionnaire four weeks earlier. After correlating the students and their attitudes toward specific topics, it was arranged that the chosen students would give speeches that ran counter to their positions on the issues in question. Following the public communication, their attitudes would be measured again. (Appropriate steps were taken to ensure that the students did not know that the dependent variable was their set of attitudes.) The results indicated that, to a significant degree, students who actively participated in counterattitudinal advocacy changed attitudes to a much greater degree than did students who only listened to speeches. In summarizing the results of this study, Insko observed, "when people play certain roles they tend to take on the attitude consistent with those roles" (1967, p. 220).

Similar studies have been conducted specifically with an eye to testing dissonance theory's predictions. In one case (Harvey and Beverly, 1961), a group of admittedly antialcohol college students was exposed to a proalcohol communication. Afterward, the students were asked to summarize the main arguments in the communications they had heard. One half of this group of respondents was further asked to write its own proalcohol communication. It was found that those who wrote the messages changed attitudes more than those who merely summarized the main arguments they had passively heard.

As a result of such studies, it is widely recognized that counterattitudinal advocacy can affect attitudes profoundly. You might think of the effects of these changes as impact that proceeds inward from outward behavior to changes in internal set. Dissonance theory predicts that such changes will occur because, by changing attitudes, a person brings into line inner inclinations and outward performance.

Taken together, the research both on the impact of group discussion and on counterattitudinal advocacy suggests that a major tool in persuasion is active audience participation. Self-persuasion is a real and documented phenomenon. Zimbardo and his colleagues assert unequivocally that "one of the most reliable [conclusions] in this area of attitude change [is that] active participation is more effective in changing attitudes than is passive exposure to persuasive communications" (1977, p. 127). A speaker who overlooks this powerful persuasive tool is making a grave error. In Student Activity Option 5.8, you are invited to think of ways in which you as a persuader might structure active participation into your talks.

Cognitive dissonance theory has exerted tremendous influence on the field of attitude change. It has generated a great deal of research and has undergone refinements and improvements over the past three decades. It remains one of the more carefully scrutinized conceptualizations, perhaps because it is the first theory of attitude change to offer a comprehensive explanation of persuasive effects.

Popularity alone is no measure of the worth of a theory. However, Festinger's formulation has at least two other significant features. First, among attitude change theories, cognitive dissonance is unique in its capacity to generate nonobvious predictions and to have them verified by research. To summarize: (1) under conditions of forced compliance, the smaller the reward, the more attitude change occurs and (2) under similar conditions, a disliked communicator will produce more attitude change than will a well-liked communicator. Both these surprising predictions have been verified, bearing testimony to the predictive power of cognitive dissonance theory.

The second feature of the theory is that it predicts that different amounts of dissonance will be created by the performance of specific behaviors. Thus there is no simple correlation between the performance of a specific behavior and the production of changes in beliefs, attitudes, or intentions. Performance of the same behavior can generate different amounts of change (or none at all) under different circumstances.

Despite its impressive advantages, dissonance theory is open to important and basic criticisms. The first set of criticisms has to do with the manner in which dissonance theory is stated. The second set concerns the theory's failure to consider the magnitude of dissonance felt at any given time. Other fundamental objections have to do with the theory's openness to disconfirmation and with the fact that often the results of experimental manipulations can be explained without reference to dissonance theory.

To reiterate, unlike congruity principle, which is stated quantitatively, Festinger's formulation is verbally stated. While this in itself is not necessarily bad, language is always open to vagueness and imprecision. Indeed, at the heart of dissonance theory are such ambiguous and vague concepts as *dissonance* and *cognitive element*. Festinger claims that two cognitive elements are in dissonant relationship to one another when the obverse of one follows from the other. But as Insko reports (1967, pp. 282–83), the words *follows from* may have several meanings. Is a logical consequence implied—that is, one idea logically follows from another? Or would one thing follow from another because of cultural mores, as when arrest follows from the commission of a victimless crime? Or perhaps one behavior would follow from another because one's past experience has led to such an association. Since it is clear that *follow from* can mean different things, *dissonance* is an imprecise concept, the experience of which remains somewhat vaguely accounted for.

The term *cognitive element* is also an imprecise concept. As we saw in Chapter Three, it is rare for a belief not to give rise to an attitude. Dissonance theory, however, fails to distinguish clearly among beliefs, attitudes, and intentions; nor does it specify the relationships among them. For example, the intention "I do not want to get pregnant" is rooted in beliefs about pregnancy and in attitudes toward it. Both beliefs and attitudes in turn are likely tied to a woman's past experiences and present circumstances. What precisely are the interconnections among all of these cognitive elements? Which elements are involved—the intention alone? the intention and the belief that lays beneath it? the attitudes that stem from the beliefs? And what about persuasive effects? Do changes in intentions always imply changes in attitudes? in beliefs? to the same degree? All these matters are left unspecified in dissonance theory. Hence, it is rightly criticized for vagueness and imprecision.

The second set of criticisms may sound familiar. When contrasting balance theory and congruity principle, I reported an advance over Heider's formulation because Osgood and Tannenbaum were able to take into account the amount of pressure toward congruity. Dissonance theory takes a step backward in this area, because it fails to consider (or to provide any way of measuring) the amount of dissonance. It has been found, as I have reported, that such factors as volition and commitment have a bearing on how much dissonance is felt. Nevertheless, precise measures of the magnitude of dissonance are lacking as are precise formulations of factors contributing to the magnitude of dissonance.

Another criticism of dissonance theory is that Festinger's formulation fails to specify why one method of restoring consonance is chosen over another. Why, for example, would you revoke a decision rather than seek out points of cognitive similarity among the alternatives? Why would you change your attitudes rather than minimize the importance of the beliefs being challenged by a persuader? One of the flaws of balance theory as well is that it fails to give adequate reasons why one method of restoring balance is chosen over another. Heider merely predicted that a person's attitudes toward one or the other object of judgment would undergo a turnabout but did not say *why* one would change rather than the other. Congruity principle offers some explanation for which of the three methods of restoring congruity would be utilized. (Recall that the degree of polarity has much to do with which attitudes would change and to what degree.) Although dissonance theory is a vast improvement over both balance theory and congruity principle, because it enumerates many more options for reducing dissonance and for restoring consonance, it still represents a regression since the exact reasons for the election of one dissonance-reducing option over another are not specified by the theory.

Cronkhite (1969, p. 59) notes further that dissonance theory generates so many explanations for a phenomenon that it cannot readily be disproved. And, one of the criteria for a good theory is that it is capable of being disproved (see Chapter Three). With some dismay, Cronkhite reports that as a mental exercise, Festinger once showed how every conceivable outcome of an experiment could be explained by dissonance theory. When a theory can predict every possible outcome, however, it cannot be disproved, and when a theory cannot be disproved, it possesses basic flaws. It is like explaining every possible behavior—acts of loving and caring no less than acts of hatred and vengeance—as a function of repressed hostility toward one's mother. (Indeed, Freudian psychoanalysis has been criticized on the same grounds as dissonance theory.)

Cronkhite observes, too, that most research findings reported by students of dissonance theory can be explained without reference to Festinger's creation. Thus dissonance theory seems to Cronkhite a superfluous addition to the pool of attitude-change theories. I personally do not consider this a serious flaw. In the early stages of theory development, it is important to generate as many alternative explanations as possible. Festinger cannot be faulted for having come up with a new and different way of accounting for the same phenomena since the task of researchers is not to discourage the formulation of alternative explanations, but to decide which of those explanations is best.

In general, dissonance theory is far from perfect. Yet it is an important contribution to our understanding of attitude change. Perhaps in the end its most important feature is that it specifies many strategies by which people seek to avoid dissonance and to minimize or eliminate it when it occurs. Dissonance theory includes a far more comprehensive listing of such strategies than the listings provided by any of the formulations that preceded it. While it certainly is in need of refinement, dissonance theory represents an advanced and thought-provoking account of attitude change.

Student Activity Option 5.8
Cognitive Dissonance

INSTRUCTIONS
Following are several activities that can help you appreciate more fully Festinger's theory and its implications. With the consent of your instructor, consider working with a group and actually conducting some of the activities suggested. The readings that follow these activities are well worth your time and effort.

1. This is an individual activity. First reread the section on cognitive dissonance theory, then answer these questions. Have you ever been in a situation that

created a great deal of dissonance? What was the situation? How did you deal with it? What strategies did you use to reduce dissonance? Were your efforts successful? Did you employ any strategies that were not considered in the discussion here? In your personal experience, what methods seem to work best to reduce dissonance? Other questions to consider: Are you now doing anything (or failing to do anything) that might be regarded as self-defeating or dissonance-producing? For example, are you failing to fulfill some course requirement or other responsibility? Why do you suppose you might be behaving as you are? (Some interesting, and perhaps frightening, explanations might be provided by Fyodor Dostoyevsky, *Notes from Underground.* See especially Part One, Sections IV–XI.) Have you ever intentionally put yourself in a dissonance-producing situation? Why? Review the situation. What benefits, if any, were derived from the experience? What were the psychic costs? Would you do it again if you had the choice? What can be said of the person who never experiences dissonance? Can such a person exist? What precautions would have to be taken in order to live in a state of constant consonance?

2. Here is a relatively simple study that can be done with the consent and cooperation of your instructor and of several classmates.

Select a group of college students randomly. Show the students photographs of several hair styles and instruct them to rank the styles in the order of their personal preferences. Keep accurate records of each person's ratings. After the rankings have been completed, arrange to have a woman, a supposed expert on hair styles, talk to the group. It will be the job of the "expert" to demonstrate that the styles fall into a very definite order of esthetic quality. She is to present her own ranking, arguing that based on her many years of experience as a hairdresser, it is beyond doubt that intelligent, refined, and sensitive people would rank the styles as she has done. Following the talk, have the speaker leave the room. The students should then complete a questionnaire (that you have made up previously) designed to measure their perceptions of the speaker, her credibility, expertise, etc. Then redistribute the photos once again and ask the students to rank them. See whether the rankings change. You should find that those students who thought the speaker most credible changed their rankings most. Similarly, those who thought least of the speaker should change their rankings least.

While the subject matter of this study has to do with hair styles, the same process could be utilized with different subject matter—a ranking of novels, followed by the "expert" opinion of a "professor" of literature, judgments of art works, followed by the informed judgments of an art "professor," and so on. Whatever content your study deals with, be certain to keep careful records to ensure that you can correlate (1) the audience members' initial rankings, (2) their judgments of speaker credibility, expertise, etc., and (3) their postcommunication rankings.

3. This exercise gives you the opportunity to involve your audience actively in your persuasive efforts. For each of the following situations, write several ways in which you might involve your audience actively.

    a. You are a defense attorney. The charge against your client is based on one critical bit of evidence—the first hand testimony of an eyewitness. You are sure that this witness did not see what he thinks he saw. Your task is to convince a jury of five men and seven women that a person's perceptions are not always accurate. How might you convince the jurors, involving them actively in the process of persuasion?

b. You are planning a speech on a topic that is usually considered technical—mathematics, simple statistical procedures, or basic laws of chemistry or physics, for example. How might you convince your audience that your supposedly technical subject is within the easy grasp of any reasonably intelligent individual?

c. You are to address a group of hard-line racists. Your task is to have them begin to challenge some of the narrow views they hold. Interestingly, your hard-liners are almost all experienced speakers, and they all enjoy an argument. How might you involve them actively in counterattitudinal advocacy?

SUGGESTED READINGS

Boulding, Kenneth (1965) *The Image:* Ann Arbor: University of Michigan Press.

Brehm, J. and A. Cohen (1962) *Exploration in Cognitive Dissonance.* New York: John Wiley.

Cronkhite, Gary (1969) *Persuasion: Speech and Behavioral Change.* Indianapolis: Bobbs Merrill, pp. 56–60.

Festinger, L. A. (1957) *A Theory of Cognitive Dissonance.* Stanford, California: Stanford University Press.

Festinger, L. A., H. Riecken, and S. Schacter (1956) *When Prophecy Falls.* Minneapolis: University of Minnesota Press.

Fishbein, M. and I. Ajzen (1975) *Belief, Attitude, Intention and Behavior: An Introduction to Theory and Research.* Reading, Massachusetts: Addison-Wesley Publishing Company.

Insko, C. (1967) *Theories of Attitude Change.* New York: Appleton-Century-Crofts, pp. 198–284.

Janis, I. and B. King (1954) "The Influence of Role-Playing on Opinion Change," *Journal of Abnormal and Social Psychology* 49: 211–18.

Karlins, M. and H. L. Abelson (1970) *Persuasion: How Attitudes and Opinions Are Changed.* New York: Springer Publishing Company. See pp. 19–21, 62–67.

Lewin, K. (1952) "Group Decision and Social Change," pp. 459–73 in G. E. Swanson, T. M. Newcomb, and E. L. Hartley, eds. *Readings in Social Psychology.* New York: Holt.

Zimbardo, P., E. Ebbesen, and C. Maslach (1977) *Influencing Attitudes and Changing Behavior,* 2nd ed. Reading, Massachusetts: Addison-Wesley Publishing Company.

SUMMARY

From this chapter you have gleaned the essence of five typical approaches to the study of attitude change. Reinforcement theory, with its roots in learning theory, was reported to be the first systematic attempt to understand persuasive effects. Though hardly a theory in any formal sense, the work of Hovland and his associates provided basic conceptual tools with which the study of attitude change could be approached systematically. The Yale group emphasized the importance of attention, comprehension, acceptance, and retention.

Social judgment theory was born of a desire to understand better the internal processes that operate when an auditor yields to a persuasive message.

The chief conceptual tool contributed by social judgment theory was the concept of latitudes of acceptance, rejection, and noncommitment. Although crude and very narrowly focused, social judgment theory does penetrate into the inner space of psychological yielding and makes the phenomenon understandable.

Balance theory was specifically formulated to account for the results of psychological imbalance. It rests on the assumption that human beings seek to maintain harmony among the attitudes they possess. When imbalance occurs, steps will be taken to restore harmony. Though Heider's theory oversimplifies a complex reality, it was the first systematic attempt to explore the balance-imbalance phenomenon.

Congruity principle, a quantitatively stated formulation, specifies in great depth the precise manner in which congruity can be reestablished if it is disrupted. Osgood and Tannenbaum went far beyond Heider, offering a more detailed account of attitude change as a result of psychological imbalance. Their principle reflects reality more accurately, for it takes into account the fact that attitudes differ in strength. Further, according to congruity principle, attitudes toward both objects of judgment can change when the objects are linked in such a way as to cause incongruity. The principle asserts that the degree of attitude change depends on the polarity or strength of the original attitude. Though congruity principle has been only partially validated, and though it possesses many basic flaws, it represents a significant improvement over balance theory.

Dissonance theory reflects reality still more accurately. While its verbal (nonquantitative) statement leaves it open to charges of vagueness and imprecision, dissonance theory provides a comprehensive enumeration of the many strategies by which consonance, once disrupted, can be restored. The only approach reviewed here that is formally stated as a theory, Festinger's brain child is remarkable for its ability to generate nonobvious predictions, some of which have been validated by research.

It must be stated that none of these theories, taken collectively or individually, represents a final statement of the truth about attitude change. Each theory is flawed, and each is but a preliminary step to understanding the phenomenon of persuasion. While none offers a set of sure-fire techniques for persuasion, each in its own way can help you to understand the circumstances under which people's attitudes change. By judiciously applying the principles generated by these noninterventive theories, you can anticipate audience reactions, prepare strategies, and maximize your persuasive potential.

PART THREE

Practice and Criticism of Persuasion

Chapter 6

Strategic Persuasion

A strategy is a carefully chosen plan or series of maneuvers designed to achieve a specific goal. In all undertakings, from warfare and chess to persuasion, strategy plays a crucial role. It is always one of the last subjects studied, for the study of strategy assumes a familiarity with the basics of a field. For example, a chess player who begins a study of strategy must already have mastered the moves appropropriate to each piece on the board. The player must be familiar with the ways a game can end and with the simple techniques for capturing an opponent's pieces. After such thoroughgoing competency is achieved, strategy can afford a systematic, theoretically derived game plan chosen for specific reasons to achieve a specific result.

This chapter deals with persuasive strategy. I am assuming by now a thorough familiarity with the process of speech preparation. I will show in detail the ways in which theory may be applied to practice in order to help you achieve persuasive results.

In the first part of the chapter, I discuss general principles, derived from persuasion theory and research, that apply across a broad spectrum of persuasive situations. In the second part, I show the applications of theory to planning for persuasion, specifically audience analysis. I discuss both individual and group influences on auditors' behavior, and point out the importance of such audience features as degree of homogeneity, group feeling, and common focus. Audience analysis is described as a purposeful activity undertaken to help bridge the gap between the audience's initial position and that of the speaker. Specific suggestions are offered for planning arguments that will effectively bridge that gap. In the third part, I detail several specific presentation strategies, offering suggestions about the placement of arguments and the inclusion of arguments on both sides of an issue.

213

I. General Principles

Research in persuasion has allowed us to derive several basic principles applicable to a wide variety of persuasive communication situations. These principles help us think about the way people behave when exposed to persuasive messages—whether they are being urged to buy a product, to vote for a particular political candidate, or to accept the advances of a member of the opposite sex.

The first of these principles is that a person's internal set can be compared to a physical or social system. An internal set consists of an interlocking and interdependent network of components that are in dynamic balance and that tend to be self-sustaining. Let us examine each element in this statement in detail.

A system is made up of components. Regardless of whether you talk about the solar system, the cardiovascular system, your car's electrical system, or any other physical system, the elements or components that make it up can always be identified. The components are the individual pieces that together make up an organized whole. If the pieces merely fit together, like the pieces in a puzzle or the furniture grouping in a room, they constitute a static system. If the elements function together, as do the components of your cardiovascular system, then the system is said to be dynamic. The elements of static and dynamic systems are balanced and interdependent—that is, a change in one component brings about corresponding changes in other components.

Social systems, all of which are dynamic, are also balanced and interdependent. Whether you are talking about a family, a small, problem-solving group, or an entire society, it is always possible to identify the individuals who constitute the components of the system. It is possible, too, to observe that the members of a social system are interdependent, so that if one member cannot function well, the others take up the slack. For example, when a parent is ill, other members of the family take over the chores to compensate for the disability in order that the goals of the system can be achieved. (It makes more sense to speak of goals when talking about a social system. Nevertheless, it is also possible to use the term *goal* loosely when talking about a physical system, as when we say the goal of the cardiovascular system is to provide oxygen to the body's cells, while removing waste products.)

Psychologically, your internal system consists of your network of beliefs, attitudes, and intentions. All are interdependent, like the components of your auto or your cardiovascular system. All function together in orienting you toward reality, providing a frame of reference, and otherwise providing the basics of a psychological stability upon which effective functioning depends. It is important to remember that your cluster of beliefs, attitudes, and intentions forms a true network. It is an interlocking whole, each part of which is in dynamic balance with every other part (see Chapter Two).

Because the components in your internal set exist in dynamic relation to one another, a change in any one component of the system results in adjustments and corresponding changes in other components. For example, suppose you hold attitudes toward solar energy that are mixed, though predominantly negative. As Fishbein and Ajzen's scheme suggests, these attitudes are based on beliefs. Your opposition may be based in part on the belief that solar energy is technologically impractical. If you were persuaded that solar energy is in fact technologically practical, it is likely that your attitudes would become less negative, perhaps even mildly positive.

Given the interdependence of the components of your internal set, you may wonder about the impact of changes in beliefs about and attitudes toward related subjects.* For example, what would happen to your attitude toward solar energy if your beliefs about nuclear energy changed? If you became convinced that nuclear energy is unsafe, would that make you more inclined to favor solar energy? The answer is maybe, because by a usually unconscious process related to the defense mechanism of isolation, a person can separate two ideas that under normal circumstances would be associated with each other. An auditor who does this is resisting persuasion; in such cases, it may be necessary for the persuader to make the association for the auditor, to bring the two seemingly unrelated ideas into psychological contact. Provided that connections are made, however, it may safely be said that no part of your internal network is entirely divorced from other parts. A change in one element of the system may be made to reverberate throughout the entire ideational and attitudinal structure.

It is extremely important that you be aware of the interdependence of the components of your auditors' psychological systems. When a direct attack on their attitudes would provoke resistance, for example, you may make the strategic choice to change the attitudes indirectly by altering the beliefs upon which they rest. If you know your auditors oppose solar energy because they believe it to be technologically impractical, you would be wise to concentrate your efforts on changing that belief, without in any way attempting by direct effort to change their attitudes. In this way, you would avoid provoking the resistance a direct attack might engender, while slowly undermining a central belief upon which the opposition rests.

Dynamic systems are self-sustaining. What does it mean to say that a person's internal set is self-sustaining? To answer, let me draw an analogy to liv-

---

*The question of relatedness is important, because two cognitive components unrelated in one person's mind might be linked by associations in a second person's mind. Thus, it is unlikely that most of us would change our attitudes toward solar energy as a result of a change in our attitude toward the use of insecticides by farmers. However, there might be a corresponding change in the mind of a person who links the two subjects beneath a broader area of concern we might label ecology.

ing organisms. You may recall from biology that living organisms are open systems, that is, they maintain themselves in the face of a changing environment. An open system exists within an environment upon which it depends for survival. Basic life processes involve taking in material from the environment, acting on it in some manner (digesting it, for example), and generating output. An organism acts on input in fairly predictable ways, according to a sort of biological agenda akin to a computer program, which provides instructions on how the organism is to process input. While this input-processing-output is going on, an open system maintains itself. It continues to exist as an ongoing, discrete organism.

The term *homeostasis* is used in biology to refer to the process whereby balance is maintained and continuity is ensured in the face of a changing environment. For example, as your body temperature rises on a hot day, you perspire. The effect of perspiring is to reduce your body temperature, thereby maintaining a balance upon which your survival depends.

In the psychological realm, the same processes operate. Your internal psychological system is open, you continually interact with your environment. New ideas bombard you constantly as you read, watch television, listen to the radio, and talk with people. By such means, input is constantly entering your psychological system in the form of ideas that you process according to a learned program. (This, by the way, is one of the features that distinguishes us from the computer: Our programs are learned and can be unlearned.) You generate output in such forms as talking and behavior. Your output is a consequence of the input you receive and of how you process it.

Just as your physical organism maintains its identity despite new input, so does your psychological self resist significant changes in structure. Your *self* consists of a pattern of relatively stable, predictable, and consistent ways of perceiving and coping with reality. This response pattern resists change because in a fundamental sense it is you. When this pattern changes radically, as it sometimes does under intense psychological pressure (see Chapter One), people are inclined to say things like "She isn't herself!"

CONCRETE PREDICTIONS

These insights about self-sustaining components lead to more concrete predictions about the ways people behave in persuasive situations. For example, people seek to avoid experiencing cognitive imbalance, inconsistency, or dissonance. More prosaically, people try to avoid unsettling input. They defend against or resist messages that threaten to upset their psychological balance. This process is sometimes under conscious control; more often it is automatic.*

---

* Except to point it out, I will not deal here with unconscious resistance in the psychoanalytical sense. The interested reader should see one or both of the following books: Anna Freud (1966)

Two corollaries can be identified. One corollary is that the more basic the belief challenged and the more crucial it is to your psychological system, the more strenuously you will resist contradictory messages. For example, if you have always believed that Presidents tell the truth, it is likely that you would resist strenuously a message to the effect that any one President has lied to the American people (see Chapter Five).

The second corollary is that the more direct the challenge, the greater will be your resistance. This is especially so if the idea under attack is one your audience holds dear. In cases like this, a brash confronting style can often work against a speaker. Far more often, success is achieved by a subtler, more gradual approach.

In Student Activity Option 6.1, you are invited to consider basic strategy in addressing several different audiences.

Student Activity Option 6.1
Basic Strategic Planning

INSTRUCTIONS

In each of the following situations, an audience holds the indicated attitude statement. Beneath each attitude statement is a set of three supporting beliefs. Assuming you must change the audience's attitude, describe how you would go about it. Would you attack the attitude directly? Why or why not? Would you attempt to modify the content or the strength of each belief? Why? Would you address any one belief in particular? Why or why not?

For optimal learning value, it is important that you have a rationale for each strategic choice you make. If time and your instructor permit, engage in a discussion during which you and your classmates share your strategic decisions and the reasons why you made them.

In arriving at your answers, consider such factors as these: (1) your audience's latitudes of acceptance, rejection, and noncommitment; (2) your audience's level of ego involvement; (3) the tenacity with which your audience clings to its position.

1. *Audience:* A group of private pilots

Attitude Statement: We oppose Federal Aviation Administration efforts to limit landing and takeoff rights by private aircraft at major metropolitan airports during heavy traffic periods.

Belief Statements:
1. Airport facilities, paid for by taxpayers, ought to be available without restrictions to those who pay for them.
2. Private pilots are safe flyers.

The Ego and the Mechanisms of Defense. New York: International Universities Press; Gertrude and Rubin Blanck (1974) *Ego Psychology: Theory and Practice.* New York: Columbia University Press.

3. Radar, radio, and other mechanical equipment aboard private aircraft is equivalent in safety and reliability to that aboard large commercial aircraft.

2. *Audience:* A group of high school students

Attitude Statement: The destruction of American Indian culture and tradition is of little consequence.

Belief Statements:
1. American Indian culture is primitive.
2. Tradition in general is of little importance.
3. We have little to learn from the American Indian.

3. *Audience:* A group of businessmen

Attitude Statement: We oppose legislation that imposes safety and health standards in business.

Belief Statements:
1. Such legislation increases costs to consumers by adding as much as 50 percent to the cost of production.
2. Such legislation represents an unacceptable intrusion by government into the private sector.
3. The business community can be trusted to maintain adequate safety and health standards because of its own economic self-interest.

4. *Audience:* A group of rural residents

Attitude Statement: We oppose federal aid to cities.

Belief Statements:
1. The major urban centers of this nation contribute little to the quality of life in rural America.
2. Big cities live beyond their means.
3. Big cities manipulate their budgets.

A second major general principle of persuasion is that the recipient of a persuasive message will seek to reduce dissonance or imbalance and to restore consonance or balance only when (a) unable to avoid exposure to input that runs counter to beliefs, attitudes, or intentions; and (b) efforts to resist, undertaken as soon as the recipient is exposed to unsettling input, are unsuccessful. In other words, recipients will seek to reduce imbalance and to restore consonance only when they experience imbalance or dissonance.

Thus, the persuasion process can be described as a process of creating and managing dissonance. In Figure 6.1, I sketch a simplified model of a two-

Phase One:	Phase Two:
Creating Imbalance	Establishing a New State of Balance

Subphase One

1. Assessment of audience's prior state
2. Survey of available resources
3. Strategic planning and message construction (inducements to change)

Subphase One

1. Strategic planning
2. Estimate of strength and directional tendency of pressure toward congruity
3. Estimate of which balance-restoring mechanisms are most likely to be used by audience

Subphase Two

1. Message presentation

Subphase Two

1. Message preparation (inducements)
2. Message presentation

Figure 6.1. Simplified Model of a Two-stage Persuasion Process

stage process of persuasion: During the first stage, the efforts of the persuader are geared toward creating imbalance. During the second, the efforts are geared toward managing dissonance—that is, creating a new state of balance incorporating the changes in beliefs, attitudes, and/or intentions sought by the persuader.

CREATING IMBALANCE

How can a persuader overcome initial resistance and create imbalance? To answer it is necessary first to restate that imbalance can mean (1) changes in belief content, strength, or both; (2) changes in attitudes (evaluations); and (3) changes in intention content, strength, or both.* These distinctions are important, for as a persuader you can select any of these—individually or in various combinations—as the target of your change effort. Strategic planning means very deliberate decision-making. The planner makes decisions on the basis of information, careful inference-drawing, and available resources. A knowledge of the exact changes you wish to make is essential to strategic planning.

To determine the most efficient approach to overcoming initial resistance and creating imbalance, you need to ask yourself two sets of questions. The first set consists of questions that can guide you in deciding where to intervene. The second set includes queries that provide useful data on the kinds of inducements most likely to bring about the intended results.

In deciding where to begin your change effort, consider such matters as these: What component of your audience's internal set is most open to change? most vulnerable? least well supported? Which components are crucial or pivotal to your audience's attitudinal structure? Which components are

---

*Imbalance can also result from changes in behavior (see Chapter 5). Here, however, I will concentrate on speech-making as the primary vehicle for persuasion.

held with the least tenacity? Do you wish to bring about a change by altering your audience's evaluations of different objects of judgment? For example, if your auditors hold only neutral or mildly positive attitudes toward you, and if it is important that they evaluate you positively, you might elect to change their evaluations of you as an inducement to accept what you say.

While these questions are suggestive rather than exhaustive, they clearly indicate that deciding where to intervene in order to create imbalance is a strategic decision that must be made with your goals and with a thorough assessment of your audience clearly in mind.

What about inducements to change? Once you have decided where to intervene, how do you decide what inducements to use? Here again, decisions about inducements must be made in light of your objectives, your knowledge of the audience, and your assessment of available resources.

In general, inducements can be either logical or nonlogical. Logical inducements include hard evidence (facts, statistics, and such) and chains of reasoning that together constitute arguments. Research indicates that such logical inducements (if purely logical inducements can be said to exist) are rarely sufficient to bring about change (Bowers, 1963; Carmichael and Cronkhite, 1965). Other inducements are therefore necessary. These include the sort of proof traditionally regarded as emotional because it makes use of the feelings, wants, desires, and needs of the audience. Emotional proofs include not only blatant emotional appeals ("Buy this product to increase your sex appeal") but also softer forms of evidence, including authoritative testimony and endorsements by well-known public figures. The implication is that the audience will identify with the person or institution making the endorsement, and feel confident that they will be correct in opting for what the persuader recommends.

Nonlogical inducements also include the sort of proof regarded as personal by traditional rhetoricians. These inducements arise from what a speaker is or appears to be in the eyes of the audience. In other words, you yourself constitute an inducement to change. The esteem in which you are held and the credibility your opinions are afforded are among the factors that constitute inducements to believe or disbelieve what you say. To paraphrase Ralph Waldo Emerson, what you are thunders so loudly that your audience cannot hear what you say.

It is important to make one final point regarding the creation of imbalance. A speaker is well advised to be aware of how much dissonance he or she is creating. Too much dissonance, and you run the risk of being rejected early on, before securing a fair hearing. Too little, and your audience comfortably ignores you. Optimum dissonance seems to unsettle an audience just enough so that the members question previously accepted beliefs, convictions, and evaluations. Once such an opening is provided—ideally, most subtly and unobtrusively—you have laid the foundation for bringing about significant and long-lasting changes in your audience's internal set.

Under normal circumstances, it is impossible to know just how much dissonance your audience is experiencing, but careful audience assessment and keen observation can provide important clues. The more completely you know your audience, the better your estimates of reactions to what you will say. The more attuned you are to the feedback the audience provides, the more likely you are to judge the responses accurately.

MANAGING DISSONANCE

Once a persuader has succeeded in creating imbalance, the task becomes that of managing dissonance. For convenience, we can divide this task into two parts. First, the persuader must gauge the strength of what Osgood, Suci, and Tannenbaum call pressure toward congruity. Here, I am using this term in a less strict and nonmathematical sense than before, as meaning a pressure to restore balance and reachieve consonance. Second, the persuader must be aware of and responsive to the balance-restoring options open to the listeners.

Pressure toward congruity

An audience in which imbalance has been created can be compared to a sewing needle that has been moved just far enough away from a magnet so that the magnetic field is incapable of drawing it back. However, the slightest nudge will push the needle back within the magnetic field, which will then draw the object instantaneously toward the magnet. In the same way, an auditor is almost always ready to revert to his or her prior position. The least rationale will often justify this reversion—a proof the auditor regards as inconclusive, something you do that makes the listener doubt your sincerity, a source you cite who is not held in high regard. Only by anticipating audience reactions can you prevent the action of the invisible psychological forces that inexorably draw your auditors back to the position they held before.

The development of persuasion theory allows us to formulate these ideas more scientifically. Researchers tell us that pressure toward congruity can vary from weak to strong. Pressure toward congruity can also tend toward the restoration of the prior state of balance, or toward the establishment of a new balanced state.

The strength and directional tendency of pressure toward congruity are related to the magnitude of the dissonance felt. The factors affecting the magnitude of dissonance were discussed in Chapter Five and are briefly enumerated in Figure 6.2. For instance, the contestability of the imbalance-generating information is one factor affecting magnitude of dissonance: The more contestable the information, the less dissonance felt and the greater the pressure to restore consonance by reverting to the prior position. In other words, if a speaker presents easily refuted information, it would be very simple for the auditor to ignore what is said (even if it is momentarily effective) and return to the position held prior to hearing the information.

Theorists other than Festinger have also helped us understand the factors

Type of Dissonance-producing Situation	Determinants of the Magnitude of Dissonance Felt
Choice	1. Importance of the cognitive elements between which the choice is made;
	2. cognitive similarity of the alternatives;
	3. functional equivalency of the alternatives;
	4. freedom with which the choice is made.
Discrepant Information	1. Importance of the cognitive element contradicted by the discrepant information;
	2. extent to which the discrepant information directly contradicts prior belief;
	3. contestability of the discrepant information;
Encountering Someone Who Disagrees with You	1. Extent to which the person is well liked and/or well respected;
	2. importance and extent of the disagreement;
	3. extent to which the disagreement is resolvable by observation and testing;
	4. weight of the facts and evidence on both sides;
	5. amount of social support felt by the audience.

Figure 6.2. Summary of Factors Affecting Amount of Dissonance Felt

affecting the strength and directional tendency of pressure toward consonance. Cronkhite, for example, discusses tenacity as one such factor. The more firmly the original conviction was held, the greater will be the pressure to revert to the prior state of balance. The less firmly held the original conviction, the weaker will be the pressure to revert. In this second case, there may be considerable pressure to establish a new state of balance incorporating the ideas advanced by the speaker. In general, the more compelling the inducements offered by the persuader and the less firmly held the audience's original convictions, the greater will be the pressure to establish balance not by reverting to the prior position, but by changing beliefs, attitudes, or intentions in the direction advocated by the speaker.

The strategic persuader assesses the strength and directional tendency of the audience's pressure toward congruity and responds to it directly, with his or her goals clearly in mind.

Awareness of balance-restoring options

An important tool in the speaker's armamentarium is the knowledge of the options open to an audience once the auditors experience dissonance. In the planning process, the wise speaker determines which of those options is most likely to be selected. The estimate can be made in light of such factors as the audience's prior knowledge of the speaker and its attitudes toward him, its attitudes toward the sources of prior convictions, and the cognitive similarity between the ideas offered by the speaker and those held prior to the speech. A brief review of the options open to an audience appears in Figure 6.3.

Type of Dissonance- producing Situation	Strategies Used to Reduce Dissonance
Choice	1. Seek out areas of cognitive similarity between cognitive elements; 2. revoke prior choice; 3. seek out data that support prior choice; 4. downplay or avoid data indicating an incorrect choice was made.
Discrepant Information	1. Minimize importance of cognitive element(s) contradicted by discrepant information; 2. defensively misperceive the discrepant information; 3. change prior beliefs; 4. compromise or otherwise bring discrepant cognitions into harmony.
Encountering Someone *Who Disagrees with You*	1. Seek out social supports; 2. downplay areas of disagreement; 3. convert opponents; 4. change attitudes toward or beliefs about source of prior convictions; 5. change attitudes toward or beliefs about source of the dissonance-producing message; 6. change beliefs or attitudes.

Figure 6.3. Summary of Strategies Used to Restore Consonance

Once the persuader reviews the audience's options and determines the ones most likely to be used, he or she can structure appeals to increase the likelihood that dissonance will be resolved in the speaker's favor. For example, knowledge of persuasion theory tells you that one way an audience reduces dissonance is by seeking evidence and arguments that support beliefs held prior to receipt of the contradictory information. If a speaker gauges that the audience will use this ploy, he or she might elect to include such arguments in the talk. By interpreting the evidence so that it supports his or her position, and by refuting opposing arguments, the speaker would blunt possible negative impact of the evidence.

The persuader also knows that social supports or the lack of them are crucial variables in persuasion. Thus, in assessing the possible impact of the change you are advocating, and in planning for the acceptance of your proposed change, you would be wise to ask such questions as these: How will persons with whom my auditors have social ties see their change? Are my auditors likely to receive support for their change? (If not, it is likely that change will be extremely short-lived.) Will it be necessary for me to provide my audience with social supports? (For example, many self-help groups maintain a network of open phone lines so that in times of stress a member can contact another person in the group for support.) By assessing the social impact of the change and by gauging the need for social supports, you can make a realistic appraisal of an important and often overlooked dimension of your persuasive needs.

In Student Activity Option 6.2, you are invited to use your knowledge of pressure toward congruity and of the strategies used to restore consonance in order to plan strategically for persuasion.

Student Activity Option 6.2
Managing Dissonance

INSTRUCTIONS

Refer to the four situations described in Student Activity Option 6.1. (Your instructor may provide you with other situations as well, or you may wish to make up your own.)

Assume in each case that you have decided to change the attitude statement by challenging each of the belief statements. Assume further that your persuasive efforts have begun to succeed and that you have successfully overcome resistance to changing each belief. As a result, your audience is experiencing dissonance. For each belief statement, answer the following questions: (1) How strong might be the audience's pressure toward congruity? Why? (2) In what direction would it tend? Why? (3) What strategy or strategies would your audience be most likely to use in its attempt to restore consonance? Why? (4) How might you decrease the likelihood that the audience will revert to its prior position? Why have you made your choices?

II. *Audience Analysis*

In addition to providing general principles that apply across a broad spectrum of persuasive situations, theory and research can also generate guidelines useful in undertaking an analysis of the audience. These guidelines can help, for example, in identifying key variables and in stimulating us to think about their impact. More specifically, the guidelines can alert you to what to look for in analyzing an audience—namely, those factors that can make a difference in the way an audience perceives, interprets, and reacts to your talk.

Here I wish only to suggest some of the more important variables that have been found to play a part in listeners' reactions to persuasive messages. In no sense is the discussion intended to be exhaustive. I hope that as a result of what you will read, you will feel inclined to search the literature to determine other key variables that have been identified.

WHAT PERSONALITY VARIABLES AFFECT PERSUASION?

The behavior of audience members in persuasive situations is always in accord with their personality traits and configurations. Researchers have investigated the impact of such traits as extroversion, intelligence, authoritarianism, and tolerance of ambiguity on the way people react to persuasive
messages. One research study (Carment, Mills, and Cervin, 1965) indicates
that more intelligent* and extroverted persons tend to be more persuasive
but less persuadable when arguing with an opponent with whom they disagree. Hovland, Janis, and Kelley (1953) have suggested that more intelligent
persons tend to be more persuadable when exposed to messages containing
impressive logical arguments. Wright and Harvey (1965) suggest that authoritarian individuals tend to change peripheral beliefs (those of little importance
in their cognitive sets) quite readily, while they change core or central beliefs
very rarely and very little. A number of researchers (Janis and Field, 1959;
Linton and Graham, 1959) have reported that persons with high self-esteem
are more difficult to persuade than persons whose self-esteem is low.

WHAT MAKES PEOPLE LISTEN?

Much research has been done to determine why people listen, or fail to listen, to others. A knowledge of research findings in this area can provide you
with important guidelines in planning your speech and in deciding how to
deliver it.

For example, we know that giving attention involves both selecting and
focusing. We know that the individual plays an active, determining role in the
process of perception. A person does not passively receive information as a
sponge soaks up water but filters, selects, and distorts the information in accord with his or her needs, interests, and psychological disposition (Hastorf,
Schneider, and Polefka, 1970).

Barker (1971) reports several variables that play a role in the audience's listening behavior. Research findings indicate that high levels of ego involvement (or, if you prefer, low levels of objectivity) tend to reduce comprehension. While there is no simple relationship between comprehension and
yielding, if accurate comprehension is an important goal in your speech, then
the more ego-involved your audience, the more you must strive to ensure
comprehension by such devices as restatement and repetition.

Another variable affecting listening is the audience's motivation. You can
verify this from your own experience. If your instructor announces a quiz on

---

* Intelligence here is defined as the capacity to learn, to make critical distinctions, and to draw
inferences—all of which constitute easily measurable behaviors.

material to be covered during a particular class period, it is likely that you will listen carefully. Similarly, if you know that you must apply what you have learned during a presentation, and if successful application is important to you, it is very likely that you will listen with care.

There are also relationships between listener fatigue and the ability to listen effectively, the intervening variable being attention span. As a person's fatigue increases, the attention span tends to grow shorter. As that happens, the person's ability diminishes to listen and to report accurately on what is heard.

Barker mentions several other variables, among them intelligence (more intelligent listeners tend to score higher in listening ability), verbal ability (listeners who score high on verbal ability tend to score higher as listeners), and the experience of having had a course like this one (which correlates positively with improved listening ability).

Over some of these variables you have control. You cannot control the intelligence level of your audience, unless you preselect your auditors. Nor can you easily control your listeners' verbal ability. But you can, for example, speak to auditors when they are not exhausted and when their attention span (and hence their ability to listen) is still adequate. You can also control your rate of speaking. While a speed of 135 to 175 words per minute is average for most speeches, there is no set rate at which a speech should be presented. Such factors as message content, length of speech, and size of the audience make a difference in the rate at which you should speak. In general, the more technical the material and the less familiar it is to your audience, the slower you must go. Similarly, while a rapid rate of delivery may be appropriate in a short message, as a message increases in length, not only must you reduce the average speed, but also vary the rate of speaking from one section of your talk to another. Weighing such factors can help you decide on an optimum overall rate of speech, as well as on an optimum rate of speech within sections.

Still other factors affect listening, among them message variables. Research indicates that emotional messages, those that strike a responsive emotional chord in your auditors, tend to be listened to more carefully than nonemotional or coldly rational messages. This does not mean that you should avoid logical presentations or that you must lard your speech with mawkish appeals. But it is a fact of human nature that we tend to pay more attention to stories containing human interest than we do to stories that lack it. Editors, for example, include in newspapers the human-interest sidelights of major stories—the photo of an abandoned doll lying face down in a mud puddle in an Iowa town swept by a tornado, the story of one man's experiences during a *coup d'état*. People are more likely to attend to these stories and photos because they conjure up feelings of a personal nature.

The perceived quality of the material included in a speech also plays a role in determining how carefully people listen. If you use material that your auditors judge to be of high quality, they are more likely to hear you out than if you use material that they evaluate as poor quality. It is important to emphasize that what matters here is not the objective quality of the data you present or the sources you cite, but the way the audience perceives and judges it. This is an important distinction to keep in mind.

In Student Activity Option 6.3, I suggest other areas for study, and provide you with sources to consult in gathering additional information.

Student Activity Option 6.3
Auditors as Individuals

INSTRUCTIONS

What other findings have been reported on the peculiarities of auditors? Research one or both of the following questions and make a report to your classmates.

1. In what ways, if any, do the following variables affect the behavior of individuals in persuasive situations: (a) field dependence/independence? (b) ascendance/submission? (c) internal/external control? (d) self-concept? (Consult your instructor for other personality variables, or examine the literature in persuasion to find more.)

2. What do the research findings indicate about the general personality feature of persuasibility? Does such a feature exist? Can its action be predicted? In what way(s) has research in this area undergone a change in the past 20 years?

SUGGESTED READINGS

Barker, L. (1971) *Listening Behavior*. Englewood Cliffs, New Jersey: Prentice-Hall.

Carment, D., C. Miles, and V. Cervin (1965) "Persuasiveness and Persuasibility as Related to Intelligence and Extraversion," *British Journal of Social and Clinical Psychology*, 4: 1–7.

Devine, T. (1967) "Listening," *Review of Educational Research* (April), 37: 152–58.

Hastorf, A., D. Schneider, and J. Polefka (1970) *Person Perception*. Reading, Massachusetts: Addison-Wesley.

Hovland, C., I. Janis, and H. Kelley (1953) *Communication and Persuasion*. New Haven: Yale University Press.

Janis, I. and P. B. Field (1959) "A Behavioral Assessment of Persuasibility," pp. 21–54 in C. Hovland and I. Janis, eds. *Personality and Persuasibility*. New Haven: Yale University Press.

Karlins, M. and H. Abelson (1970) *Persuasion: How Opinions and Attitudes Are Changed*. New York: Springer Publishing Company. See especially Chapter Five, pp. 83–105.

Keller, P. (1969) "Major Findings in Listening in the Past Ten Years," *Journal of Communication*, 10: 29–38.

Kiesler, C., B. Collins, and N. Miller (1969) *Attitude Change*. New York: John Wiley. See especially the discussion of the effects of ego involvement.

Linton, H. and E. Graham (1959) "Personality Correlates of Persuasibility," pp. 69–101 in C. Hovland and I. Janis, eds. *Personality and Persuasibility*. New Haven: Yale University Press.

McGinnies, E. and L. Rosenbaum (1965) "A Test of the Selective Exposure Hypothesis in Persuasion," *Journal of Social Psychology*, 66: 237–40.

Steiner, I. and H. Johnson (1963) "Authoritarianism and Conformity," *Sociometry*, 26: 21–34.

Wright, J. and O. Harvey (1965) "Attitude Change as a Function of Authoritarianism and Punitiveness," *Journal of Personality and Social Psychology*, 1: 177–81.

HOW DO GROUPS INFLUENCE AUDITORS?

Common sense reveals that auditors respond not only as individuals but also as people subject to group influences. How do group influences affect auditors' responses to persuasive messages?

It is possible to view the problem of group influence from more than one perspective. You may address an audience that possesses a group identity—a campus organization, Elks Club, or civic organization, for example. In cases like these, the group's ideology, history, and shared concerns provide you with important information with which to anticipate auditors' responses to your message.

On the other hand, your audience may be drawn more or less at random; the members may possess nothing in common except an interest in your topic. This sort of situation is very different from that in which an audience has a group identity. Loyalties to extraaudience groups (many of which may be unknown to you) also play a role in affecting your audience's reactions to your talk. Individual audience members may possess social supports for beliefs, attitudes, and intentions not shared by their fellows. (In a sense, your class constitutes such a group, or at least it did early in the semester. Class members likely have been drawn from a variety of disciplines, and a wide range of extraclass groups might be represented.) The more completely you know your audience, the better you are able to anticipate its responses to what you say.

Finally, audience members may be seen as being under the influence of outside reference groups. These are groups of which auditors are not members, yet the groups set a standard or provide a model according to which auditors wish to fashion themselves. The upper class may constitute such a reference group. So too may sports heroes, actresses, and clergy. When you know that audience members are strongly influenced by reference groups, you possess important information with which to anticipate their responses.

Regardless of the type of group involved—membership (inside or outside the audience) or reference—research indicates that groups exert varying degrees of influence on individuals. Several variables determine the direction and extent of this influence. For example, individuals rely on group support in forming or at least in stating opinions. It has also been shown that groups that an individual finds very attractive exert more influence than those groups he or she finds less attractive (Hare, 1962). If a speaker is perceived as outside a group that is important to auditors, both the speaker and the message stand a greater chance of being rejected (Iwao, 1963). Sampson and Insko (1964) have shown that under specific sets of circumstances, individuals will change their judgments to make them similar to those of a person they like. They will also change their opinions so that they are unlike those of persons whom they dislike. Another basic finding is that the more a person values his or her membership in a group, the greater its influence, and the more resistant a person is to messages arising from outside the group (Charters and Newcomb, 1952). Further, if you have been a member of a group for some time, and if you intend to maintain membership for some time to come, that group will exert more influence over you than one which you have only recently joined or which you intend to leave. Saliency—the extent to which a fact is uppermost in a person's mind—seems to make a difference, too. Although there is disagreement, it appears that groups exert more influence on members when membership is salient. Thus, a group's spirit or a sense of group identity can be used as a lever in persuasion.

AUDIENCE COMPOSITION: FACTORS AFFECTING
AUDIENCE RESPONSES

In an interesting book on audience analysis, Clevenger (1966) mentions several factors—the degree of homogeneity among them—that affect the direction and extent of an audience's influence on its members. You should bear in mind several questions: Is the audience made up of only one group, or are there subgroups divided along ethnic, socioeconomic, political, or other lines? Do you wish to reach all of the audience? Would you be content to persuade only a segment of the audience? What is your target group? Why have you selected them? Some speakers characteristically aim their addresses at the opinion-shapers in their audience, for such people can exert influence that goes far beyond the impact of any one speech.

What is the extent of group feeling in the audience? Do the auditors see themselves as sharing membership in a highly valued group? Does the audience share some common concern? Is its attention focused on one or on a few subjects? If, for instance, a recent tragedy has alerted auditors to some lurking danger in their community, they will be united in their concern to eliminate the problem. If they share no common concerns, it may well be your job to create concern and thereby to motivate your hearers to act.

Clevenger mentions another factor affecting audience influence on its members that he calls polarity, by which he means the extent to which a speaker is seen as occupying a position or role that is complementary to or opposite the audience's own. A high degree of negative polarity in audience perceptions of the speaker can compound the persuasive problem, for it is well known that a speaker espousing ideas that flatly contradict an audience's prior position is very likely to fail. One major task of the persuader in such a situation is to seek out and talk about areas of common ground with the listeners. Only when the speaker succeeds in building those mutual bridges can he or she fruitfully begin the process of persuasion.

Student Activity Option 6.4 ——————————————
The Audience as a Group

INSTRUCTIONS
Included in this exercise are several questions dealing with how to gauge and influence group factors that may operate in persuasive communication situations. Answer the questions and, with the consent of your instructor, hold a class discussion during which you share your answers with your classmates. Several representative readings follow the questions.

1. Conduct a survey in your class to see how many groups are represented. How important do your classmates consider their membership in these groups? How has their membership affected their responses to speeches they have heard?

2. Answer each of the following questions regarding group variables:
Audience homogeneity
  a. How can the extent of group homogeneity be gauged?
  b. Under what circumstances might a speaker want to address a subgroup in an audience? When would he or she not want to?
Group feeling
  a. How can a speaker manipulate the degree of group feeling among the members of an audience?
  b. Under what circumstances is group feeling likely to be heightened? minimized?
Reference groups
  a. How can reference groups be used as a lever in persuasion?

3. Have you ever seen an audience change its attitude toward a speaker during a talk? Perhaps a friendly audience grew hostile, or vice versa. Perhaps an attentive audience grew restless, or an inattentive one became increasingly fascinated. What factors account for the shift? How can your insight into the situation help you and your classmates in planning and presenting persuasive messages?

SUGGESTED READINGS
Allport, F. (1962) "A Structuromatic Comception of Behavior, Individual and Collective: I. Structural Theory and the Master Problem of Social Psychology," *Journal of Abnormal and Social Psychology*, 64: 3–30.
Asch, S. (1952) *Social Psychology*. Englewood Cliffs, New Jersey: Prentice-Hall.
Bem, P., M. Wallach, and N. Kogan (1965) "Group Decision-Making Under Risk of Aversive Consequences," *Journal of Personality and Social Psychology*. 1: 453–60.
Berne, Eric (1963) *The Structure and Dynamics of Organizations and Groups*. New York: Grove Press.
Brager, G. and S. Holloway (1978) *Changing Human Service Organizations: Politics and Practice*. New York: The Free Press, a Division of Macmillan Publishing Company, Inc.
Charters, W. and T. Newcomb (1958) "Some Attitudinal Effects of Experimentally Increased Saliency of a Membership Group," in E. Maccoby, T. Newcomb, and E. Hartley, eds. *Readings in Social Psychology*. New York: Holt, Rinehart, and Winston.
Cronkhite, G. (1969) *Persuasion: Speech and Behavioral Change*. Indianapolis: Bobbs-Merrill. See especially Chapter Seven, pp. 129–71.

Crutchfield, R. (1955) "Conformity and Character," *American Psychologist,* 10: 191–98.
Gerard, H. and G. Rotter (1961) "Time Perspective, Consistency of Attitude and Social Influence," *Journal of Abnormal and Social Psychology,* 62: 565–72.
Hare, A. (1962) *Handbook of Small Group Research.* New York: The Free Press, a Division of Macmillan Publishing Company, Inc.
Iwao, S. (1963) "Internal vs. External Criticism of Group Standards," *Sociometry,* 26: 419.
Sampson, E. and C. Insko (1964) "Cognitive Consistency and Performance in the Autokinetic Situation," *Journal of Abnormal and Social Psychology,* 58: 184–92.
Wallach, M. and N. Kogan. (1959) "Sex Difference and Judgement Processes," *Journal of Personality,* 27: 555–64.
——— (1961) "Aspects of Judgement and Decision-Making: Interrelationships and Changes with Age," *Behavioral Science,* 6: 23–36.
——— (1965) "The Roles of Information, Discussion, and Consensus in Group Risk-Taking," *Journal of Experimental Social Psychology,* 1: 1–19.
——— and D. Bem (1962) "Group Influence on Individual Risk-Taking," *Journal of Abnormal and Social Psychology,* 65: 75–86.
Wyer, R. (1966) "Effects of Incentive to Perform Well, Group Attraction and Group Acceptance on Conformity in Judgemental Task," *Journal of Personality and Social Psychology,* 4: 21–26.
Zeff, L. and M. Iverson (1966) "Opinion Conformity in Group Under Status Threat," *Journal of Personality and Social Psychology,* 3: 383–89.

PURPOSES SERVED BY AUDIENCE ANALYSIS

Now that you know some of the ways individual and group factors may affect audience reactions to your persuasive speech, we can turn to the specific ways in which an understanding of your audience may be useful. In general, four crucial purposes are served by an analysis of your audience: It can help you choose a topic (when this is necessary), formulate your goal(s), determine proof requirements, and both assess and evaluate available resources.

1. *Choosing a topic*

In the vast majority of situations outside the classroom, the topic about which you speak will be determined by the circumstances, your expertise, the needs of the audience, or all three. For example, if you were an expert on hang gliding and you were invited to address a group of beginning gliders, your general topic would clearly be dictated by circumstances. There would be a degree of freedom, of course; you might talk about basic flying techniques, safety considerations, equipment checks, or other subjects of interest to beginners. Nevertheless, your subject would largely have been chosen for you.

In those cases where your subject is not decided by circumstances, however, a knowledge of your audience can help you determine what you will talk about. In deciding, you might ask yourself such questions as these: What might be of interest to this particular audience? Given my background and expertise, about what subject might I talk most meaningfully to this particular audience? Or again, given the occasion upon which I am being asked to address this group, and given the group's makeup and ideology, what subject might go over best? By answering such questions, and by checking your answers with some representative members of the planned audience, you can arrive at a decision about your topic.

2. *Formulating goals*

When I talk about formulating a goal for your persuasive speech, I am discussing the effect you intend to achieve. Effective persuaders have their goals clearly in mind. They know what they wish to achieve and they work consciously toward that end. But it is important to recognize that persuasive messages often spark unintended effects. For example, a politician who faults the government for waste may intend to generate concern among the constituency. Without meaning to, however, the speaker may also turn people away from government, and perhaps even erode his or her support. Thus, while this section focuses on intended effects, it is important that you anticipate unintended effects as well. To the extent that it is possible, efforts must be made to minimize undesirable unintended effects.

In choosing your goals for persuasion, several factors must be borne in mind. The first factor is your audience's state of information. It is generally believed that the less auditors know about your subject, the more time must be spent informing them, and the less time is available for directly persuasive efforts. To a degree, this is true; when your audience requires background, you must certainly provide it. But it should also be remembered that you may inform audience members in such a way as to predispose them to accept your position. For example, in telling your audience about the dangers associated with chemical waste dumps in large urban centers, it is also possible to "inform" the members about the kinds of chemicals stored there by providing a descriptive account of the uses and dangers of each. The effective persuader overlooks no opportunity.

A second factor to be borne in mind in choosing your goal is the audience's overall position regarding your subject. Do the auditors support what you are proposing? Do they oppose it? How strongly? To what degree are they involved in the positions they hold? What sort of commitments have they made to their present position? What is their motivation in maintaining their present position? In considering questions like these, you can arrive at a realistic estimate of the strength as well as of the kinds of opposition you are likely to encounter.

A third factor influencing your choice of goal is the number of times you will speak before this audience. If you will speak to the members only once, and if their overall position is very different from the one you are arguing, then it is unlikely that you can reasonably expect to achieve an ambitious goal. Because you will need to spend a considerable amount of time laying the groundwork for a persuasive appeal, it is unlikely that much time will be left to make significant inroads into your audience's psychological set.

On the other hand, if this appearance is only one of many, you can pursue an incremental approach to persuasion, changing your audience's set a little at a time. Research has shown that a message delivered by a high-credibility speaker has a residual effect on an audience over a time (Hovland and Weiss, 1951). In the literature this is called a "sleeper effect." Timing your speeches so as to make use of this sleeper effect can do much to increase the likelihood of success of an incremental approach to persuasion.

Goals may be stated and conceptualized in a number of ways. Most speakers find that the purpose of a talk is best phrased as a specific response sought from the audience. Thus, in planning, they might ask themselves; "Given this audience's state of information, beliefs, attitudes, and such, what can the auditors reasonably be expected to do or to believe by the time my speech is done?" The answer to such a question is seen as a specific response sought from your audience. Success is measurable by considering the extent to which the desired goal is attained (see Chapter Three).

The conceptualization of goals sought may also vary. If you were to use the scheme offered by Fishbein and Ajzen, you might conceive of your goals as changes in (1) belief content, (2) belief strength, (3) attitudes or evaluations, (4) intention content, (5) intention strength, or (6) behavior. Each of these changes is clearly different; each requires different strategies and techniques.

Simmons offers an alternative scheme (1976, pp. 99–100). He lists three broad categories of goals, the first of which he calls hostility reduction. (This might more accurately be called opposition-reduction, since not all opposition coincides with hostility.) Objectives in this category include reducing overt opposition (making an openly hostile audience less hostile) and reducing private opposition (that is, instilling doubts or uncertainty in the minds of opponents). The second category he calls conversion goals, which means not only converting opponents, but bringing over to your side those who are either uninformed, apathetic, or genuinely undecided. The third set of goals he labels intensification. For example, a speaker might choose to reinforce favorable beliefs, attitudes, or intentions. The speaker might seek to make a private commitment public, as when a preacher asks the believers in the congregation to come forward and accept Christ. The speech maker might increase behavioral commitments (for example, he or she might urge a group of committed citizens to work harder in their efforts to secure passage of a given bill) or simply reinforce already existing commitments and thus prevent backsliding.

Regardless of how goals are arrived at, conceptualized, or formulated, it is critically important that you learn to choose realistic ones. Given your audience's initial position, its state of information, and its attitudes (toward you and toward the information you are to present), what can you realistically hope to accomplish? Given the audience's latitudes of acceptance, rejection, and noncommitment, what goals can you hope to attain? Unless you answer such questions honestly, you run the risk of setting overly ambitious and unattainable objectives.

3. Determining proof requirements

A critically important purpose of audience analysis is to help you determine what inducements you must offer to bring the audience around to your way of thinking. These necessary inducements I call proof requirements. To determine inducements, you must have an appreciation of the components that make up your audience's internal set.

To illustrate how to determine proof requirements, I will make use of the Toulmin scheme (see Chapter 2), for it is especially useful and consistent with the Fishbein and Ajzen scheme on which I will rely here.

Suppose you are an opponent of nuclear power, and you are asked to speak at an energy-awareness conference sponsored by a college. Your audience consists of middle-class, reasonably well-educated people. Most are parents; most own their own homes. They have come to the conference because they feel a need to know more about the energy crisis and how to respond to it. You may infer that, like most people, they are neither strongly opposed to nor strongly in favor of nuclear power. They are most likely to be mildly in favor of nuclear power since it seems to represent an inexpensive, renewable source of energy.

You recognize that the gap between your position and theirs is substantial, and that you will almost certainly encounter resistance as you set out to transform this group of neutrals into active opponents of nuclear power. The resistance is likely to be less strong than it would be if you were addressing a group of proponents of nuclear power; nevertheless, it will be substantial. Your next step, therefore, is to determine the origins and components of your audience's resistance to change.

The best way to determine their components of resistance is to think thoroughly but not rigidly about the ideas, unsupported beliefs, or untested judgments that make up your audience's cognitive set. In this case, you might bear in mind that your audience consists of enlightened contemporaries who have faith—or who want to have faith—in technology. They are also likely to have heard the reassurances of the Nuclear Regulatory Commission and government officials and are inclined to believe them, for the auditors are inexpert and feel they can only trust persons who are in a more informed position.

The audience also has heard about nuclear accidents, however, the Three Mile Island incident chief among them. And the auditors may have encountered the testimony of informed persons who have come out strongly against nuclear power.

These ruminations might lead you to recognition of several key beliefs that constitute the building blocks of your audience's cognitive set:

- The government wouldn't let nuclear power plants be built if they weren't safe.
- Nuclear power is safe.
- The emissions from nuclear power plants are carefully monitored and maintained at acceptable levels.

- Three Mile Island was not a catastrophe; no serious consequences are yet to be documented.
- Government officials and their assurances can be trusted.
- Alternatives to nuclear power are prohibitively expensive, impractical, and unrealistic.
- Nuclear power accounts for a substantial portion of power generated in the United States.

The decision as to which of these beliefs to undermine is a strategic one. Suppose you wish to attack your audience's belief that nuclear power is safe. You know that in large measure this belief rests on the auditors' trust of government officials who have issued assurances. You feel that this belief is not held with great strength, so that it represents a good point of entry. If you can cause the audience to doubt the credibility of the government officials whose reassurances constitute the basis of the belief, then the structure may begin crumbling. (I am assuming, of course, that you will do more than undermine your audience's faith in official assurances. This example represents only one of several main lines of argument you might advance in your speech.)

Schematically, your audience's line of thought looks like this:

(**Data**) Government officials have ———— (**Claim**) Nuclear power
    assured me that nuclear   is safe.
    power is safe.

(**Warrant**) Government officials' assurances
are worthy of my belief.

Seeing your audience's line of thought schematically opens up several possibilities. One possibility is to challenge the warrant by citing instances in which government officials (perhaps the very officials now offering assurances) were guilty of misleading the public, covering up facts, or offering reassurances prematurely, out of ignorance. The strategy of challenging the warrant directly might work with an audience that is vaguely cynical and distrustful of government. But with a middle-aged, suburban audience of loyal and likely conservative Americans who have been conditioned to trust, this strategy might backfire.

Another option is less directly confrontive. You could grant the trustworthiness of the officials in question but introduce rebuttal material that detailed circumstances under which official assurances might not be trustworthy, for reasons having nothing to do with the honesty or good will of the officials. For example, you might offer as rebuttal the contention (which you would need to support) that nuclear power and its long-range effects are so little understood that official assurances ought properly to be questioned or ought not to be accepted blindly. Thus:

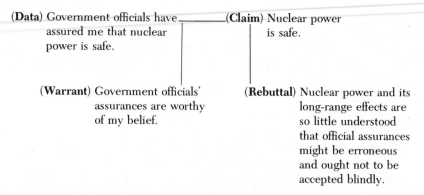

(**Data**) Government officials have assured me that nuclear power is safe.

(**Claim**) Nuclear power is safe.

(**Warrant**) Government officials' assurances are worthy of my belief.

(**Rebuttal**) Nuclear power and its long-range effects are so little understood that official assurances might be erroneous and ought not to be accepted blindly.

The effect of the rebuttal is to create dissonance, to unsettle the closed system that allows the audience to be comfortable in its acceptance of official assurances. Once dissonance is created, the audience would react in predictable ways. The auditors might reject you as untrustworthy and not credible; they might denigrate the evidence you cite; they might accept the information you offer but downplay its significance. Their range of options is large, but it is finite. It is now your task to anticipate their responses and to plan strategically for them in order to increase the likelihood of your success.

4. *Selecting supporting material*

Once you have sketched out your arguments and those of your audience—in other words, once you've determined proof requirements—you should have a fairly clear idea of what you must establish. Your next task is to gather and select supporting material. As a student in this class, you already know the mechanical procedures of how to gather supporting materials and how to measure their logical adequacy. Therefore, I will go on to present several important findings on the use of evidence and on the manner in which appropriate source material can be selected.

Research has established that information alone does not change attitudes (Haskins, 1966). While evidence is useful, the inclusion of good (i.e., logically appropriate) evidence bears no necessary positive correlation to audience attitude change. McCrosky's summary (1969) of the experimental findings on evidence indicates that three principal variables influence the impact of evidence: (1) the initial credibility of the source (if the source is initially perceived as being highly credible, the inclusion of good evidence has little if any impact on immediate audience attitude change), (2) message delivery (if the message is delivered poorly, the inclusion of good evidence has little if any impact on immediate audience attitude change), and (3) familiarity with the evidence (if the audience is familiar with the evidence, it has little if any immediate impact on audience attitude change).

None of these findings indicates that evidence is useless or that it should not be used. Hence, the question of selecting the best material still remains.

Once you have a variety of supporting materials at your disposal, therefore, upon what basis do you choose between one item and another? Freely (1976) has formulated a set of questions for testing the audience acceptability of evidence. Note that these questions have nothing to do with the logical adequacy of evidence, only with its acceptability to a particular audience.

Here are Freely's questions:

1. *Is the evidence consistent with the beliefs of the audience?* The more consistent the evidence, the more likely it is to win uncritical acceptance. Note that evidence may be consistent with one set of beliefs while being inconsistent with another. For example, your audience might believe that official assurances are only good when the subject is well understood by the person offering the assurance. Hence, if you were to cite evidence establishing the fact that nuclear power and its effects are little understood, your evidence would be consistent with one audience belief ("official assurances are only good when the subject is well understood") but inconsistent with another ("official assurances are worthy of my belief").

Freely recognizes that it is not always possible to avoid citing evidence that is inconsistent with important audience beliefs. However, when evidence is inconsistent, it is essential that the persuader anticipate audience resistance and counter it. This tactic may require acknowledging the distastefulness of the evidence while establishing both its noncontestability and such features as the objectivity and competence of the source.

2. *Is the source of evidence acceptable to the audience?* Uncritical acceptance is often given to evidence drawn from a source perceived by your audience as highly credible or prestigious. Conditional acceptance is given when the source cited is without special prestige or credibility in the mind of the audience. If evidence is drawn from a source regarded as not credible or of low prestige, it is likely to be rejected regardless of its intrinsic merits. To the extent that you are able, therefore, it is advisable to cite only sources likely to be regarded highly by your audience. When you cannot do so, it is essential that you enhance the prestige, credibility, and trustworthiness of the sources you do cite.

3. *Is the evidence suited to the level of the audience?* The more the evidence is beyond your audience, the less impact it is likely to have. The evidence may even backfire if, for example, audience members feel you are trying to confuse or mislead them with an impressive array of apparent gobbledygook. An awareness of your audience's level of expertness and sophistication can help you determine which evidence is too technical or beyond its understanding. Since it is sometimes necessary to rely on highly technical data, it is advisable to pay special attention to making the information understandable. You are already aware of the tools used for making data accessible: Various forms of definition, comparison and contrast, analogy, and well-conceived visual aids are but a few of the devices you have studied in a more basic communications course.

4. *Is the evidence consistent with the motives and attitudes of the audi-*

ence? The more the evidence is consistent, the greater the likelihood of its having a positive impact. The less it is consistent, the greater the likelihood of its encountering resistance and possibly sparking a boomerang effect. If you know, for example, that your auditors consider the health and safety of their offspring as vitally important, then evidence you cite that ties opposition to nuclear power to the safety and health issue is likely to win acceptance, provided that it meets the criteria set down in the preceding paragraphs.

(5.) *Is the evidence documented for the audience?* The more verifiable the evidence cited, the more likely it is to win acceptance and to induce change. Vague and indefinite references ("I read somewhere that . . .") work against a persuader. Fleshler, Ilardo, and Demoretcky (1974) found in one study that "message documentation was the primary variable that determined evaluations of message and speaker [other variables included credibility-manipulating introductions afforded speakers and certain audience personality traits]. Concrete message documentation resulted in significantly more positive evaluations of the message and the speaker." (Note that positive evaluations of the message and the speaker technically constitute intervening variables in the persuasive process.)

In Student Activity Option 6.5, you are invited to use your knowledge of audience analysis in a number of hypothetical situations.

Student Activity Option 6.5
Planning for Persuasion

INSTRUCTIONS
In each of the following situations, you are asked to make a variety of strategic choices. Indicate which ones you would make and why. If time and your instructor permit, discuss your answers with your classmates.

1. What special problems might you encounter in each of the following cases? How would you deal with them?
   a. You must convince a group of fundamentalist, conservative clergy that First Amendment rights must be safeguarded. Your source? *Playboy.*
   b. You must demonstrate before a traffic court that you are not guilty of having committed the traffic violation for which you are to be fined. Your evidence? The testimony of your girlfriend or boyfriend, who was in your car with you at the time.
   c. You must demonstrate the need for a national health-care program before a group of conservative Republicans. The source of your data? *The New York Times.*
   d. You must convince a group of Catholic women, predominantly young mothers, of the undesirability of prayer in the public schools. Your sources? Supreme Court rulings and the writings of Madelyn Murray O'Hare.
   e. You must convince a group of scientists that the God theory of creation

should be taught alongside the theory of evolution in the schools. Your sources? Opinions of fundamentalist religious organizations and of conservative boards of education.

2. As a speaker at an energy-awareness conference sponsored by a college, you must convert a group of middle-class parents and homeowners into active opponents of nuclear power. Following are several lines of thought, outlined according to the Toulmin model. Discuss how you might go about changing your audience's way of thinking. Note that in each case, several alternatives are available. First, list them; then discuss which alternatives you would choose and why; then discuss the way you would proceed from that point.

a. (Data) The government wouldn't let _____**(Claim)** Nuclear power is safe.
nuclear power plants be
built if they weren't safe.

        (Warrant) The government places safety considerations above
                pragmatic ones.

What options are open to you?

Which would you choose and why?

How would you undermine the claim? What logical and nonlogical inducements would you include? What special considerations would you make in planning your strategy?

b. (Data) The Nuclear Regulatory   _____**(Claim)** Emissions from nuclear
        Commission assures me that   plants are carefully
        emissions from nuclear   monitored and main-
        plants are carefully   tained at acceptable
        monitored and maintained   levels.
        at acceptable levels.

        (Warrant) Nuclear Regulatory Commission assurances are worthy
                of belief.

What options are open to you?

Which would you choose and why?

How would you undermine the claim? What logical and nonlogical inducements would you include? What special considerations would you make in planning your strategy?

c. **(Data)** I know of no serious conse-⎯⎯ **(Claim)** No serious consequences
quences of the Three Mile   of the Three Mile Island
Island accident that have   accident have been
been documented.   documented.

     (Warrant) If there were serious consequences of the Three Mile
     Island accident, they would be documented and I would
     know about them.

What options are open to you?

Which would you choose and why?

How would you undermine the claim? What logical and nonlogical inducements would you include? What special considerations would you make in planning your strategy?

3. Since World War II, the Soviet Union has set out to destroy the last remnants of Latvian culture. This situation concerns you greatly, since, as a person of Latvian descent, you know the rich heritage that will be destroyed if the Soviets are allowed to continue on their present course. You are to give a speech on Soviet destruction of Latvian culture to a group of classmates at your college. They know little about Latvian culture or heritage and they tend to be somewhat apathetic, especially about issues that seem so far away and about which they feel so powerless.
What goal would you set for yourself in addressing this audience? (Assume you will speak to them only once.)
Why would you choose that goal?
To what extent would you aim your speech at changing the audience's state of information? beliefs? attitudes? intentions? behavior?
How might you overcome the passive resistance generated by apathy and inertia? (List at least three tactics you might use and explain why you would choose them.)

4. You wish to convince your classmates to major in the field in which you are majoring.
List three beliefs your audience likely holds about your field. Give reasons why your audience might hold these beliefs.
How might these beliefs affect auditors' attitudes toward your field?
Which, if any, of their beliefs or attitudes would you want to change?
How would you go about changing a belief or an attitude? More specifically, what goal would you set for yourself? Why? How would you go about achieving that goal?

SUGGESTED READINGS

Fleshler, H., J. Ilardo, and J. Demoretcky (1974) "The Influence of Field Dependence, Speaker Credibility Set, and Message Documentation on Evaluations of Speaker and Message Credibility," *The Southern Speech Communication Journal*, 39 (Summer), 389–402.

Freely, A. (1976) *Argumentation and Debate: Rational Decision-Making,* 4th ed. Belmont, California: Wadsworth Publishing Company, Inc.

Haskins, J. (1966) "Factual Recall as a Measure of Advertising Effectiveness," *Journal of Advertising Research,* 6: 2–8.

Hovland, C. and W. Weiss (1951) "The Influence of Source Credibility on Communication Effectiveness," *Public Opinion Quarterly,* 15: 635–50.

Kelman, H. and C. Hovland (1953) " 'Restatement' of the Communicator in Delayed Measurement of Opinion Change," *Journal of Abnormal and Social Psychology,* 48: 327–35.

McCrosky, J. (1969) "A Summary of Experimental Findings on the Effects of Evidence in Persuasive Communication," *Quarterly Journal of Speech,* 60 (April), 169–76.

Simmons, H. (1976) *Persuasion: Understanding, Practice, and Analysis.* Reading, Massachusetts: Addison-Wesley Publishing Company.

Watts, W. and W. McGuire (1964) "Persistence of Induced Opinion Change and Retention of the Induced Message Contents," *Journal of Abnormal and Social Psychology,* 68: 233–41.

III. *Presentation Strategies*

Once your audience analysis is completed and you have at your disposal well-chosen material with which to induce persuasion, your next task is to give conscious, deliberate thought to how to present your material. This consideration requires a knowledge of the presentation options open to you as a persuader and of the likely consequences of selecting each one.

In discussing the three topics of attention, language, and organization, my aim is to familiarize you with representative research findings and to show you how research and theory can be useful in planning presentation strategy. My discussion is not intended to be exhaustive, and I urge you to form the habit of consulting recent periodicals in order to be up-to-date on the results of current research, and applying these findings to your persuasive efforts.

ATTENTION

A knowledge of what is involved in the processes of giving and withholding attention can help you learn how to secure the attention of your audience. You may recall that James A. Winans (Chapter 2) contended that "persuasion is the process of inducing others to give fair, favorable, or undivided attention to propositions." Reinforcement theory includes attention as a key component in the persuasion process, together with comprehension, acceptance, and retention (see Chapter Five). Knowledge of the dynamics of attention is therefore a basic tool for the persuasive speaker.

Attention is a process of selecting and focusing. At any given moment, you are bombarded by a host of stimuli, both external and internal. As you read this page, you may find yourself distracted by the sound of music next door or by voices outside. You may feel vaguely overheated, or your stomach may twinge occasionally as a Big Mac makes its way into your bloodstream. But if you are truly attending to what you are reading, then out of the many stimuli upon which you could choose to focus, you are concentrating on the words on this page. Upon what basis do you attend? To begin answering the question, complete Student Activity Option 6.6.

Student Activity Option 6.6
Stereophonic Speaking

INSTRUCTIONS
For this activity, your instructor should choose two volunteers from the class who are each given a topic for a two-minute impromptu speech. (Each student should have one minute to prepare the talk.) At the proper time, both speakers are to walk to the front of the room, position themselves on opposite sides, and present their speeches simultaneously. After the speeches, you are to complete the following questions and then discuss your answers with your classmates.

1. Which speaker did you listen to? Why? (Did your giving of attention depend on the subject of the speech? the delivery?)

2. Did you attend to only one speaker, or did your attention shift from one to the other?

3. Was there a pattern in your shifting of attention?

As Student Activity Option 6.6 demonstrated, the giving and withholding of attention is a function of identifiable factors both in the stimulus and in the receiver. Moreover, careful introspection will confirm what one set of theorists contends—that at any moment, an individual is likely to focus on certain stimuli, to be dimly aware of others, and to be unaware of still others (Morgan and King, 1971). Put another way, attention can be said to exist on a continuum, with stimuli in focus on one end, stimuli to which no attention is paid on the other, and stimuli of which we are only dimly aware between the two. The continuum is constantly undergoing change, so that at times our attention span is sharply narrowed and at other times it is broadly attuned. Stimuli of which we may be unaware at one moment may intrude themselves upon us at another.

There are degrees of conscious attentiveness; however, our unconscious minds attend to everything. During a deep, hypnotically induced regression, it would even be possible for you to remember the furnishings in your nursery. It is thus only our conscious mind that focuses. This fact leads to interesting insights for you as a persuader: You should keep in mind that you are always conveying messages through indirect suggestion—by the way you look, the clothes you wear, the sound of your voice, and so on. Such cues, while seemingly not attended to consciously, do affect an audience's perception of you, and they do color audience responses. It is one thing to say to your audience explicitly, "I am a person who is meticulously attentive to detail." Such an explicit statement might seem self-inflating and provoke unfriendly responses. However, if the statement is made silently, not by anything you say but by the way you look or by the precise manner of your expression, the message will be conveyed without risking an undesirable audience response.

One psychologist (Mehrabian, 1968), considering this phenomenon, has speculated that much is communicated without words. If the total impact of an interaction equaled 100 per cent, says Mehrabian, then 38 per cent of that impact would be attributable to how the message is conveyed (the words used, for example); 55 per cent would be attributable to how a speaker looks while conveying the message; and only 7 per cent would be due to what was actually said, the content of the message. While Mehrabian's guestimates are hardly exact science, they do reflect widespread scientific opinion that listeners, without being consciously aware of it, attend to nonverbal messages. Because of the importance of nonverbal communication in persuasive speaking, I urge you to try to be aware of the messages you convey nonverbally.

Broadbent (1957) has offered an interesting mechanical model of attention that captures important truths about the processes by which conscious attention is given or withheld. This model is depicted in Figure 6.4.

The two branches of the Y represent channels through which input—for example, eyes, ears, or olfactory sense—enters the processing system. In Broadbent's model, small metal balls representing sensory input are dropped into the branches of the Y. To influence behavior, input must enter the central channel, the straight stem of the Y. A hinged flap at the entrance to the central channel can swing freely, but it can only admit one ball from one channel at a time. If two balls reach the hinged flap at precisely the same moment, the flap will jam and neither will enter the straight stem of the Y.

Using this model, it is possible in very simplified fashion to consider situations perceivers encounter frequently, and to begin predicting the action of variables involved in attending. For example, if two competing stimuli of equal strength simultaneously enter the system, and if neither one is of more interest than the other, both will be blocked. This is the situation that may have occurred when you completed Student Activity Option 6.6. If both speakers spoke equally loudly, if each was the same distance from you, and if their subjects were of equal interest, you probably focused on neither one. But if one speaker was closer to you, or spoke more loudly, or if the subject of the speech was of more interest to you, then your attention was probably

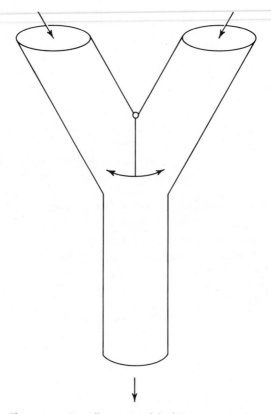

Figure 6.4. Broadbent's Model of Human Attention

drawn that way. Note that the strength of the stimulus depends not only on its own characteristics (loudness, for instance), but on the predispositions of the listener (interests, needs, and biases).

Not only can the weight of the ball vary (a heavier ball—representing a stimulus of greater strength—would push the hinged flap aside, even if a lighter one were to reach the flap at the same instant), but the flap can be set open to one side and closed to the other, thus ensuring the input of some data at the exclusion of other data. Similarly, when a listener is predisposed or "primed" for a certain message, he or she receives certain data to the exclusion of other data.

Broadbent's model suggests, too, that the timing of the two messages can be varied. A slight delay in input can give one stimulus the advantage, while still allowing both to enter. In the stereophonic speaking exercise, you may have attended to the speaker who began first, only to give your attention to your other classmate when some internal factor or some quality of the stimulus drew you away.

Broadbent's model is hardly rigorous science, but it can help you remember that attention is a process of selecting and focusing. It can also remind you to be aware of the major variables—both in the stimulus and in the receiver—that influence the giving and withholding of attention.

Here I want to discuss the more important factors of external and internal factors affecting attention, and to show their application to persuasive speaking.

External factors

External factors—intensity, contrast, novelty, and variety—are characteristics of the stimulus. *Intensity* refers to the strength of the stimulus. In your speeches, intensity refers not only to loudness, but to the potential impact of what you say. Vivid, concrete, and colorful language has more intensity than bland, abstract language. Thus, the speaker who talks about a *sports car* is likely to have less impact than one who talks about a *candy-apple-red Datsun 280Z with mag wheels and pinstriping.*

Contrast implies difference. In a neutral perceptual field, attention will be drawn to what stands out. A one-inch-diameter black circle in the middle of a stark white 3'x5' canvas will attract attention. A single star in a black night sky or a shriek on a silent street corner stand out against the field in which it occurs. In your speeches, you can utilize contrast both in your delivery and in your content. You can vary the loudness of your talk as well as its rate and pitch. You can make use of silence as a contrasting device.

A good example of the use of contrast in speech content occurred in a student speech on the use of defoliant by a major utility to clear the way for construction of power lines. It was a powerful defoliant, the same kind used during the Vietnam war to clear acres of jungle. In themselves, the facts this student gathered were not terribly exciting, since such defoliants are characteristically used to clear away brush and trees in developing sections of the country. But the speech was constructed in such a way as to create tremendous audience concern. The student used the method of contrast, the same sort of technique used by a film maker who opens a film by juxtaposing two scenes that seem to have no relationship to each other. The film is edited so that the viewer sees perhaps thirty seconds of one scene before the setting shifts abruptly and unexpectedly, and a seemingly unrelated series of events unfolds. After a few minutes of juxtaposition, the two apparently unrelated scenes are brought together. My student began the speech by describing the takeoff of a B-52 bomber from an air base in South Vietnam. We followed the pilot up into the blue, then abruptly the scene shifted to a suburban community not far from the college where the speech was being given. We were taken on a walk through the attractive countryside. Then suddenly we were back in the cockpit of the jet as the pilot prepared to drop his payload. As he was about to press the little red button, we returned to the nearby suburb and watched a young family preparing for a picnic. The scenes shifted back and forth like this until eventually the speaker drew them together. He had so effectively drawn the mental picture that the thought of using a wartime defoliant on the beautiful nearby countryside seemed horrible. Having aroused powerful emotions in his audience, he continued with his appeal. The speech was exceptionally effective; its effectiveness was largely determined not by the facts offered by the speaker but by his use of contrast in presenting them.

Novelty is a third factor affecting attention. The wise speaker makes use of the unexpected and the unfamiliar. A fresh perspective can often draw audience attention. Original examples, fresh statistics, humor, original visual aids, audience participation, and live demonstration are but a few of the ways you can utilize the novel to gain and hold your audience's attention.

Variety is also a central factor in gaining and holding attention. It has been said that the function of the artist is to make us see old, familiar things as though we were seeing them for the first time. There is an important principle in this concept: That which is familiar and unvarying tends to fade from consciousness. Thus, the sound of the wheels of your car driving over evenly spaced tar strips along a highway tends to disappear from attention. We are likely to become aware only when a regular and unvarying stimulus ceases to appear in the regular way.

To apply the knowledge of the importance of variety in persuasive speaking, you can vary the pacing of your speech, going more quickly at some points and slower at others. You can vary pitch, volume, and other vocal and speech qualities. You can make use of slides, visuals, and audiotape— anything that will serve to break up the monotony of the unchanging.

I often advise my students to vary their forms of support in order to avoid monotony. A good mix of statistics, testimonials, anecdotes, comparisons, and examples is more likely to hold your audience's attention than an unending sequence of any one form of support.

An additional, important, but often overlooked way of building variety into your speeches is to ensure that your talk builds to the climaxes as you go along. An interesting speech is characterized by "hills and valleys." There are points at which emotions should be aroused and excitement levels high. At other points, an audience must be able to catch its breath, to take a mental break in order to regroup and begin building again toward another climax. In an effective speech, the audience is quite clearly under the control of the speaker. The auditors are led gradually along, through a variety of hills and valleys, to the climax of the speech.

A fourth source of variety in a speech is the language used. In a really excellent speech, sentence length and structure vary a great deal. For dramatic effect, the speaker may use short, pithy utterances—for example, "Germany. 1936. A small beer hall in Munich." The staccato effect of such a style can serve to gain and hold attention. So, too, can the juxtaposition of formal and informal language, the use of direct dialogue, and the use of questions.

Internal factors

Internal factors affecting attention are tied to the inner state of the attending individual. They include constant factors such as sex (Mazanec and Mc-Call, 1976), relatively constant factors such as character traits (Berelson and Steiner, 1964), and changing factors such as needs, interests, and expectancy set, or readiness to respond (Berelson and Steiner, 1964). The more your speech meets the current concerns, needs, interests, and expectancy sets of your audience, the more likely it is to give voluntary attention. When your auditors are only potentially interested in your topic, it may be necessary to create the expectancy set you desire and to generate the interest you require. This is done exceptionally well in the following student speech:

> "I've had glasses thrown at me. I have been kicked in the abdomen when I was visibly pregnant. I have been kicked off the bed and hit while lying on the floor—again while I was pregnant. I have been whipped, kicked, and thrown, picked up again and thrown down again. I have been punched and kicked in the head, chest, face, and abdomen more times than I can count."
>
> And I'm very lucky. Because these aren't my own words, but instead the words of Helen Montgomery. Hers is a cry that may seem dramatic and far removed from the real world, but instead is echoed every day by 28 million American women who are victims of the least reported crime in the United States—wife beating.
>
> Helen Montgomery is not an exception; for, as the FBI crime reports estimate, at some time in their marriage, one out of every five women will be beaten by her husband. Could this happen to your best friend, your sister, mother, or even you?
>
> Your immediate response is probably "Never." For as Del Martin, author of the book *Battered Wives*, suggests, the average woman feels that she cannot discuss her problem with anyone—she is too embarrassed and humiliated. So perhaps the question to ask is not "Can it happen to someone you know?" but instead, "Has it already?"*

By making her listeners aware that the problem of wife abuse is not distant but one that deserves their immediate attention, this student succeeds in generating interest and in manipulating internal factors that account for the granting of attention.

An expectancy set, or readiness to respond, can be created by setting up your audience deliberately. For example, by sketching a problem at the beginning of a speech and by demonstrating its importance and seriousness, a speaker can create in the hearers a readiness to listen to the proposed solu-

---

*Excerpt from a speech entitled, "Wives, Mothers, and Victims," by Shawn McGee, Ball State University, Indiana, coached by Jacqueline Brown, pp. 13 –16 in Winning Orations of the Interstate Oratorical Association, 1978, Copyright © 1978 by the Interstate Oratorical Association. Used by permission.

tion. In the speech on wife abuse, this is exactly what the speaker does. In the last third of her speech, she offers concrete suggestions for dealing with the problem. But had she not established that a serious and little-recognized problem exists, it is doubtful that her auditors would have been amenable to her suggestions.

More prosaic methods for creating expectancy sets exist as well. A speaker can create a readiness to respond by using verbal pointers; "This is important!" "Now listen!" are examples. By such devices as these, you can cue your audience to important points you wish to convey.

Regardless of the methods you use, it is important to realize that attention is given or withheld both in response to characteristics of the external stimulus and in response to factors internal to your audience. By manipulating each of these so as to generate the desired response, you increase the likelihood of succeeding as a persuader.

Student Activity Option 6.7
Attention

INSTRUCTIONS
Complete one or more of the projects outlined below. With your instructor's consent, report your findings to your classmates.

1. Study a number of different advertisements from radio, television, or print. How is attention secured in each ad? Which of the external factors affecting attention are employed? In what ways are internal factors manipulated? Do you see any relationship between the limitations of the ad (for example, an ad in a magazine does not have the advantages of temporal duration, action, or musical accompaniment that a TV ad might use) and the kinds of attention-getting devices used? What sort of appeals are used with most frequency? Does the type of appeal depend on the kind of product advertised?

2. Discuss the focusing of attention with one or more of the following professionals: an architect, an artist, the chairperson of an organization run by Robert's Rules of Order, a musician, a teacher. Ask in what ways each person uses his or her special skills to ensure that attention is focused in desirable directions.

3. Study a number of photographs of mass gatherings. Determine how the attention of the audience was focused in each situation.

SUGGESTED READINGS
Berelson, B. and G. Steiner (1964) *Human Behavior: An Inventory of Scientific Findings.* New York: Harcourt, Brace & World.

Berscheid, E. and E. Walster (1969) *Interpersonal Attraction.* Reading, Massachusetts: Addison-Wesley Publishing Company, Inc.

Broadbent, D. (1958) *Perception and Communication.* London: Pergamon.

Eisenberg, A. and R. Smith (1969) *Nonverbal Communication.* Indianapolis: Bobbs-Merrill.

Hastorf, A., D. Schneider, and J. Polefka (1970) *Person Perception.* Reading, Massachusetts: Addison-Wesley Publishing Company, Inc.

Mazanec, N. and G. McCall (1976) "Sex Factors and Allocation of Attention in Observing Persons," *Journal of Psychology,* 93: 175–80.

Mehrabian, A. (1968) "Communication Without Words," *Psychology Today* (September), 3.

Mehrabian, A. and M. Williams, (1969) "Non-verbal Cue Concomitants of Perceived and Intended Persuasiveness," *Journal of Personality and Social Psychology,* 13: 37–58.

Minnick, W. (1968) *The Art of Persuasion,* 2nd ed. Boston: Houghton-Mifflin and Company.

Morgan, C. and R. King (1971) *Introduction to Psychology,* 4th ed. New York: McGraw-Hill Book Company.

Schmidt, L. and S. Strong (1971) "Attractiveness and Influence in Counseling," *Journal of Counseling Psychology,* 8: 348–51.

Strong, S. (1968) "Counseling: An Interpersonal Influence Process," *Journal of Counseling Psychology,* 15: 215–24.

Strong, S. and L. Schmidt (1970) "Expertness and Influence in Counseling," *Journal of Counseling Psychology,* 19: 81–87.

LANGUAGE

Relatively little hard research has been done on the impact of language—word choice, style, sentence length, and structure—on audience attitude change. However, it is possible to report a few scientific findings and to restate the advice of sophisticated observers.

We know that the transmission of meanings involves several processes (see Chapter Three). We use language when we encode a message, or put it into a form for the purposes of transmission. But the words we choose serve many additional purposes. Words are symbols, which means that they convey meanings at several levels. At one level, words are denotative, or representational: They stand for something other than themselves. At another level, words are connotative, figurative, evocative, or expressive: They convey emotional nuances. Thus, to refer to an unemployed person as an able-bodied person out of work conveys a different impression from referring to the same person as a welfare sponge.

Words also define relationships between people (Watzlawick, Beavin, and Jackson, 1967). The words you choose reveal the way you feel about the person to whom you are speaking and the way you perceive the relationship between you. In a real sense, words are a bridge between speaker and audience; they indicate the extent to which common ground is shared. As more than one careful observer has noted, the extent to which you share language, and all that it implies, with audience members is directly related to your capacity to influence them. In the words of Kenneth Burke, "You persuade a man only insofar as you talk his language by speech, gesture, tonality, order, image, attitude, idea, identifying your way with his."

We have already discussed the desirability of using concrete, vivid, and intense language, as well as the importance of introducing variety into speech style. An additional bit of advice can be offered with respect to the familiarity of language. Even advanced speakers err by using language that is too complex or difficult to follow. The indiscriminate use of jargon, technical verbiage, and pedantic vocabulary adversely affects not only comprehension of the message but attitudes toward the speaker as well. The techniques you learned in a more basic communications course—definition, repetition, and restatement, to name three—are critically important if you wish to ensure that the language you use accurately conveys the meanings you wish to get across.*

Some descriptive research has been conducted on the impact of language. These studies (for example, Silvestri, 1969) describing the stylistic features of outstanding orators can help you gain insight into the kinds of language used by speakers noteworthy for their effectiveness. In themselves, of course, the studies do not tell you what to do, but they do point the way to models you can emulate. Several experimental studies have identified features of oral style (Horowitz and Newman, 1964; DeVito, 1965); others have indicated that the use of an oral style improves intelligibility (Thomas, 1956); still others have investigated the effects of using obscene language. For example, Mulac (1976) found that using obscene language tends to lower audience ratings of speakers (regardless of sex). Speakers who use obscene language are judged to be of lower sociointellectual status; their speeches are also judged to be of lower esthetic quality.

In Student Activity Option 6.8, you are invited to examine in more depth the subject of language in persuasion.

Student Activity Option 6.8 _____
Language

INSTRUCTIONS
Complete one or more of the following activities. The list of readings provides a fertile field for ideas on the effective use of language.

1 Consult the work of Flesch or Klare. Learn the readability formula and apply it to some sample of written or spoken language. Report on your results.

2. Prepare two drafts of a speech on a topic of your choice (for example, why the sky looks blue, how electricity works, why a curve ball curves). Prepare one speech for presentation to a college level audience, the other for a group of third graders. How would the language of each speech differ? What special concerns would you have in addressing a group of youngsters?

---

* Research on readability (Flesch, 1963; Klare, 1963) has provided methods for testing the ease with which your language can be understood. The interested reader might wish to consult Flesch's work for a simple formula for measuring readability.

3. Analyze the speeches of a contemporary speaker. What stylistic features can you identify? Does the speaker seem to use style consciously, for effect? Is there a consistency of style from speech to speech?

SUGGESTED READINGS

Bowers, J. (1963) "Language Intensity, Social Introversion, and Attitude Change," *Speech Monographs*, 30: 345–52.

Bowers, J. and M. Osborne (1966) "Attitudinal Effects of Selected Types of Concluding Metaphors in Persuasive Speeches," *Speech Monographs*, 33: 147–55.

DeVito, J. (1965) "Comprehension Factors in Oral and Written Discourse of Skilled Communicators," *Speech Monographs*, 32 (June), 124–28.

Flesch, R. (1963) *How To Write, Speak and Think More Effectively*. New York: New American Library.

——— (1951) *The Art of Plain Talk*. New York: Harper and Row.

Haley, J. (1973) *Uncommon Therapy: The Psychiatric Techniques of Milton H. Erikson, M.D.* New York: W. W. Norton. See especially pp. 120–35.

Horowitz, M. and J. Newman (1964) "Spoken and Written Expression: An Experimental Analysis," *Journal of Abnormal and Social Psychology*, 68: 640–47.

Klare, G. (1963) *The Measurement of Readability*. Ames: Iowa State University Press.

Mulac, A. (1976) "Effects of Obscene Language Upon Three Dimensions of Listener Attitude," *Communication Monographs*, 43 (November), 300–307.

Silvestri, V. (1969) "Theodore Roosevelt's Preparedness Oratory," *Central States Speech Journal*, 20 (Fall), 182–85.

Thomas, G. (1956) "Effect of Oral Style on Intelligibility of Speech," *Speech Monographs*, 23 (March), 46–54.

Watzlawick, P. J. Beavin, and D. Jackson (1967) *Pragmatics of Human Communication: A Study of Interactional Patterns, Pathologies, and Paradoxes*. New York: W. W. Norton.

ORGANIZATION

Here I want to turn to more specific and pointed questions of strategy. I will address myself to a variety of relatively narrow queries that can conveniently be grouped under the heading of organizational strategy.

1. *What is the impact of organization on audience attitude change?* It has been established without question that effective organization does influence audience responses to a communicator and to a message. Sharp and McClung (1966) found that badly organized messages result in unfavorable attitudes toward a communicator. Inasmuch as unfavorable attitudes toward a communicator influence attitude change negatively, we may infer that poor organization has at least an indirect adverse effect on the amount of attitude change produced by a speech. One bit of evidence (Smith, 1951) suggests that disorganized messages produce significantly less attitude change than organized ones. Interestingly, however, the finding is not uncontested. A number of studies have failed to demonstrate that any tie exists between message disorganization and listener comprehension (for example, Beighley, 1952). A few studies have demonstrated that well-organized speeches are retained better by listeners (Thompson, 1960; Darnell, 1963). As you know, there is no necessary tie between retention and attitude change; nevertheless, these studies

suggest that a well-organized speech may significantly improve your chances of success as a persuader.

2. *Should the strongest arguments in a speech be placed first, last, or in the middle of the talk?* Research on this question has clearly established the inadvisability of putting the strongest arguments in the middle of the speech. However, no definitive study has established the desirability of primary over final placement. Some researchers (for example, Cromwell, 1950) have reported that placing the strongest arguments last produces most attitude change. Others (Gilkinson, Paulson, and Sikkink, 1954) have reported mixed results. Still others (Gulley and Berlo, 1956) have reported no significant differences stemming from the primary or final placement of the argument. Retention appears to be aided by placing the strongest arguments last (Tannenbaum, 1954). On the basis of their reading of research findings, Karlins and Abelson speculate that audience interest in the subject may be a key variable in determining placement of the strongest arguments. The less interest felt, they observe, the more desirable it is to place the strongest arguments first.

3. *Should the speaker present one or both sides of an argument?* This question requires a somewhat detailed answer, because many variables operate in determining the effectiveness of one-sided vs. two-sided presentations. Perhaps the most important of these variables is the audience's initial position on the topic of the speech. A number of researchers have reported that one-sided presentations seem to be most effective when the audience is in initial agreement with the position taken by the speaker (Hovland, Lumsdaine, and Sheffield, 1949; McGinnies, 1966). When an audience is opposed to the position advocated, two-sided argument presentations produce more attitude change (Hovland, Lumsdaine, and Sheffield, 1949; McGinnies, 1966). When the audience is neither strongly in favor of the position advocated nor strongly opposed to it, other factors come into play, such as the audience's level of education and state of information. In general, the better-educated and more well-informed the audience, the more likely the members are to respond well to two-sided presentations. Karlins and Abelson (1970, p. 25) speculate that under these conditions, a two-sided presentation at least gives the impression of objectivity. It also flatters the auditors, who are treated as a collection of informed and mature individuals. Finally, by preparing a two-sided communication, a speaker can be sure that he or she has anticipated any objections likely to arise.

Another factor in determining the effectiveness of one- or two-sided presentations is the degree to which the audience is likely to be aware of arguments that can counter to the speaker's position. The more obvious these arguments are to the audience, the more it is incumbent on the speaker to present them (Thistlewaite, Kamenetsky, and Schmidt, 1955). For example, during the summer of 1979, President Jimmy Carter gave a speech on the topic of energy. The Three Mile Island nuclear accident had occurred only a few months before. Carter's failure to mention nuclear power as one way out of the energy crisis was viewed as a massive cop-out by his opponents. Even an auditor sympathetic with Carter could not fail to note the omission. As Carter's experience indicates, the failure to raise issues clearly in the mind of your audience can have a severely adverse effect. As a speaker, therefore, you would be wise to prepare a two-sided presentation, except in those rare cases when your audience is wholly supportive of the thesis you are arguing.

An additional benefit follows from presenting both sides of an issue. McGuire and Papageorgis (1961) have found that by exposing an audience to your opposition's arguments during your talk, you will actually render those arguments less effective than if the audience hears them later. They compare this phenomenon with medical inoculation; it is as though the mind builds "antiarguments" just as the physical organism builds antibodies as a result of inoculation. In any event, a two-sided presentation can act as an insurance policy, guaranteeing that your listeners will not easily succumb to arguments advanced on the opposite side of the issue you argue.

4. *When a speech is organized according to a problem-solution sequence, should the problem or the solution be stated first?* This question is easily answered. Although research findings are not uncontested (see, for example, Cohen, 1957; Leventhal and Singer, 1966), it appears that statement of the problem followed by statement of the solution produces most attitude change.

Despite the availability of these research findings, there is no simple way to decide how best to organize your speech materials. As I have indicated before, human behavior is multidetermined; it is influenced by a host of variables. Hence, it is virtually impossible to say that under all circumstances a given alternative will always work or always fail. All a conscientious persuader can do is to plan as thoroughly as possible, basing strategic decisions on the information, research findings, and theoretical perspectives that seem to hold the greatest likelihood of success under the widest set of circumstances.

Student Activity Option 6.9
Organization

INSTRUCTIONS
The following readings focus on the effects of message organization on speech effectiveness. Read and make a report on one or more of them.

SUGGESTED READINGS

Beighley, K. C. (1952) "An Experimental Study of the Effect of Four Speech Variables on Listener Comprehension," *Speech Monographs*, 19: 249–58.

Cohen, A. R. (1957) "Need for Cognition and Order of Communications as Determinants of Opinion Change," pp. 102–120 in C. I. Hovland, et al., *The Order of Presentation in Persuasion*. New Haven: Yale University Press.

Cromwell, H. (1950) "The Relative Effect on Audience Attitude of the First versus the Second Argumentative Speech of a Series," *Speech Monographs*, 17: 105–22.

Darnell, D. K. (1963) "The Relation Between Sentence Order and Comprehension," *Speech Monographs*, 30: 97–100.

Gilkinson, H., S. F. Paulson, and D. E. Sikkink (1954) "The Effects of Order and Authority in an Argumentative Speech," *Quarterly Journal of Speech*, 40: 183–92.

Gulley, H. E. and D. K. Berlo (1956) "Effect of Intercellular and Intracellular Speech Structure on Attitude Change and Learning," *Speech Monographs,* 23: 288–97.

Hovland, C. I., A. A. Lumsdaine, and F. D. Sheffield (1949) *Experiments on Mass Communication (Studies in Social Psychology in World War II,* VOL. 3). Princeton: Princeton University Press.

Hovland, C. et al. (1957) *The Order of Presentation in Persuasion.* New Haven: Yale University Press.

Leventhal, H. and R. P. Singer (1966) "Affect Arousal and Positioning of Recommendations in Persuasive Communications," *Journal of Personality and Social Psychology,* 4: 137–46.

McGinnies, E. (1966) "Studies in Persuasion: III. Reactions of Japanese Students to One-sided and Two-sided Communications." *Journal of Social Psychology,* 70: 87–93.

McGuire, W. "Inducing Resistance to Persuasion," *Advances in Experimental Social Psychology,* 1: 191–229.

McGuire, W. J. and D. Papageorgis (1961) "The Relative Efficacy of Various Types of Prior Belief-Defense in Producing Immunity Against Persuasion," *Journal of Abnormal and Social Psychology,* 62: 327–37.

Sharp, H. and T. McClung (1966) "Effects of Organization on the Speaker's Ethos," *Speech Monographs,* 33: 182–83.

Smith, R. G. (1951) "An Experimental Study of the Effects of Speech Organization Upon Attitudes of College Students," *Speech Monographs,* 18: 292–301.

Thistlewaite, D., D. DeHaan, and J. Kamenetsky (1955) "Attitude Change Through Refutation and Elaboration of Audience Counter-Arguments," *Journal of Abnormal and Social Psychology,* 51: 2–12.

Thistlewaite, D., J. Kamenetsky, and H. Schmidt (1956) "Refutation and Attitude Change," *Speech Monographs,* 23: 14–25.

Thompson, E. (1960) "An Experimental Investigation of the Relative Effectiveness of Organization Structure in Oral Communications," *Southern Speech Journal,* 26: 56–69.

SUMMARY

In this chapter you have been introduced to the basics of persuasion strategy. In the first part, several general principles were shown to derive from persuasion theory and research. A person's internal set was described as an interlocking and interdependent network of beliefs, attitudes, and intentions. In any persuasive situation, people will resist messages that threaten to upset their internal balance. The more basic the belief challenged and the more direct the challenge, the more strenuous will be the person's efforts to resist. Only when an individual cannot avoid exposure to unsettling information, and only when efforts to resist are unsuccessful, will the individual seek to reduce imbalance or to restore balance. Hence, the process of persuasion can be described as one of creating and managing dissonance. Specific suggestions were made for creating dissonance, as well as for estimating and responding to pressure toward congruity. The management of dissonance was discussed in terms of anticipating audience reactions and responding to them systematically.

In the second part of the chapter, I was concerned with audience analysis. Factors affecting an audience's perceptions of and reactions to your persuasive speeches were sketched. These factors included personality variables, group affiliations, and characteristics of the audience itself (degree of homogeneity, extent of group feeling, and degree of speaker-audience polarity). You learned that an audience analysis can help you choose a topic (when this is necessary), formulate your goal(s), determine proof requirements, and select supporting materials.

In the third part of the chapter, specific presentation strategies were offered. Factors affecting attention were discussed in depth, and specific suggestions were offered with respect to gaining and holding attention. A few general principles regarding the use of language were offered, and I reported on research findings on organizational strategies.

Chapter 7

Speech Evaluation and Speech Criticism

In this chapter we turn to speech criticism,* a subject that may hold special interest for you. Speech criticism is an intellectually stimulating undertaking requiring insight and sensitivity best derived from broad knowledge and extensive practical experience. It is a subject with many variations, and one that can occupy a lifetime's work. This chapter is designed to introduce you to the rudiments of the subject. In the first part, I define speech criticism and discuss its many variations. In the second part, I present the perspectives and tools required to conduct speech criticism intelligently.

I. Nature and Kinds of Criticism

What is speech criticism? To answer the question, it is necessary first to place the subject in context—that is, to determine what makes the act of criticism different from other kinds of intellectual endeavors. Next, it is necessary to distinguish speech criticism from criticism of other kinds. Making this distinction will involve examining the different kinds of judgments of speech critics.

Criticism, regardless of the type, involves the analysis and evaluation of some critical object. It assumes the existence of some set of methods for the

*It is possible to analyze critically many types of persuasive messages, including not only speeches, but print advertisements, poetry, and television commercials, to name a few. This chapter is limited in its focus to speech criticism. Nevertheless, many of the principles discussed here can be applied with equal validity to the criticism of other persuasive messages as well.

conduct of critical inquiry. In these respects, speech criticism is much like other forms of criticism. In fact, most critical undertakings share common concerns and methods. What sets critical undertakings apart from one another is the object that is the focus of study. In the case of dramatic criticism, the critical object is a work written for the stage, while the literary critic focuses efforts on a literary work, whether poetry, fiction, history, biography, essays, or writings of still another sort.

The critical object in speech criticism is the speech. This statement can be mistaken to mean that the speech critic need only scrutinize the text of a speech and render an evaluation based on this closet analysis. The truth is quite different, for the speech critic knows that a speech is not given in a vacuum. A speech is a product of a particular combination of historical circumstances, including audience, speaker, and occasion. It is very much a product of its time. Hence, adequate critical study of a speech requires careful examination of the total speech situation: By whom was the speech delivered? on what occasion? to whom? under what circumstances? with what effect?

This last question on the effect of a speech may prompt you to wonder about how speech criticism differs from purely scientific inquiry, for scientists, too, can study a persuasive message and their concern is also with effect. According to two students of criticism (Wellek and Waren, 1956), several features distinguish the work of the scientist from that of the literary or rhetorical critic. These distinctions are presented in schematic form in Figure 7.1. Note that these two undertakings are set apart by two distinguishing features: first, the functions of each; and second, the amount of attention given the style or manner in which the results of the inquiry are reported. Of the two, function is of more importance and of greater interest to us.

The scientist is particularly concerned with determining causal relationships. He or she concentrates on identifying variables and on assessing the effects of manipulations of particular variables. The scientist makes no judgments of an esthetic nature; instead, the concentration is on assessing effects. By contrast, the critic's function is broader. He or she is not so much concerned with measuring effects and establishing causal relationships as with determining the meaning of an event or a critical object. Put another way, criticism is a humanistic undertaking, with roots that are broader than those of the scientist.

The second functional distinction noted in Figure 7.1 concerns the scientist's nonevaluative task. The scientist's work is theoretical and pragmatic in nature, and the goal is primarily to understand the phenomenon under investigation. Secondarily, the scientist may be concerned with determining what works. In either case, he or she is rarely if ever concerned with making esthetic judgments or drawing evaluative conclusions about the quality of the object under investigation. Whereas the scientist stops at the analytical phase of inquiry, the critic goes beyond that point into the realm of evaluation and decision-making. The task of the critic is to render a judgment, to assess the worth of the object under investigation.

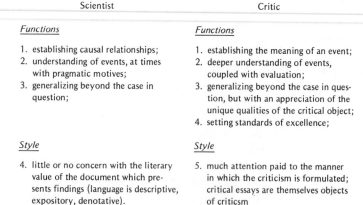

Scientist	Critic
Functions	*Functions*
1. establishing causal relationships; 2. understanding of events, at times with pragmatic motives; 3. generalizing beyond the case in question;	1. establishing the meaning of an event; 2. deeper understanding of events, coupled with evaluation; 3. generalizing beyond the case in question, but with an appreciation of the unique qualities of the critical object; 4. setting standards of excellence;
Style	*Style*
4. little or no concern with the literary value of the document which presents findings (language is descriptive, expository, denotative).	5. much attention paid to the manner in which the criticism is formulated; critical essays are themselves objects of criticsm

Figure 7.1. The Scientist and the Critic

Finally, the scientist is invariably concerned with generalizing beyond the particular case in question. As we saw in Chapter Three, scientific findings must be generalizable—that is, capable of generating principles that apply in a large number of situations in addition to the one studied. The critic may be said to have concerns beyond the particular case in question too. However, the critic also seeks to secure an appreciation of the unique qualities and merits of the object under investigation.

The critic performs another function not performed by the scientist; the critic establishes by his or her work a standard of excellence against which future performance is judged. The critic possesses the knowledge required to make a judgment about the quality of a work; in assessing quality, he or she makes explicit the basis upon which the judgment is rendered. It is but a short step from judging and assessing quality to providing criteria against which future performances are to be judged.

The second category serving as a basis of distinction in Figure 7.1 is the attention paid to style in presenting findings. The scientist is little interested in the manner in which the results of the inquiries are reported. Clarity, brevity, and precision are the scientist's only concerns. Scientific language is descriptive, expository, and denotative. The writing style used in a professional journal article is typically bland; it does not call attention to itself, nor is much effort made to present ideas in an interesting or appealing way. By contrast, most critical undertakings are themselves subject to scrutiny. Hence, outstanding criticism is a sort of literature; students examine the critical works of noteworthy commentators in order to learn how to conduct and present criticism.

Rhetorical criticism has as its critical object the speech, but it is also identifiable by five different kinds of judgments that are incorporated into the rhetorical judgment. Two of these judgments I have already mentioned: First, the rhetorical critic makes judgments of effectiveness. The critic answers such questions as these: Did the speech succeed or fail? Did it have the effect sought? Different critics assign varying degrees of importance to judgments of effect. Of those persons emphasizing their importance, perhaps the most eloquent was Herbert Wichelns, who wrote simply that rhetorical criticism is "not concerned with permanence nor yet with beauty. It is concerned with effect."

Second, rhetorical criticism also makes judgments of literary or esthetic quality. Despite Wichelns' rather extreme pronouncement, I believe the rhetorical critic is also concerned with permanence and beauty. Consider, for example, the speeches of Martin Luther King, Jr., or of Winston Churchill. No one can deny that speeches such as "I Have a Dream" were eminently effective. In addition, however, they are esthetically pleasing objects. Speeches like those of Churchill and Martin Luther King, Jr., leave a lasting imprint on the psyche.

Rhetorical judgment incorporates three other sorts of judgments, including philosophical judgment. The critic evaluates the ethics of oratory, answering questions like these: With what degree of honesty did the speaker argue the case? Were important facts omitted or distorted? Did the speaker convey a false impression or mislead the audience in any way? These ethical considerations are central to rhetorical criticism, for rendering a rhetorical judgement on the basis of effectiveness alone could lead to erroneous conclusions. No one can deny, for example, that Hitler's speeches were effective. But were they ethical? Judged by any human standard, the ideas presented in his speeches were morally repulsive, the products of a sick mind. In rhetoric, the ethical value is higher than that of effectiveness. It is one of the critic's jobs to assess the worth of a speech in the light of ethical criteria.

A closely related judgment made by the rhetorical critic can be called a logical judgment. One of the tasks of the rhetorical critic is to assess the logical strength of the arguments advanced by the speaker. What proofs were used? Of what quality were they? To what extent does the speaker reveal a thorough familiarity with the important evidence having bearing on the case presented? Questions like these point the critic in the direction of an evaluation of the logical probity of the speech under consideration.

The final judgment made by the rhetorical critic is an historical one. It is the critic's function to assess the place of the critical object in the sequence of events that we call history. Of what was the speech a product? In what ways did the historical trends of the times give birth to it? In addition, what influence was exerted by the speaker and his or her message? There can be no doubt that in every age, speakers serve to echo public opinion. However, truly eloquent orators do more; they articulate the hopes and dreams of their age. They help form and marshall opinions and so help to shape the course of future events. To render judgments about the historical impact of speakers and their messages is an important function of the rhetorical critic.

TYPES OF RHETORICAL CRITICISM

Rhetorical studies are as varied as the interests of the people who write them. In fact, there is disagreement within the field on how best to categorize rhetorical studies. Three such schemes of categorizing are presented here. Taken together, they provide an exhaustive summary of the types of studies most frequently undertaken.

Thonnsen, Baird, and Braden (1970) identify four types of criticism, the first of which they call *impressionistic*. This is both the most common and the least systematic type of rhetorical criticism. It is the sort of criticism usually incorporated into an historical personage's biography. A few passing references to the person's speaking style and preparation methods may be supplemented by a very subjective and episodic recounting of one or more famous addresses. Any judgment made in the course of such criticism is rooted only in the writer's uninformed personal preferences. No objective or systematic study points the way to the critical conclusions. You may encounter this sort of criticism in weekly newsmagazines, and in daily newspapers. Thonnsen, Baird, and Braden consider this the least satisfying of the four types of critical studies they summarize.

Analytical studies, a second type of rhetorical criticism, are empirically oriented and descriptive in nature. They hardly resemble criticism in the traditional sense, since they offer no judgments as to the quality of the work under investigation. Instead, these studies substitute content analyses, enumerate the frequency with which certain appeals or arguments appear in the speech, and otherwise provide raw descriptive data about the critical object. Analytical study is more scientific than critical, according to the distinctions made in Figure 7.1

Thonnsen and his associates label *synthetic* those studies that report the results of exhaustive fact-gathering relative to a particular speech, speaker, and occasion. The critic's function in undertaking such a study is to gather and to report on abundant material. Who was the speaker? Upon what occasion did he or she speak? under what circumstances? to whom? with what effect? Virtually all of the critic's efforts are expended gathering such data. What the critic fails to do, however, is to offer any judgment about the quality or value of the critical object. The synthetic study is a data-oriented examination. According to Thonnsen et al., the synthetic critic emphasizes historical and empirical functions, but fails as a critic because he or she does not perform the task essential to all criticism—to render a verdict.

The fourth type of study, *judicial* criticism, is, in the view of Thonnsen and associates, the most complete and best form of critical study. The critic gathers extensive data about every aspect of the speaking situation. He or she scrutinizes the speech, reporting the kinds of findings that are part of analytical studies. The critic reports also on the speaker, the occasion, and the audience. But whereas the synthesist stops short of making a judgment, the judicial critic offers an evaluation of the critical object. The judgment of the judicial critic, unlike that of the impressionistic critic, is grounded in objective knowledge and extensive familiarity with both rhetorical theory and historical content. The judicial critic makes all the following judgments: (1) judgments of effect, (2) literary and esthetic judgments, (3) philosophical or ethical judgments, (4) logical judgments, and (5) historical judgments.

While no simple statement can ably summarize the extensive work done by the conscientious judicial critic, the following sentence serves as a brief summary of the opinions offered by Thonnsen, Baird, and Braden. The judicial critic seeks to determine to what extent and using which resources of rhetorical craftsmanship a particular speaker addressing a particular audience on a specific occasion achieved the desired end, immediate or delayed.

A second classification scheme divides rhetorical criticism into biographical studies, movement studies, and case studies. Note that a study may not fall clearly into one category or another; while it may emphasize elements of one particular category, it may include elements of others as well.

Biographical studies, the type most frequently conducted, are of three sorts. The first is the historical biography, or a biography with a rhetorical slant. It deals with the historical personage's rhetorical training, experience as a speaker, patterns of preparation, performance style, and related subjects. (A good example of the historical biography is Louis A. Mallory's "Patrick Henry," pp. 580–602 in W. N. Brigance ed. (1943) *A History and Criticism of American Public Address,* II. New York: McGraw-Hill Book Co.)

Biographical studies can also be psychological rather than historical in nature. While these studies are extremely difficult to carry off, they are interesting attempts to tie together rhetorical style and personality. (One reasonably successful psychological study is Martin Malony's essay on Clarence Darrow in Marie Hocmuth Nichols, ed. (1955) *A History and Criticiam of American Public Address,* II. New York: McGraw-Hill Book Co.)

A third sort of biographical study focuses on one or a number of speeches central to the life of the historical personage. The speech in question may be the one that established the individual as a politician to be reckoned with. Or a number of speeches may be selected for study because they all deal with the same theme—currency reform or civil rights, for example. Speeches can be grouped according to time spans in a person's life, according to geographical location (for example, the speeches of Pope John Paul II during his 1979 visit to the United States), or according to other criteria. Whether one or several speeches are chosen, they are viewed as central to the life experience of the individual and are seen as significant in shaping his or her destiny. (A good example of this sort of study is Bernard J. Brommel (1966) "The Pacifist Speechmaking of Eugene V. Debs," *Quarterly Journal of Speech* (April), 52: 146–64. Another example is Russel Windes, Jr. (1956) "Public Address in the Career of Adlai E. Stevenson," *Quarterly Journal of Speech,* (October), 42: 225–233.)

Biographical studies traditionally have been the cornerstone of rhetorical criticism. Lately, they have begun to be supplemented by other kinds of rhetorical-critical studies, among them *movement* studies, which incorporate several goals. One goal is to trace the birth and evolution of a movement (say, the gay rights drive) by analyzing typical or critical speeches delivered at different times. Another goal is to show the crosscurrents that unite movements occurring simultaneously but following different tracks—for example, the gay, black, and women's liberation movements of the 70s and 80s. (Movement studies include Leland Griffin "The Rhetorical Structure of the Antimasonic Movement," in Donald C. Bryant, ed. (1958) *The Rhetorical Idiom: Essays in Rhetoric, Oratory, Language, and Drama*. New York: Cornell University Press.)

A third type of rhetorical investigation is the *case* study, the examination of a particular event with special emphasis on the speech-making and rhetoric it occasioned. (A 1969 study of the student uprisings at Columbia University is James R. Andrew (1969) "Confrontation at Columbia: A Case-Study in Rhetoric," *Quarterly Journal of Speech* (February), 55: 9–16.)

It is important to note that within these broad categories, considerable differences can exist. Biographical and other sorts of studies may be conducted from differing theoretical vantage points. For example, a traditionalist might conduct a rhetorical analysis from an Aristotelian perspective while a more contemporary-minded critic might base his or her writing on the rhetorical theories of Kenneth Burke. There is an enormous variety of alternative investigatory styles opened to the rhetorical critic.

The final classification scheme of rhetorical studies is to group them according to which of the four elements in the speaking situation they emphasize. The studies can focus on the speaker, the audience, the occasion, and the speech. In addition, Ernest J. Wrage (1947) has proposed that rhetorical criticism constitutes an investigation into social and intellectual history, tracing the evolution of ideas, values, and cultural trends. This rather lofty goal is well worth pursuing since oratory often serves as an accurate mirror of the times from which it springs.

Finally, there are no hard and fast rules for classifying rhetorical studies. I have offered these three systems of categories in order to suggest the enormous variety of studies that can be conducted under the umbrella of rhetorical criticism.

Student Activity Option 7.1 _____
Criticism Alternatives

INSTRUCTIONS
Following are three sets of readings on the subject of rhetorical criticism. The readings in Group One offer general discussions of rhetorical criticism; those in Group Two are examples of different types of studies; and those in Group Three are anthologies containing speeches for analysis.

Choose one or more items from any group and report on what you read. You may wish to survey in more depth the kinds of criticism students of rhetoric can conduct. If you are practically inclined, you may actually conduct such a study, using the format spelled out in one or more of the following readings.

SUGGESTED READINGS

Group One: Rhetorical Criticism

Baird, A. Craig (1956/1968) "The Study of Speeches," pp. 39–52 in William A. Linsley (1968) *Speech Criticism: Methods and Materials.* Dubuque, Iowa: William C. Brown.

Black, Edwin (1965) *Rhetorical Criticism.* New York: Macmillan.

Campbell, Karlyn K. (1971) *Critiques of Contemporary Rhetoric.* Belmont, California: Wadsworth Publishing Co.

Cathcart, Robert (1966) *Post-communication: Criticism and Evaluation.* Indianapolis: Bobbs-Merrill.

Croft, Albert J. (1956/1968) "The Functions of Rhetorical Criticism, pp. 108–118 in William A. Linsley (1968) *Speech Criticism: Methods and Materials.* Dubuque, Iowa: William C. Brown.

Hesseltine, Willaim B. (1961/1968) "Speech and History," pp. 92–98 in William A. Linsley (1968) *Speech Criticism: Methods and Materials.* Dubuque, Iowa: William C. Brown.

Hillbrunner, Anthony (1966) *Critical Dimensions: The Art of Public Address Criticism.* New York: Random House.

Linsley, William A. (1968) *Speech Criticism: Methods and Materials.* Dubuque, Iowa: William C. Brown.

Nichols, Marie Hocmuth (1955/1968) "The Criticism of Rhetoric," pp. 53–75 in William A. Linsley (1968) *Speech Criticism: Methods and Materials.* Dubuque, Iowa: William C. Brown.

Parrish, Wayland (1954/1965) "The Study of Speeches," pp. 76–91 in William A. Linsley: (1968) *Speech Criticism: Methods and Materials.* Dubuque, Iowa: William C. Brown.

Thonnsen, Lester, A. Craig Baird, and Waldo W. Braden (1970) *Speech Criticism,* 2nd ed. New York: The Ronald Press Company.

Wellek, Rene and Austin Warren (1956) *Theory of Literature.* New York: Harcourt, Brace & World.

Wichelns, Herbert (1925/1965) "The Literary Criticism of Oratory," pp. 7–38 in William A. Linsley (1968) *Speech Criticism: Methods and Materials.* Dubuque, Iowa: William C. Brown.

Group Two: Sample Studies

Graham, Mary W. (1963) "The Lyceum Movement and Section Controversy," pp. 108–114 in J. Jeffrey Auer, ed. (1962) *Anti-slavery and Disunion, 1858–1861: Studies in the Rhetoric of Compromise and Conflict.* New York: Harper and Row.

Reid, Loren D. (1957) "The Education of Charles Fox," *Quarterly Journal of Speech,* 43 (1957): 357–64.

VanDeusen, Glyndon (1958) "Some Aspects of Whig Thought and Theory in the Jacksonian Period," *American Historical Review,* 63 (January, 1958): 305–332.

Wichelns, Herbert A. (1943) "Ralph Waldo Emerson," pp. 501–25 in W. N. Brigance, ed. (1943) *A History and Criticism of American Public Address,* II. New York: McGraw-Hill Book Company.

Wolfarth, Donald L. (1961) "John F. Kennedy in the Tradition of Inaugural Speeches," *Quarterly Journal of Speech,* 47 (April, 1961): 124–32.

Group Three: Anthologies

Brigance, W. N., Nichols, et al. (various dates) *A History and Criticism of American Public Address.* New York: McGraw-Hill Book Company.

Bryant, Donald C., and Carroll C. Arnold, Frederick W. Haberman, Richard Murphy, and Karl R. Wallace (1967) *An Historical Anthology of Select British Speeches.* New York: The Ronald Press Company.

Linsley, William A. (1968) *Speech Criticism: Methods and Materials.* Dubuque, Iowa: William C. Brown.

Wrage, Ernest J. and Barnett Baskerville (1960) *American Forum: Speeches on Historic Issues, 1788–1900*. New York: Harper.
———(1962) *American Forum: Speeches on Twentieth Century Issues*. New York: Harper.

II. *Perspectives and Tools*

An awareness of the complex relationships among theory, practice, and criticism provides an important perspective for the speech critic.

In Chapter Two, I presented a learning model for persuasive speaking in which I indicated that practice always precedes theory, and that successful practice can be accounted for in different ways. The most reasonable and constructive attempts to account for successful practice utilize sound theory, rooted in careful observation and measurement of speaker behavior. I also observed that once theory has developed sufficiently, it can contribute to successful practice. For example, by identifying variables in persuasion, and by showing the relationships among variables, the theorist can contribute indirectly to improved practive. Thus, a mutual or circular relationship exists between theory and practice; each contributes to the other.

Criticism is similarly related to both practice and theory. Like theory, criticism follows practice, criticism can also contribute to effective practice. You have already seen that criticism provides standards for performance, particularly in the ethical and logical components of rhetorical judgment. Perhaps in no other areas can the influence of rhetorical criticism be felt more directly. Less directly, the critic, like the scientist, heightens the practitioner's awareness of those elements in specific speaking situations that have contributed to (or failed to contribute to) effective practice. Thus, practice and criticism exert mutual influence on one another.

Theory and criticism contribute to each other as well. On the one hand, theory forms the basis for criticism since the critic must work from a theoretical base. He or she brings to any analysis the working assumptions and insights provided by a particular theoretical orientation. As noted, rhetorical criticism can be conducted from an Aristotelian, traditional, or contemporary perspective. On the other hand, however, the theorist has much to learn from the critic. In one author's words (Cathcart, 1966, p. 7), "the careful and thorough critic will find areas of human communication not adequately accounted for by existing rhetorical theory. He will discover where old theories no longer apply, and he will evolve new theory to account for unexplained matters."

From the premises advanced thus far, you can infer that the most important tool available to the critic is a knowledge of theory—not just a general knowledge of the rudiments of a theory, but a thorough familiarity with its gaps, flaws, and weaknesses. One of the main functions of criticism is to bridge the gaps, to correct the flaws, to shore up the identified weaknesses of a theory (while also helping to expose formerly unidentified weaknesses). Edwin Black, writing nearly two decades ago, was among the earliest and most eloquent students of rhetorical criticism to call for the expansion of the critic's functions to include contributing directly to persuasion theory. In his excellent volume, *Rhetorical Criticism: A Study in Method* (New York: Macmillan Book Company, 1965), Black states that the goal of criticism is to explain how effective rhetorical discourses work. He does not consider rhetorical biography adequate as criticism unless such work accounts for successful practice. He would disagree with Ernest Wrage, who says that rhetorical criticism ought to constitute a sort of lesson in social and intellectual history. Instead, Black argues that criticism ought to advance our understanding of the persuasive process. In short, it should contribute directly to the development of persuasion theory.

The bridge between theory and criticism includes three central concerns—observation, judgment-making, and generalization or hypothesis formulation.

OBSERVATION

Much of the critic's effort is expended on careful scrutiny, including gathering facts about the speaker, the occasion, the audience, the speech itself, and the short- and long-range effects of the speech. The critic may need to pay special attention to one or more of the elements in the rhetorical situation. For example, if a speaker faces a particularly hostile audience and succeeds in winning it over, then the critic would want to pay special attention to the composition of the audience, its unexpected readiness for change, and similar matters. Regardless of where the emphasis is placed, however, the critic pays particular attention at all times to both the speaker's behavior and the consequences of that behavior. For, if we attribute changes in the audience to what the speaker does, then these observations are at the heart of rhetorical criticism.

JUDGMENT-MAKING

This is the point at which the critic makes an informed judgment about the speech. In light of what is known about the speech (including the background, occasion, audience, and so on), the critic attempts to relate what is done by the speaker to the consequences of the speech. In what ways did the audience react to the speech? Did the members behave in ways intended by the speaker?

In both the observation and the judgment-making phases of the critical process, it is crucially important that the rhetorical critic define all key terms operationally. Suppose, for example, that a critic observes that one factor contributing to the effectiveness of a successful speech was the speaker's sincerity. Just what is meant by *sincerity* in this context? What does it mean for a speaker to be sincere? What cues were sent off by the speaker that resulted in the audience's judgment that he or she was sincere? Were the cues nonverbal—facial expressions? dress? posture? Were they vocal—tone of voice? vocal quality? intensity? Were the cues written into the language of the speech, originating in the turn of a phrase or the choice of one mode of expression over another? The answers to such questions are an essential part of the critical process, because without adequate answers, the critic fails to provide information that can be useful to other practitioners or to theorists.

Another caution must be entered with respect to observation and judgment-making. The conscientious critic tries to isolate variables so that critical observations pertain to the impact of one variable at a time. While practically, of course, this is virtually impossible, a basic knowledge of statistics facilitates more sophisticated observations. Factor analysis and multiple regression analyses, for example, are tools that ought to be part of every sophisticated rhetorical critic's armamentarium. If they are not yet part of your stock in trade, you are forced to do your best with the resources available to you. However, it is incumbent on the serious rhetorical critic to acquire the knowledge and skills demanded by the trade.

GENERALIZATION OR HYPOTHESIS-FORMULATION

Having now formulated a number of simple propositions with respect to the speech and its effects (for example, "The speaker appeared to be sincere" or "The speech was effective"), the critic proceeds to the next step of formulating generalizations or hypotheses that are capable of being tested empirically. In Chapter Three, I defined an hypothesis as a tentative statement of a relationship between two variables. At this point in the critical process, the critic formulates hypotheses—for example, "Speakers who appear to be sincere are more effective than those who do not." Such statements (with all key terms defined operationally) are capable of scientific testing in accord with the methods briefly outlined in Chapter Three.

As you can see, if the rhetorical critic follows the recommendations spelled out here, he or she can contribute to theory directly, by generating hypotheses capable of being tested in the laboratory. Of course, a number of potential problems arise. First, what happens if the hypothesis generated by the critic has already been tested by the scientific community? If that is the case, one of two things can occur. If the hypothesis has already been validated, then the critic can confidently assert that a relationship exists between apparent sincerity and speech effectiveness; further, on the basis of this established relationship, the critic can truly account, at least in part, for the speech's effectiveness. On the other hand, if the hypothesis has been tested and invalidated, and if the critic is satisfied that past research has been well conducted and has yielded accurate findings, then he or she may need to revise the estimate of the reasons for the speaker's success. More likely than not, it will be possible to replicate past research or to design another study that is more sharply focused and that may qualify past research findings. The process of refining and sharpening the focus of research findings is an important part of scientific study. The critic who forces such rethinking contributes in a significant way to the development of theory.

A second potential problem with rhetorical criticism is that the specific circumstances surrounding a particular speech may make generalization to other speech situations impossible. For example, the analysis of a televised campaign speech delivered by a 35-year-old Quaker of Scotch-Irish descent to an audience of American voters in 1952 may be so tied to a particular, narrow set of circumstances—many of which are incapable of being duplicated in the laboratory—that it would seem to yield few generalizable conclusions. In my view, this is a serious problem but not an insurmountable one. Provided that the critic specifies the circumstances of the original speech, and provided that he or she extrapolates from the study those factors that seem to be true of speech-making in general, it may be possible to formulate hypotheses that have bearing on speech situations similar to (though not necessarily identical with) the one in question.

Student Activity Option 7.2 is designed to give you a chance to conduct this sort of critical inquiry.

Student Activity Option 7.2 _____
Criticism

INSTRUCTIONS
Learning by doing is the best kind of learning, especially when learning skills. In this five-step activity, the entire class is to cooperate in sharpening each other's ability to observe, to make connections between speaker behaviors and audience responses, to make critical judgments, and to begin formulating scientific hypotheses.

1. Each student in the class is to prepare a four- to six-minute persuasive speech on a topic of his or her own choosing.

2. On the assigned day, the scheduled speakers should present their talks. (It is not advisable to schedule more than five speakers during any 50-minute class period.) Classmates are to take notes during each talk, paying special attention to what the speaker does (incuding both verbal and nonverbal aspects of the performance) and to the effect the behavior seems to have.

3. Absolutely no oral comments or criticisms, from teacher or students, are allowed following each speech. Instead, each student is to prepare a set of writ-

ten observations about each speaker and speech. The written observations should answer these questions:

    a. Was the speech persuasive? Did it succeed in bringing about a change in the beliefs, attitudes, intentions, or behavior of the audience? (You may wish to measure such changes in accord with the methods discussed in Chapter Three.) In judging the persuasiveness of the speech, you are to rely primarily on your own personal reactions to the talk. Did it work for you? Were your beliefs changed?

    b. What did the speaker do (or fail to do) that seems to account for the observed effect? In other words, what speaker behaviors seem to be related to your reaction to the speech? (It is important to be as specific as possible in defining speaker behaviors. Avoid imprecise statements such as "The speaker seemed to be an expert." Rather, ask yourself what the speaker did that made you feel he or she was an expert. Did the speaker furrow his or her brow when speaking? Did the speaker document arguments carefully, suggesting careful preparation? Questions like these point away from ill-defined statements toward concrete, quantifiable data.)

4. Although it is important to take careful notes on each speaker's presentation, select only four or five of your classmates' speeches to form the basis on which to complete this assignment. Selection of the speeches should be made according to criteria such as these:

    a. Which speeches contained clearly identifiable speaker behaviors that seemed to correlate most directly with observed effects?

    b. Which speeches seemed particularly effective, or ineffective?

    c. Which speeches seemed unique, or at least different in some clearly identifiable way?

5. Review your notes on each of the speeches you have selected. Prepeare a written report on each talk. Consult with your instructor regarding the form of this report, and on such matters as length, due date, etc. In the report you prepare, include the following:

    a. Your judgment about the speech. Was the speech extremely effective? moderately effective? ineffective? Did it have a boomerang effect, making the audience (you) feel precisely the opposite of the way the speaker intended?

    b. The reasons for your judgment. What was it the speaker did that resulted in the observed effect? (Remember to spell out specific, concrete behaviors.) You should specify more than one behavior per speech. You may wish to focus on speaker behaviors that had to do with the speaker (posture, facial expression, etc.) or with the speech (arguments used, kinds of evidence, language, etc.). Try for as complete an analysis as possible in describing what the speaker did that contributed to or accounted for the observed effect. Note, too, that you may wish to specify effects. For example, a speech you judge to be moderately effective overall might have had other, less global effects. Perhaps the speaker made you feel you could trust his or her honesty; perhaps the speaker made you angry at one point; or perhaps he or she came across as lacking in confidence, despite the overall good performance. Again, the more specific you can be in pointing to observed effects, the better. Prepare a set of descriptive statements that link speaker behavior with observed effects. For example, "The speaker looked at the audience members' eyes approximately 75 per cent of the time while speaking. The result of this behavior was to make me feel the speaker was earnest." Or "The speaker laughed nervously throughout the talk. The result of this behavior was that the audience tended to disregard what the speaker had to say."

c. Formulate a set of four or five generalizations (or hypotheses) pertaining to persuasive speaking for each speech you have studied. The number of generalizations should correspond to the number of descriptive statements you prepared in paragraphs a and b. These generalizations should be specific, descriptive statements that seem to be true of speeches and speech-making in general. For example, here is the progression from a descriptive statement tied to one speaker and a particular speech to a generalization applicable to many speakers and speeches:

Example 1

Specific descriptive statement

"The speaker looked at the audience members' eyes approximately 75 per cent of the time while speaking. The result of this behavior was to make me feel the speaker was earnest."

Generalization

"Speakers who look at the audience members' eyes approximately 75 per cent of the time while speaking are perceived as earnest by their auditors."

(If the sex of the speaker seemed to be a factor here, you might wish to mention it in your generalization.)

Example 2

Specific descriptive statement

"The speaker laughed nervously throughout the talk; the result of this behavior was that the audience tended to disregard what the speaker had to say."

Generalization

"Speakers who laugh nervously throughout their talks are likely to create in their audience a tendency to disregard what they have to say." (Be as specific as possible. Does "the tendency to disregard what the speaker has to say" lend itself to more specific definition? Under scrutiny, perhaps "the tendency" breaks down to such factors as these: the speaker is perceived as insincere; the audience becomes uncomfortable for the speaker and stops listening to the message; the speaker is perceived as lacking confidence. There are many more ways of specifying audience reactions. How many can you think of? Remember to strive for measurable, quantifiable audience reactions.)

Here is another example, tied to the content of a speech and drawn from a recent student paper.

Example 3

Specific descriptive statement

I thought the speaker was fair because he acknowledged the arguments of his opponents.

Generalization

Speakers who acknowledge the arguments of their opponents are perceived as fair by their audience.

Be certain to couch your generalizations in descriptive terms. Avoid prescriptions, which begin with words like "you should" or "speakers should." In general, avoid giving advice and stick to simple, descriptive statements that show the connections between specific speaker behaviors and precise observable effects.

Following the submission of your written work, it may be possible for your instructor to discuss your generalizations and those of your classmates. Perhaps some members of the class would be interested in surveying the persuasion literature to determine what researchers in the field have found out about the generalizations formulated by your class. You may even elect to do a paper about research findings bearing on one or more of the generalizations you formulated.

As you have seen, it is possible to bridge the gap between criticism and theory by applying the methods discussed here. It is important to emphasize, however, that such work constitutes only part of the enterprise called rhetorical criticism. The critic does far more than generate hypotheses for scientific testing as the critic's range of concerns is broader than that of the scientist. The critic makes judgments that are esthetic, philosophical, logical, and historical. A complete rhetorical analysis is a comprehensive report on all significant aspects of a rhetorical act.

To guide you in your rhetorical criticism, I have drawn up a guide to speech analysis that is intended to call your attention to many of the important considerations that must be made by the rhetorical critic.

GUIDE TO SPEECH ANALYSIS

1. The Speaker
   - pertinent biographical facts
   - reputation as a speaker, as a person
   - effect of a speaker's personality and character upon audience
   - relation of speaker to question under discussion

2. The Audience
   - state of information of the audience
   - relation of audience to question, its interest, prejudice, etc.
   - is speech directed to this audience only or to a larger one?
   - effect of speech on this audience, a remote audience

3. The Occasion and Setting
   - historical background of question under discussion
   - immediate cause for discussion
   - physical setting
   - psychological setting (climate of opinion, etc.)

4. The Speech (or Speeches)
   - general purpose (to persuade, to entertain, etc.)
   - specific purpose
   - speaker's personal purpose
   - methods of fulfilling the purpose of the speech
     a. logical proof
        evidence, forms of support: preponderance of one type? why?
        reasoning employed: preponderance of one type? why?
        beliefs of audience as premises
        reliance upon speaker's authority, etc.
     b. refutation
     c. ethical proof
        speaker's credibility, trustworthiness, etc. revealed in speech and
           used as a sort of proof
     d. emotional proof
        are motives used to arouse feeling? allay hostile feeling? circumvent
           or anticipate prejudice and bias? what attempt was made to secure
           a fair hearing? to arouse and hold attention?
     e. arrangement of material
        introduction, approach, etc.
        placement of arguments
        is purpose stated at outset? does it emerge?
        how does the speaker conclude?
     f. style
        vividness, clearness, figure of speech, effective phrases, loaded
           words, rhetorical devices, etc.

5. Criticism
   - judgments of effect: does the speaker use all the available means of per-
     suasion? what contributes to the effectiveness of the speech?
   - literary aesthetic judgments: of what enduring value is the speech? why?
   - philosophical-ethical judgments: was the speech ethical?
   - logical judgments: was the message logically sound? of what quality were
     the proofs presented?
   - historical judgments: what was the historical impact of the message?

SUMMARY

This chapter was designed to introduce you to the rudiments of speech criticism, which is a form of intellectual inquiry that has as its focus a persuasive message. A distinction was made between the work of the critic and that of the scientist. The two differ in functions, concern with style, and by the presence or absence of judgment-making. The rhetorical judgment was made up of judgments of effect as well as esthetic, philosophical, logical, and historical judgments. I reviewed types of rhetorical studies—impressionistic, analytical, synthetic, and judicial, as well as biographical studies, movement studies, and case studies. I then discussed the relationships between criticism and practice on the one hand, and between criticism and theory on the other. A scheme was presented whereby the critic can contribute directly to persuasion theory by generating hypotheses capable of being tested scientifically. To assist you in any rhetorical criticism you undertake, a guide to speech analysis was offered.

Index